Isaiah
40–66

John A. Braun

CONCORDIA PUBLISHING HOUSE · SAINT LOUIS

CONTENTS

Editor's Preface   v

Introduction to Isaiah 40–66   1

I. Woes and judgments (1:1–39:8)*

II. Comfort and consolation (40:1–66:24)   9

   A. The sovereign Lord will rescue his people
      from Babylon (40:1–48:21)   12

   B. The Lord's Servant will redeem his people
      (49:1–57:21)   169

   C. The Lord promises his new Zion
      (Jerusalem) eternal glory (58:1–66:24)   283

   *Part One is treated in *Isaiah 1–39.*
   A more detailed outline begins on page 6.

ILLUSTRATIONS

The prophet Isaiah   vi

Jesus anointed with the Holy Spirit at his baptism   52

Jesus carries his cross to Calvary   224

The gentile wise men worship the Christ Child   317

MAP

The Middle East at the time of Isaiah   408

I, even I, am he who blots out your transgressions,
for my own sake,
and remembers your sins no more.

Isaiah 43:25

PREFACE

The People's Bible Commentary is just what the name implies—a Bible and commentary for people. It includes the complete text of the Holy Scriptures in the popular New International Version. The commentary following the Scripture sections contains personal applications, as well as historical background and explanations of the text.

The authors of *The People's Bible Commentary* are men of scholarship and practical insight, gained from years of experience in the teaching and preaching ministries. They have tried to avoid the technical jargon which limits so many commentary series to professional Bible scholars.

The most important feature of these books is that they are Christ-centered. Speaking of the Old Testament Scriptures, Jesus himself declared, "These are the Scriptures that testify about me" (John 5:39). Each volume of *The People's Bible Commentary* directs our attention to Jesus Christ. He is the center of the entire Bible. He is our only Savior.

We dedicate these volumes to the glory of God and to the good of his people.

The Publishers

The prophet Isaiah

INTRODUCTION TO ISAIAH 40–66

Centuries before Isaiah, God appeared to Moses, another leader of God's people. While Moses talked with God on the mountaintop, the Lord proclaimed his name to his servant Moses. The Lord spoke these words: "The LORD, the LORD, the compassionate and gracious God, slow to anger, abounding in love and faithfulness, maintaining love to thousands, and forgiving wickedness, rebellion and sin. Yet he does not leave the guilty unpunished; he punishes the children and their children for the sin of the fathers to the third and fourth generation" (Exodus 34:6-8). Centuries after Isaiah, the apostle John wrote simply, "God is love" (1 John 4:8). In another letter, the apostle also wrote of God's judgment upon unbelievers (Revelation). From Moses to John—from the writer of the first book of the Bible to the writer of the last—God's message remains the same. God loves the world, but he also threatens punishment to all who reject him.

Isaiah proclaimed that same message. He announced judgment upon the unfaithful, but he trumpeted the comfort God intended for the faithful. Like Moses and John, he proclaimed law and gospel. The second part of Isaiah's prophecy begins with the command, "Comfort, comfort my people" (40:1) and ends with a look at those who rebelled against the Lord: "Their worm will not die, nor will their fire be quenched, and they will be loathsome to all mankind" (66:24).

Isaiah stands between Moses and John. His prophecy stands as a high and majestic peak in the range of moun-

1

tains we treasure as God's Word. The second portion of his prophecy contains some of the most beautiful treasures God gave his people. We find more than one great height, but none rises greater and more majestic than chapter 53. Isaiah saw the crucifixion of Jesus so clearly in prophecy that it is as if he stood at the cross with John and Mary.

Other majestic truths rise from the words of God's great prophet. Believers over the centuries have gazed at the peaks of Isaiah's prophecy, praised the Lord for them, and found comfort and strength in them. As you read them, may you take your place among the multitudes of believers who have found these treasures so satisfying to their weary hearts.

Who is Isaiah, and why did he write?

We have included whatever information we have about God's prophet Isaiah in the introduction to the first volume of this commentary. Rather than repeat that information here, the author refers the reader to that section of the first volume. But we might well ask where Isaiah acquired the ideas he wrote.

Isaiah did not develop these ideas on his own. He was a prophet of God and received his message from God himself. We believe that God the Holy Spirit inspired Isaiah, giving him not just the ideas and concepts to write but also the words themselves. God used all Isaiah's experiences, talent, and vocabulary so that his prophecy is uniquely Isaiah's. At the same time, these words are God's words and come from God by inspiration.

We believe in a revealed religion, one that comes from God to us. We do not believe that Isaiah developed his message through a long, protracted period of meditation, research, and experimentation. Isaiah did not invent God nor did he fashion his ideas about God from his own imagination, intelligence, or experience. God gave the message to him just as God gave his message to all the writers of the Bible. Like Isaiah, the messages of other writers of Scripture bear the stylistic stamp of the human author, but all those messages come from God. He revealed himself to humanity through the medium of words. Isaiah's message, like the rest of the Bible, is God's self-disclosure. No human can know anything about God unless God himself reveals it.

Because we believe that God revealed himself to Isaiah, we have no doubt that Isaiah could write about the future. God can reveal the future to humans, who have only a limited knowledge of what even the next day will bring. In this second portion of Isaiah's prophecy, God's prophet saw the Babylonian captivity and the release of a remnant from that exile. Isaiah identified Cyrus as the one who would bring about the release from captivity. These events occurred as Isaiah described them but more than a century after Isaiah died. Isaiah also saw the crucified Savior "stricken by God, smitten by him, and afflicted" (53:4). The crucifixion occurred seven hundred years after Isaiah. The prophet knew that God revealed both events to him by inspiration. Isaiah could not have known of either on his own. Again and again, Isaiah punctuated his message with the phrase "This is what the LORD says" or some variation of it. We approach the words of Isaiah from that perspective. God revealed these things to his prophet.

What is different about the second portion of Isaiah?

Isaiah ties the first portion of his prophecy (chapters 1–39) to the history of his day. King Ahaz and King Hezekiah play important roles in the prophecy. King Ahaz forged an alliance with the Assyrians. But then in Hezekiah's day, the Assyrians turned on Judah, ravaged the country-side, and laid siege to Jerusalem. The first portion ends when God rescued Jerusalem by destroying the Assyrian forces at the very gate of the capital city.

Isaiah skillfully built a bridge to the second portion of his prophecy by introducing the Babylonians in chapter 39. When Hezekiah entertained the Babylonian envoys, the king showed them everything in his treasury. After they were gone, Isaiah warned Hezekiah that at some point in the future, Babylon would come and carry the people away into captivity.

The second portion of Isaiah (chapters 40–66) assumes the future after the Babylonians had already come to power. Although chapter 40 begins with the deliverance of God's people from Babylon, God stretched the prophet's vision farther into the future. Cyrus defeated Babylon and in 538 B.C. issued an edict that allowed the Jews to return to Jerusalem and rebuild the temple and city. But the name of Babylon disappears after chapter 48. In the remaining chapters, Isaiah concentrated his attention on another and greater deliverance. Isaiah foretold that a greater Deliverer would come, suffer and die for the sins of the people, and release them from the bondage of sin and death. The work of God's great Servant forms one significant feature of the second portion of Isaiah.

In the second half of his prophecy (chapters 40–66), Isaiah revealed the coming of this great Servant of the Lord. Four special sections are called the Servant Passages. They are 42:1-7; 49:1-7; 50:4-11; and 52:13–53:12. Two additional passages help us understand the work of this Servant: 61:1-3 and 63:1-6. These passages provide a wonderful look ahead at the ministry of Jesus. Interestingly, the fourth of the servant passages, 52:13–53:12, occupies the center of the prophecy. In many ways it is the high peak toward which the first chapters ascend, and from that high peak we can see the majestic grandeur of the remaining chapters.

Many biblical scholars doubt that the same prophet wrote the entire prophecy. Some suggest that one prophet wrote the first 39 chapters and another the last 27. Others suggest that two writers wrote the second 27 chapters—one of them writing chapters 40 to 55 and another writing chapters 56 to 66. The arguments these scholars marshal in defense of their position are not persuasive. We believe that one writer wrote the entire prophecy. The Great Isaiah Scroll, discovered among the other Dead Sea Scrolls, does not divide the scroll as if two authors wrote the text. Chapter 39 ends one line from the bottom of a column. Chapter 40 begins on the last line of that column without any indication of a break. Clearly the religious community that copied the manuscript did not consider Isaiah to be the product of two writers but one. This is but one argument for the unity of Isaiah and the authorship of one writer. Other arguments for a single author are included in the text of this volume and in the introduction to the first volume.

Outline

Isaiah carefully constructed the second portion of his prophecy. He created three parts of almost equal length. Each of these three parts can be divided into nine chapters. Isaiah appears to have that division in mind too. Two of the three parts conclude with the same thought: "'There is no peace,' says the Lord, 'for the wicked'" (48:22) and "'There is no peace,' says my God, 'for the wicked'" (57:21). Isaiah ends his prophecy with a variation of this thought. The Lord says, "They will go out and look upon the dead bodies of those who rebelled against me; their worm will not die, nor will their fire be quenched, and they will be loathsome to all mankind" (66:24). So the wicked never have peace. The outline below reflects that organization.

Theme: This is what the LORD says

I. Woes and judgments (1:1–39:8)*

II. Comfort and consolation (40:1–66:24)
   A. The sovereign Lord will rescue his people from Babylon (40:1–48:22)
      1. The incomparable Lord comes (40:1-31)
      2. The Holy One of Israel will help his people (41:1-29)
      3. The Lord will send his Servant (42:1-25)
      4. The Redeemer, the Holy One of Israel, delivers his people for his own sake (43:1-28)
      5. There is no god apart from Israel's King and Redeemer (44:1-23)
      6. The Lord will raise up Cyrus to set the exiles free (44:24–45:25)
      7. The Lord will do all he pleases (46:1-13)
      8. The Lord Almighty will destroy even Babylon (47:1-15)
      9. The Lord will refine his people for his own sake (48:1-22)
   B. The Lord's Servant will redeem his people from sin (49:1–57:21)
      1. The Lord will remember his people and send his Servant to save them (49:1-26)
      2. The Lord's Servant will ransom his disobedient people (50:1-11)

---

*Part One is treated in *Isaiah 1–39*.

3. The Lord's deliverance approaches (51:1-16)
4. The Lord calls his people to awake because he reigns (51:17–52:12)
5. The Servant of the Lord will suffer for God's people (52:13–53:12)
6. The Lord has deep compassion for his people (54:1-17)
7. Come, the Lord invites (55:1-13)
8. God delivers foreigners too (56:1-8)
9. Nothing can save the wicked (56:9–57:21)

C. The Lord promises his new Zion (Jerusalem) eternal glory (58:1–66:24)
1. Rejoice in the sincere worship of the Lord (58:1-14)
2. The Redeemer comes to Zion in spite of their iniquities (59:1-21)
3. The glory of the Lord rises upon God's people (60:1-22)
4. The Lord's Servant proclaims good news and makes righteousness spring up before all nations (61:1-11)
5. The Lord takes an oath to bless the redeemed (62:1-12)
6. The Lord also brings judgment on the wicked (63:1-6)
7. God's people pray for the salvation of the Lord (63:7–64:12)
8. The Lord will create a new Jerusalem for his people but will punish those who forsake him (65:1-25)
9. The Lord repays his enemies but brings enduring peace and comfort to the faithful (66:1-24)

PART TWO

Comfort and Consolation
(40:1–66:24)

Isaiah 39:5-8—a review
Judah will be carried off to Babylon

⁵Then Isaiah said to Hezekiah, "Hear the word of the LORD Almighty: ⁶The time will surely come when everything in your palace, and all that your fathers have stored up until this day, will be carried off to Babylon. Nothing will be left, says the LORD. ⁷And some of your descendants, your own flesh and blood who will be born to you, will be taken away, and they will become eunuchs in the palace of the king of Babylon."

⁸"The word of the LORD you have spoken is good," Hezekiah replied. For he thought, "There will be peace and security in my lifetime."

As we begin the study of the second portion of Isaiah's prophecy, we should not forget the end of the previous portion. We start our study here for two reasons. First, the prophecy of Isaiah is a whole. While we make a division between the first 39 chapters and the last 27, the entire prophecy is a unified whole. The first volume in this series indicated some of the bridges between the two major sections of the prophecy. When scholars catalogued what was found among the Dead Sea Scrolls, they found a complete copy of Isaiah. This Great Isaiah Scroll does not make a distinction between the first and second parts of Isaiah, as if the first part of Isaiah were one book and the second part

9

another. Both are included together (see introduction, page 5). Certainly the two parts of Isaiah are different, but the differences are not because two different authors wrote them. We can find several other reasons for the differences.

Second, Isaiah's announcement of the Babylonian captivity connects the first 39 chapters with the remaining chapters of his prophecy. At the end of the first half of the prophecy, God provided a deliverance from the Assyrian army, encamped at the very gates of Jerusalem (chapters 36,37). Because of God's intervention, Assyria was no longer a threat to Judah. But Hezekiah foolishly entertained the envoys of the king of Babylon and showed them everything in his palace. Unfortunately, a century and a half later Babylon would threaten Judah. God knew this and revealed it to Isaiah. Hezekiah learned it from God's prophet shortly after the envoys had left and returned to Babylon. In chapters 38 and 39, Isaiah turned the attention of his readers away from Assyria and toward the next threat, Babylon.

Isaiah's prophecy placed the dark cloud of captivity in Babylon on the distant horizon. The cloud would grow darker and gather power over the next century. Finally it would thunder against Judah about 120 years after the envoys left the palace of King Hezekiah. Who could see such a storm so far ahead in the future? By God's power, Isaiah did. Long before the events occurred, he predicted the rise of Babylon. Remember that Isaiah was the prophet of the Lord of hosts, the Holy One of Israel. It was a small thing for God to reveal to his prophet these future events. While many scholars doubt that Isaiah could predict the future, Bible-believing Christians accept the idea of a God who can do that and more.

The ascent of Babylon spelled great difficulty for Isaiah's own people. Babylon, the next ancient Near East superpower, would eventually come to carry everything in Judah away. As Isaiah predicted, Babylon would not spare even the descendants of Hezekiah. Some of the king's descendants would be taken away and would serve in the palace of the king of Babylon. The threat of captivity had real concrete meaning in Isaiah's day. The Assyrian army may have failed to destroy Jerusalem because of God's miraculous deliverance, but the Assyrians did not fail against Samaria. In 721 B.C., after a three-year siege, the Assyrians had conquered the capital city of Israel, the Northern Kingdom of God's Old Testament people. The population had been deported—taken captive. At the time of Isaiah's words to Hezekiah, the former kingdom of Israel was mostly deserted and everything of value had been taken away. When Isaiah spoke to Hezekiah, all this was still fresh in the king's mind, as well as in the minds of all his subjects. In the future, Isaiah warned, Judah would also be taken captive.

Such news was frightening. It was not some vague general doom to come; it was a real bleak, harsh, dark threat of God's law. God said it. Isaiah stamped this prophecy with the mark of authenticity, ". . . says the LORD." Hezekiah understood it and acknowledged that it was "The word of the LORD." Yet the Lord had another message—a message of comfort—for his people as they anticipated the captivity. Normally exile marked the end of a nation. It would not be so with Judah. They would return from captivity. The opening words of the next chapter trumpet the sweet good news of the gospel in the context of the law's harsh judgment.

As clearly as these prophecies have application to the historical circumstances of Judah, Isaiah looked far beyond the beginning and end of the Babylonian captivity. God granted him a look at the coming of the Great Servant of the

Lord. That Servant would end the captivity of all humanity to sin and death and would provide eternal joy and glory for his people. The prophetic vision of Isaiah sees two events far apart in time yet captures them in a single picture, just as Jesus pictured the destruction of Jerusalem and the end of the world in a single image (Matthew 24). With this in mind, we see not only Babylon and the return from captivity, but we see more—namely Christ and his work. We see beyond the return of the Jewish captives to Jerusalem; we see the deliverance of all God's people from their spiritual bondage and their entrance into the new Jerusalem above.

The sovereign Lord will rescue his people from Babylon

An introduction

40 **"Comfort, comfort my people,
        says your God.**
   **² Speak tenderly to Jerusalem,
        and proclaim to her
      that her hard service has been completed,
        that her sin has been paid for,
      that she has received from the LORD's hand
        double for all her sins.**

Not just once, "Comfort", but twice, "Comfort, comfort." So the Lord begins with a single repeated command. The command flows from the mind of God, and God himself directed it toward his messengers, who will announce the good news of his love. God intends this comfort for his people. He claims them, "my people." After all their unfaithfulness, all their rebellion, all their sins, they are still his people. God remains their God, faithful and gracious, as he promised to be: "The LORD, the LORD, the compassionate and gracious God, slow to anger, abounding in love and faithfulness, maintaining love to thousands, and forgiving wickedness, rebellion and sin" (Exodus 34:6,7).

The prose of the previous chapter disappears, and the poetry begins again. Without an introductory comment, we are in the midst of God's thought, "Comfort, comfort my people." Who should comfort them? Isaiah? Of course, but not only Isaiah. The command extends to more than just one person. In the Old Testament, God's message of comfort came through the prophets; in the New Testament, through the apostles. All who share the gospel carry out God's command to comfort his people. This command applies to all who serve as public ministers of God and all believers who share the gospel. All believers share the important task of bringing God's comfort to those who need it.

The second verse introduces us to the method by which the comfort was to be shared, "Speak." Through the means of human language, God transfers his comfort to others. The process is simple. The comfort originates with God, who reveals it in human language so that it can be extended to others by the same vehicle or means. The gospel comes in words, the means through which God extends his grace and mercy. "Speak tenderly," God directs. Speak to the heart and proclaim, or call out. Use your voice.

What is the message? God tells us exactly the content of the words he wants spoken. Three clauses identify the content of the message. First, the hard service of God's people is completed. Second, their sins have been paid for, and third, God's people have received abundant blessing from the Lord. Each of these clauses begins with *that.* All of these clauses announce an action that has already taken place. It's done, even though all these things lie in the future. Babylon had not yet become a powerful nation; Judah had not yet been carried away captive; Cyrus had not yet been born, much less issued an edict that allowed the Jews to return to Jerusalem; and certainly Jesus had not yet entered this world. The events God announced were so certain that God speaks as if they had already been completed. No doubt exists about this future.

The "hard service" of the first clause means military service and can also mean difficulty and trials. On the one hand, the promise means that the Babylonian captivity has come to end. The end of the Babylonian captivity brought comfort to God's people. On the other hand, sin and death forge chains of bondage for every sinner. Every sinner longs for the announcement that he or she is free from such bondage. Because Jesus has come, we are released from death. We are no longer slaves to sin. We are no longer locked in the dungeon because of God's wrath and anticipating an eternity of punishment in hell. Our hard service is completed, not because we have achieved release by our own effort or because we have done our time and satisfied the law. Our bondage is over because God has achieved our release through his Son, the Messiah.

The second clause announces the forgiveness of sins. The debt caused by every twisted and perverted deed committed by God's people and all humanity has been paid off. This does not mean that the 70 years of Judah's captivity have been enough to pay the debt that Judah's sins created. Judah could not atone for her own guilt or for the guilt of any other nation or people. But her sins have been paid for. If Judah could not pay the debt, how would her sins be paid for? The answer provides the reason why Isaiah's prophecy remains so important. Someone will come to pay for her sins. In chapter 53, Isaiah clearly describes how this will happen. The sins of Judah and all the world will be paid for by the vicarious suffering and death of the Servant of the Lord. "The LORD has laid on him the iniquity of us all" (53:6).

The third clause is twice as long as the other two and underscores the grace of God. Isaiah tells us that God's people receive a double portion from the hand of the Lord. The God of the covenant, Jehovah, the Savior-God, holds these blessings. They belong to the Lord. The blessings originate in the heart of God; he possesses them, and he dispenses them to his people. The people only receive them from the Lord's hand, and from his hand alone. The people do not deserve these blessings. They cannot be earned either by sacrifice or by suffering. Instead, God distributes them by free grace.

He offers a double portion. This is not a quantity measured out in two portions. The word *double* simply means that God's blessings are ample, abundant, and beyond expectations. The sins of God's people have deserved punishment, but God has offered forgiveness and eternal life instead of punishment. The apostle Paul grasped the meaning of this clause when he wrote, "But where sin increased, grace increased all the more" (Romans 5:20).

These three clauses not only identify the content of the message of God's heralds; they also provide a road map to follow through the remaining chapters of Isaiah's prophecy. The 27 chapters of the last part of Isaiah can be divided into three nine-chapter sections. The first section (chapters 40–48) focuses on the release of God's people from their captivity in Babylon and develops the thought that "her hard service has been completed." The second section (chapters 49–57) announces the coming of the Great Servant of the Lord, who will be pierced and crushed for the sins of the people. How appropriate that the center of this section and the center of the entire last portion of the prophecy is the

53rd chapter. The sins of the people have "been paid for" completely by the Redeemer. Finally, the last section (chapters 58–66) takes us to the grand results of the Messiah's great work. God's people receive magnificent blessings—a double portion—from God because of the suffering and death of the Savior.

The two verses provide an appropriate beginning to the study of the remaining chapters of Isaiah.

Here is your God!

³ A voice of one calling:
"In the desert prepare
  the way for the LORD;
make straight in the wilderness
  a highway for our God.
⁴ Every valley shall be raised up,
  every mountain and hill made low;
the rough ground shall become level,
  the rugged places a plain.
⁵ And the glory of the LORD will be revealed,
  and all mankind together will see it.
For the mouth of the LORD has spoken."

As dramatically as the first verse, Isaiah continues, "A voice of one calling." A human voice had responded to the command of God to speak comfort to his people, Jerusalem. The word *voice* appears three times in the next nine verses. The verses can be divided by the appearance of the word. God communicated his message through human speech—the means through which God works on the hearts of his people. God does not work through telepathy or inner illumination. He communicates his thoughts to humans through human words expressed by a human voice. No human knows the gospel of God by intuition or meditation. Humans learn of the love of God when messengers give voice to the gospel; God hasn't promised to work in any other way.

Seven hundred years after Isaiah wrote these words, John the Baptist appeared. Matthew, Mark, and Luke tell us that he came preaching, and all three cite this passage, identifying John the Baptist as the voice who calls. But John the Baptist was not the only voice that fulfilled this prophecy. All preachers have a similar calling to announce the good news of God's love for all the world. Finally, all believers respond to the Lord's call when they give voice to the gospel and witness to others.

The message of John the Baptist and every messenger of God remains, a message of repentance. Repent, for the kingdom of God is at hand. The prophecy pictures the Lord coming to his people from the wilderness. In preparation for his coming, the people are to prepare his way by removing all obstacles to his coming. The mountains, rough ground, and rugged places represent the natural condition of the hearts of the people; by nature all human hearts are hard as rock. The call of the gospel empowers human hearts to believe. Repentance is a turning away from sin and a trusting in the forgiveness God offers. That was John's message in the wilderness and the message of every believer who gives voice to the hope within. Through the words of the gospel, God knocks on the door of an impenitent, unbelieving heart and creates faith. The obstacles disappear when the Holy Spirit creates faith.

The picture recalls the coming of the Lord to deliver his people from the bondage of Egypt. God called Moses in the wilderness at the burning bush and went with him when he appeared before Pharaoh. The Lord came from the wilderness with Moses and brought his people out of Egypt to Mount Sinai in the wilderness. Isaiah's references here to the wilderness remind God's people that he will come again as he did that first time. Isaiah added a further thought. Just as the glory of the Lord appeared to the people of the exodus in order to lead them and assure them of his presence, so "the glory of the LORD will be revealed" once again. The same God will work deliverance. Of course, this is a poetic and prophetic picture, not a literal one. We do not look for the Lord's return in some remote wilderness, but we do wait for him, and by faith we have prepared our hearts for his coming. The picture here comes from an ancient custom of kings. An ancient king sent messengers ahead of his arrival, so that the road might be made level and smooth for the king's journey.

> ⁶ A voice says, "Cry out."
>   And I said, "What shall I cry?"
> "All men are like grass,
>   and all their glory is like the flowers of the field.
> ⁷ The grass withers and the flowers fall,
>   because the breath of the LORD blows on them.
>   Surely the people are grass.
> ⁸ The grass withers and the flowers fall,
>   but the word of our God stands forever."

The voice again. The word stands forcefully at the beginning of the verse with a command: "Cry out." This time God directs his command to a single messenger, perhaps Isaiah as a representative of all messengers. But precisely who is to cry out is left indefinite and vague. Once again the Lord appears to cover all his messengers in these verses. Every messenger of God is to be like Isaiah. The identity of the messenger disappears behind the news. The news becomes more important than the one who delivers it. Even the personality of Isaiah disappeared behind the glorious message he proclaimed. We know only a little about this prophet, but we know a great deal about his message.

The reappearance of the voice reminds us that the message of God comes to humans through a speaking voice. No one becomes a believer without the gospel. God the Holy Spirit works through the gospel as it is spoken or read. Without the Word, there is no faith; without the Word, sinners do not know of God's grace. No human mind could imagine what God has done out of undeserved love for sinners. No human could come to faith in the God of love without the gospel—the words that communicate God's love—just as no human mind could know sin except through the words of God's law (Romans 7:7). God has chosen to enter human hearts through the simple means of words. He commands his people, "Cry out"—preach, witness, communicate, proclaim—and he promises to work through the words of their witnessing.

The messenger asks an important question: "What shall I cry?" What follows defines a specific message—a message of law and gospel. The law comes first and destroys all human pride. Walt Whitman, the poet of *Leaves of Grass*, may have relished the idea that all men are grass, but these words are far from his belief in democratic equality. The prophet's message leaves no human glory standing before God's great majesty and power. Twice we see the word *all*. All humans and all human achievements are included. That message devastates the human mind with its pride. All of us want to consider ourselves important, and we desire to do something important. Our history books record the events of human achievement. The monuments of the ages stand as testimony to great people as surely as the arts perpetuate the thoughts and lives of significant people. But all humans are like grass, and every achievement—all their glory—is nothing more than the blossom of a flower, which blooms beautifully but soon drops its petals and dies.

The prophet repeats the thought in these verses so there is no mistake about God's message. In the face of the Lord's hot breath, both the people, who are grass, and their achievements, which are flowers, wither and fall. No matter what humans may accomplish, death still stalks every last one of us and will eventually pounce on us all and devour us. We are not to place our hopes and dreams on anything human, no matter how glorious it seems. The phrase "the breath of the LORD" perhaps recalled the hot dry winds that frequently blew across Palestine from the desert. In a short time such a hot, persistent wind could dry up everything and make life in Jerusalem miserable.

The passage sets all human thought and effort on one side and the Word of the Lord on the other. We cannot escape the idea of communication in these verses; it is the *Word* of our God that stands. *Word* corresponds very well with the word *voice* in this section. The Word of God communicates God's wrath against sin and his boundless love for all humans—law and gospel. The message is the Word of *our* God. Believers recognize their own sin and the grace of God. They confess that God has rescued them from their bondage of sin and death. All that is divine and belongs to God surpasses all that is human. Everything human fades and disappears; all that comes from God in his Word endures for all time. Finally, when the Lord returns, the earth and all that is within it will be destroyed (2 Peter 3:10). The Word of the Lord will survive even that catastrophe. It is permanent and enduring.

> [9] **You who bring good tidings to Zion,**
> **go up on a high mountain.**

> You who bring good tidings to Jerusalem,
>   lift up your voice with a shout,
> lift it up, do not be afraid;
>   say to the towns of Judah,
>   "Here is your God!"
> ¹⁰ See, the Sovereign LORD comes with power,
>   and his arm rules for him.
> See, his reward is with him,
>   and his recompense accompanies him.
> ¹¹ He tends his flock like a shepherd:
>   He gathers the lambs in his arms
> and carries them close to his heart;
>   he gently leads those that have young.

The word *voice* appears for the third time but this time not as the first word of the verse. Two ideas receive emphasis before we read the word *voice*. First, the Word of God rises far above anything human. It deserves to be proclaimed from the highest mountain. God directs the messengers who possess the "word of our God" (verse 8) to go up to a high place where their message can be broadcast to the widest audience. Second, the message they were to proclaim is "good tidings." This is the gospel—the good news of God's tender love for his people. In the verses to follow, we will learn more about that good news.

God intends the "good tidings" for his people—for Zion and Jerusalem. The messengers of God are to use their voices to proclaim the gospel to these people. The messengers are encouraged not to be fearful; the news is too wonderful and important. They are not to whisper it but to shout it from the high mountains. The people must hear the message; God works in human hearts through it.

If the breath of the Lord caused the grass and flowers of humanity to wither, why would anyone want to hear that the Lord is coming? The message is clear, "Here is your God!" But if he comes with fierce, hot judgment, humans will want to hide from him. People will call for the hills to cover them rather than face the Lord. Why would anyone want to rejoice and revel at his coming? We find the answer in the law and the gospel. Those who reject God will fear his coming, but those who believe will anticipate his coming and prepare for it, will actually look forward to it joyfully. The Lord's good news works this change, for the good news reveals not God's anger against sin and the sinner— that's the message of the law—but his compassionate and gracious heart. Both law and gospel reveal the same God. The law reveals him as fierce in judgment. The gospel reveals him as gracious and loving.

Our eyes are to look to God and see his coming. What do we see? The Sovereign Lord, that is, the powerful, gracious, and faithful God of the covenant. He controls all things and comes in power. He comes leading the exiles back home from their captivity. He leads them in triumphant procession. And he has something with him—a reward. What he has is further described as a "recompense." Both words indicate something that has been earned by the performance of some work. This reward is not what humans have stored up in God's mind or heart because of their many good deeds. Luther suggests, "Though we should all our life go about attempting to please God, we should be nothing but worms in view of his majesty" (*Luther's Works* [LW], American Edition, Volume 17, page 18). The entire Scripture announces that human works do not earn God's reward. The previous section, which identified human glory as nothing but a temporary flower, will not allow us to say that the Sovereign Lord appears with the rewards earned by any humans. No, he comes with rich blessings, which he will freely give to his people. They will no longer have the misfortune, desolation, shame, pain, and tears they deserve because of their rebellion and sin.

God clearly brings this reward with him. The reward is the result of the work that God himself performed. God has obtained the reward by the suffering, death, and resurrection of his own Son. Through that work God has achieved forgiveness of sins, eternal life, and deliverance from everything that would separate his people from him. Blood bought this reward, and God achieved it by his own work. Such blessings no human could achieve. God appears in this portrait ready to dispense these blessings to his people.

Because of his work, God has claimed us as his own, and by grace and the power of the Holy Spirit, we surround this glorious and powerful Lord as sheep surround a shepherd. As God's people, we are familiar with the picture of the shepherd tenderly caring for his flock. Jesus made use of the image (John 10), so did others like David (Psalm 23) and Ezekiel (Ezekiel 34). The powerful Lord cares for his people. He places the lambs, weak and newly born, in the folds of his garment close to his heart. Those who have young need his special care to lead them. It is no wonder that this message, these good tidings, should be proclaimed from the mountains for all to hear.

To whom will you compare God?

> [12] Who has measured the waters in the hollow of his hand,
>   or with the breadth of his hand marked off the heavens?
> Who has held the dust of the earth in a basket,
>   or weighed the mountains on the scales
>   and the hills in a balance?
> [13] Who has understood the mind of the LORD,
>   or instructed him as his counselor?
> [14] Whom did the LORD consult to enlighten him,
>   and who taught him the right way?

> **Who was it that taught him knowledge**
>> **or showed him the path of understanding?**
> [15] **Surely the nations are like a drop in a bucket;**
>> **they are regarded as dust on the scales;**
>> **he weighs the islands as though they were fine dust.**
> [16] **Lebanon is not sufficient for altar fires,**
>> **nor its animals enough for burnt offerings.**
> [17] **Before him all the nations are as nothing;**
>> **they are regarded by him as worthless**
>> **and less than nothing.**

Those who bring good tidings to Zion were to say, "Here is your God!" (verse 9). The vision of the Lord we saw in the previous verses was powerful, gracious, and tender. The remaining sections of the chapter continue to clarify the vision of the Lord. Isaiah begins with a series of rhetorical questions, all of which are intended to demonstrate God's greatness. God is the almighty creator of the universe. His power in creating the universe surpasses anything any human could imagine. Who can even measure the waters of the seas or the vastness of space? Contemporary measurement techniques are more sophisticated than those in Isaiah's day, but even light-years cannot measure the heavens, and we only estimate the volume of the oceans. Weighing the earth or its hills and mountains is a mathematical exercise that will yield an estimate—the best guess of science. Still only God knows for sure. He reigns all powerful, and we cannot even accurately measure what his power has created.

God knows all things. Isaiah asks who served as God's consultant. The answer is obvious. No one had more knowledge than God. The most intelligent human being may be acclaimed by his or her society for the great contributions made to some field of knowledge. But we measure such greatness only by comparison with other humans, not by comparison with the omniscience of God. Here is your God—the all-powerful and all-knowing Creator. These simple questions present profound truth in a forceful and dramatic way. The answers are inescapable and humbling.

Isaiah next makes a comparison. We measure nations and people differently than God does. To him, all the nations are nothing but a "drop in a bucket." That doesn't mean God thinks the nations are unimportant and worthless. His love for the world moved him to send his Son so that all who believe in him would have everlasting life (John 3:16). Here Isaiah presents the comparison in order to remove human pride and arrogance. Entire nations amount to nothing more than dust on the scales. The coastal regions of the Mediterranean—the islands—amount to nothing more than fine dust.

What could nations offer to God that would influence him? What sacrifice could any human give God that would cause him to smile? What does God need from any human or from all of them together? In the Old Testament, Lebanon was known for its timber; Solomon imported its cedars for the temple and his other building projects. Even if all the forests of Lebanon could be burned as an altar fire, it is not enough for God. If you offer all the animals of Lebanon as a sacrifice, it is nothing. The conclusion is clear, and Isaiah emphasized the truth with three terms. Before the almighty and all-knowing God, the nations are "nothing," "worthless," and "less than nothing."

> **[18] To whom, then, will you compare God?**
> **What image will you compare him to?**
> **[19] As for an idol, a craftsman casts it,**
> **and a goldsmith overlays it with gold**
> **and fashions silver chains for it.**
> **[20] A man too poor to present such an offering**
> **selects wood that will not rot.**

He looks for a skilled craftsman
to set up an idol that will not topple.

God reveals himself in this chapter as a great conqueror who has defeated his enemies, coming to his people with the blessings he has earned. In addition, he reveals himself as a tender shepherd who cares for his flock. With the questions in the previous section, God asserts that he is all powerful and all knowing. These important truths concerning God come from God himself. Because God is so much greater than human imagination, speculation, or thought, all information about God must come from God himself. In this chapter God also pictures himself as one ready to tell his creatures about himself. He reveals the content of the words of comfort he commanded in the opening verse. His messengers had voices to speak good tidings.

Without the aid of God's revelation—his Word—the human mind can only grasp some of God's invisible qualities, that is, his eternal power and divine nature (Romans 1:20). Those things humans can perceive by looking at the magnificent created world. But the natural human mind remains limited and also perverted by sin. Left to itself without the Word of God, humanity has fashioned God in the form of idols. In the First Commandment, God has expressly forbidden his people from using graven images, but that did not prevent them from creating a golden calf in the wilderness any more than it prevents the creation of false gods today. The perversity of the human mind, because of sin, drags worship of God away from his revealed Word to the imagination of the human mind and heart.

Look at what has happened. Isaiah takes us on a trip to see how idols are made. Craftsmen cast images, overlay them with gold, and decorate them with silver chains, perhaps so that their creations would not topple over. The precious metals and the care in creating the idol reveal deep devotion. Those who worship idols sacrifice for the gods they worship. Isaiah asks us to consider the poor. Even though a poor man cannot create a god as exquisite as that made of gold and silver, nevertheless he will carefully spend time selecting the best materials he can and hire a skilled craftsman to fashion his god. For the poor man, his religion requires sacrifice and devotion.

Humans through the centuries have fashioned God with their limited imaginations. In our own world, we do not create idols as Isaiah describes in these verses. Yet every time humans imagine God apart from his revelation, they create a false god—an idol. We fashion God when we teach our own opinions; we make our own idols. The gods of our contemporary world are no different in essence from the gods of the ancient world. They differ only in their outward forms. The human mind wants to create a god that rewards loving effort, kind words, and noble thoughts. The god that so many fashion today appears as a tolerant old grandfather in the sky who smiles when we do good. He forgets and excuses our moral lapses. He accepts everyone and embraces them in his fatherly arms. He does not threaten punishment for anyone except the most heinous criminal. All too many people conclude that God will not punish so many who are guilty of the same or similar sins. That's an idol as surely as the images of Baal or Dagon. Whenever we create a god who can be appeased by human behavior, we have created a god different from the one Isaiah and all the other writers of the Scriptures describe. We have fashioned a god in our image and molded him to be the way we want him to be.

²¹ Do you not know?
Have you not heard?

> Has it not been told you from the beginning?
>> Have you not understood since the earth was founded?
> [22] He sits enthroned above the circle of the earth,
>> and its people are like grasshoppers.
> He stretches out the heavens like a canopy,
>> and spreads them out like a tent to live in.
> [23] He brings princes to naught
>> and reduces the rulers of this world to nothing.
> [24] No sooner are they planted,
>> no sooner are they sown,
>> no sooner do they take root in the ground,
> than he blows on them and they wither,
>> and a whirlwind sweeps them away like chaff.

The four questions of verse 21 are blunt challenges to all who create God in their own image and make idols. God has not hidden himself. He has revealed himself from the beginning. He talked with Adam and Eve in the garden. After they sinned, he continued to speak to them and revealed the promise of a Savior to come. He spoke to Noah before and after the destruction of the sinful world by the flood. Moses brought God's revelation down from the mountain and wrote the first five books of the Bible. God made sure that what Moses and later writers wrote was *his* Word, not their own speculation. God inspired them, giving them the very words they were to write. The apostle Paul makes that point: "We speak, not in words taught us by human wisdom but in words taught by the Spirit" (1 Corinthians 2:13).

The truth has always been available. But the human mind has been so darkened by sin that it cannot imagine God as he is. Isaiah pictures God as the Creator and Ruler of the world. God sits high above the created world. He stretched out the heavens as easily as one would pitch a tent. God is not created but uncreated and eternal, without beginning and without end. He is separate and different from the world he created. He is holy, infinite, perfect, and changeless. Humans are like so many grasshoppers. Because of sin, they are nothing like God. They are finite, temporal, imperfect, subject to changes of all kinds, and mortal. What arrogance for finite creatures to fashion God! If we want to know about God, we must humbly listen to what he tells us.

God takes us and his prophet one step further. Even the great leaders of the world are nothing compared to God. The princes and rulers of this world come under the control of the God of the heavens. He controls their history. God exists far above the world he created; he rules the universe as a powerful monarch above all creation. Humans are at best a swarm of grasshoppers. Their leaders, princes, and rulers are small and insignificant compared to God, who controls the course of history. This God is very different from the old grandfather in the sky. When humans attempt to penetrate spiritual reality without God's revelation, they are doomed to create gods in their own images.

> 25 **"To whom will you compare me?**
> **Or who is my equal?" says the Holy One.**
> 26 **Lift your eyes and look to the heavens:**
> **Who created all these?**
> **He who brings out the starry host one by one,**
> **and calls them each by name.**
> **Because of his great power and mighty strength,**
> **not one of them is missing.**

Isaiah returns to the question he first raised in verse 18, but now it is a question God himself asks. God, the Holy One who is high above and separate, has always wanted his creatures to know who he is and what he has done. God now instructs men and women in the mysteries of his love for the world and its inhabitants. The messengers were

29

encouraged to say, "Here is your God!" (verse 9). What follows is a wonderful revelation of the Lord God of heaven.

First, we are directed to look to the heavens and the stars. We know the answer to the question "Who created all these?" God did, of course, but God did not simply create the world and then let it continue on its own power. He continues to care for the created world. God controls the motion of the stars of heaven. Astronomy studies the movements of the stars in the vast expanse of the universe, but God determines the movement. We talk of galaxies and planets; God controls them all. He controls the movement of the stars as a general would control his army. But God does not control them with impersonal detachment. He knows each heavenly body by name. What a contrast to those who think that the stars control their destinies and who consult their horoscopes to discover what life will bring them. God controls the stars and us; the orbits of the planets and stars do not control us.

Look up at the sky on some clear night. A look into the starry sky humbles us. Then remember that the stars of heaven have God's personal attention; not one is missing without his knowledge. He calls them all by name, as a father would call his children by name. So powerful, vast, and loving is our God.

> ²⁷ **Why do you say, O Jacob,**
> **and complain, O Israel,**
> **"My way is hidden from the LORD;**
> **my cause is disregarded by my God"?**
> ²⁸ **Do you not know?**
> **Have you not heard?**
> **The LORD is the everlasting God,**
> **the Creator of the ends of the earth.**
> **He will not grow tired or weary,**
> **and his understanding no one can fathom.**

²⁹ **He gives strength to the weary**
    and increases the power of the weak.
³⁰ **Even youths grow tired and weary,**
    and young men stumble and fall;
³¹ **but those who hope in the LORD**
    will renew their strength.
  They will soar on wings like eagles;
    they will run and not grow weary,
    they will walk and not be faint.

All too often we fail to depend on God's power and tender interest in the affairs of his created world. God's people are not beyond complaining that such a powerful and boundless God has forgotten them. Jacob and Israel are names for God's people that recall the love of God and the origins of God's Old Testament people. God cared for Jacob, blessed him, and protected him. God wrestled with him and changed his name to Israel. Then God repeated the promise that the Savior would come through his descendants. All this God did out of grace and mercy. Jacob did not deserve any of it. When Jacob's descendants became the nation of Israel and left Egypt, God continued to care for them. God marked every phase of their history with his gracious care.

In view of the way God cares for the stars of heaven and in view of the care God had demonstrated in the past for his people, their complaints were groundless. If God can call the stars by name, he certainly could care for his people. If God had demonstrated such love for the ancestor of his people, he would continue to care for them. God had pledged himself to his people; he had bound himself to them by promise. No matter what difficulties they faced, he was powerful enough to care for them. He loved them too much to abandon them.

This message was important for the Jews who would be led away captive by the Babylonians. In the midst of their tears and heartache, God wanted them to remember that he was in control and continued to love them. The stars proved it as well as their own history. The lesson is just as important for us to remember. We are God's people by faith in Jesus Christ, but we are no less prone to complain when things go badly. God loves us not just when all goes well. He loves us always. He has his own reason for allowing trouble, pain, and tears into our lives. Remember that he is almighty and all knowing. We are not. We can trust him to do the best for us. He loves us too much to do anything less.

Once again, two questions appear: "Do you not know? Have you not heard?" The questions direct us back to what God reveals about himself in the Scriptures. That's where we can discover who God is. There God reveals himself as "the LORD," Jehovah, the God of free and faithful grace. That name reappears in these verses after a short absence. (That special name for God was last used in verse 14.) This covenant-God reveals himself to be the true God. "The LORD is the everlasting God."

The Lord reveals four important truths about himself. First, he is the Creator. He has unlimited power and uses that power for the benefit of his creatures. He gave them life and provided a beautiful world in which to live. Second, he does not become tired or weary. His power was not exhausted by creation nor does he grow tired with the continuous care of the world he called into existence. Third, he is beyond human ability to grasp and understand. He is holy. Humans know there is a god; the psalmist says, "The fool says in his heart, 'There is no God'" (Psalm 53:1). But the full truth about God lies beyond our empirical investigation. God must reveal himself if we are to know anything about him beyond the fact that he exists and he is great.

Fourth, God gives strength to the weary and weak. God turns himself toward his creatures. He gives blessings to them out of love for them.

Humans are much different. We are creatures, not the Creator. We grow weary and weak. We can understand some things, but we are often confused and ignorant. We must learn; God knows all things. Without the Lord, the best humans will stumble and fall. The young appear to be tireless and energetic; yet they too will certainly grow weary and stumble. To such limited creatures, God promises to give strength.

How can we receive such a gift from the Lord? "Those who hope in the LORD will renew their strength." Faith in the Lord brings this strength. When we rely on human strength, we will stumble. When we trust in the Lord for strength, he gives it. Not only will believers receive strength; they will renew their strength. They will arise from the ashes of grief and suffering to run and walk again. Believers are pictured as eagles soaring in the blue sky. Eagles ride the air currents as they stretch out their wings and soar. God promises to be the wind beneath the wings of his people. What wonderful comfort for all "who hope in the LORD"! The entire life of God's people—their walking, running, and soaring—is filled with the boundless and tireless strength of God. Even in death, they mount on eagle's wings and soar to God in heaven, where God gives them joy forever.

The Lord proves that he is superior to the idols of the nations

41 "Be silent before me, you islands!
Let the nations renew their strength!
Let them come forward and speak;
let us meet together at the place of judgment.

² **"Who has stirred up one from the east,**
   calling him in righteousness to his service?
He hands nations over to him
   and subdues kings before him.
He turns them to dust with his sword,
   to windblown chaff with his bow.
³ **He pursues them and moves on unscathed,**
   by a path his feet have not traveled before.
⁴ **Who has done this and carried it through,**
   calling forth the generations from the beginning?
I, the LORD—with the first of them
   and with the last—I am he."

The opening verses of this chapter turn our attention away from "those who hope in the LORD" (40:31) to the nations and islands who worship idols. The Lord addresses these nations, suggesting that they summon all their strength and then come before him. He has an important issue to discuss with all those who worship idols. God has commissioned Isaiah to serve as recording secretary of the proceedings. The readers of Isaiah's record are to listen, learn, and find comfort. The scene appears to be some kind of court for settling differences. The Lord's first words are like the words of a presiding judge calling the court to order. "Be silent!" Then the Lord invites the nations to present their arguments in this place of debate and judgment. The evidence will speak for itself, or God will make his arguments and clearly present his case. Although he invites the nations to present their case, they never present an argument. They do speak but only to one another. God's truth is never in doubt; no human argument is strong enough to stand before God's absolute truth.

Something has happened that requires discussion, debate, and truthful analysis. Someone has arisen in the east. He appears as a conqueror who subdues kings and turns the swords and bows of his enemies to dust and chaff.

He triumphs and gains victory as he carries out campaigns against his enemies. Who is this conqueror? At first, the answer seems clouded in some mystery. A more important question must be answered first.

Before we know the identity of this conqueror, God asks, "Who has stirred up one from the east?" In other words, who's responsible? The Lord answers that question emphatically: "I, the LORD . . . I am he." He is "the LORD," that is, the God of the covenant, Jehovah, the God of free and faithful grace. He revealed himself to Moses as "I AM" (Exodus 3:14). He is absolute being, who always is. At no time can we say that God was, that is, that his time has passed; he existed in the past, but he has not stopped being who he is. Nor can we say that God is not yet what he will be. He will be the same in the future as he is today and as he was in Isaiah's day. He is. He always is and can never be subject to the cycle of time he himself has created. He is the first—the One who created the first humans. He is the last—the One who will be when the last humans cease to be. Like Isaiah, the apostle John served as a recording secretary for this same Lord. John heard him say, "I am the Alpha and the Omega, the First and the Last, the Beginning and the End" (Revelation 22:13). This God is free to do whatever he chooses; he is I AM, the Lord of all history—the first and the last. Not only is he free to do whatever he chooses, but he remains the same—constant and sure through every uncertainty.

This Lord claims responsibility for calling forth the conqueror, the "one from the east." Who is this one? Some suggest Christ; some, Abraham; but the clearest answer comes later in Isaiah. In this chapter, the conqueror remains identified by no more than the description of the opening verses, but later God will clearly identify him as

Cyrus (44:28; 45:1). Cyrus, known as Cyrus the Great, founded the Persian Empire and became ruler of Persia in about 559 B.C. Quickly, he conquered the surrounding nations and conquered Babylon in 539 B.C.

The debate, which Isaiah records here, seems to take place when Cyrus had already achieved several conquests, perhaps the victory over the Medes (549 B.C.) and Lydia (546 B.C.). All these events occurred about 150 years after the time in which Isaiah lived and wrote. When Isaiah wrote (about 700 B.C.), Babylon had not yet become a Mideastern superpower. How could Isaiah know about Cyrus, who would defeat the Babylonians? Because many Bible scholars think it was impossible for Isaiah to know about Cyrus, they suggest that someone other than Isaiah wrote the entire last part of the prophecy—someone who lived much later and thereby knew of Cyrus. But we must not bring God down to our level and expect that he can do only what we think. Because the Lord is the eternal I AM, time does not mean to him what it means to his creatures. God transported Isaiah to some point in time far into the future and revealed these events to him. If we believe that the Holy Spirit gave the apostle John such a vision of the future, it is not difficult to believe that the same Spirit gave Isaiah a similar opportunity.

God had a very important reason for revealing the coming of Cyrus to Isaiah and to the people of Isaiah's day. The Lord had clearly told King Hezekiah that the Babylonians would come to destroy Jerusalem and carry Judah off into captivity. But that was not the end of the story. Judah would not disappear into the masses of Semitic people and the chaos of conquest and defeat. A remnant would return from captivity and rebuild Jerusalem and Judah. The announcement of the coming of Cyrus was intended to comfort God's people before and during their captivity in Babylon. These promises became bright lights of hope in the dark days of captivity. God revealed these proceedings for the benefit of his people.

The history books of the world are filled with stories of the great contributions of many men and women. Why does Cyrus deserve to be included in God's Word? Why not also Julius Caesar, Lord Admiral Nelson, George Washington, Mao Tse-tung, or the thousands of others who are noted in the record of human history? God asks the question "Who has stirred up one from the east?" God also identifies the reason for calling up this conqueror: The Lord had called him "in righteousness to his service."

Righteousness characterizes God's faithfulness toward his people in accomplishing their deliverance and in destroying their enemies. Cyrus had a special role in carrying out God's plans for his people. God made a promise that the Messiah would come, but he had not yet appeared in Isaiah's day. He would not appear even in the future days of the Babylonian captivity. The righteous plan of God meant deliverance for the whole world and required some champion or conqueror. Even if Cyrus did not understand fully, God chose him to play a role in bringing the Savior into the world. Judah was released from captivity. A remnant returned to Palestine. Cyrus issued the edict that released Judah from bondage. Centuries later the Messiah was born of the house of David, in David's royal city, Bethlehem. Other world leaders may be important, but none of them had the same direct impact on the history of God's plan to save a world of sinners.

> **⁵ The islands have seen it and fear;**
> **the ends of the earth tremble.**

> **They approach and come forward;**
> 6   **each helps the other**
>   **and says to his brother, "Be strong!"**
> 7 **The craftsman encourages the goldsmith,**
>   **and he who smooths with the hammer**
>   **spurs on him who strikes the anvil.**
> **He says of the welding, "It is good."**
> **He nails down the idol so it will not topple.**

According to the vision God gave to Isaiah, the conqueror has begun his campaigns and already defeated kings and nations. What is the reaction to this development? First, Isaiah tells us that the nations tremble at the conqueror's approach and prepare to resist. The nations adopt three strategies for resisting him. First, they come together to help one another. Second, they encourage one another to be strong; third, they create idols.

The enemies of God's purposes speak in these verses, but they do not speak to the Lord in his place of judgment. Instead, they speak to one another. First they say, "Be strong!" These words are spoken by humans to humans; they are little more than wishful thinking. The words have no underlying support and do not come from any position of strength. They come from weak, fearful humans who face difficult circumstances together. One human tells another; the encouragement rises to nothing more than a pep talk. Keep these words in mind when reading the encouragement God gives to his people. The contrast is important.

We find another interesting contrast in the other words spoken by the unbelieving nations. They encourage their craftsmen to create idols. These idols appear to be bigger and better gods that they hope will help them resist the coming of the conqueror. The Lord God appeared weak and ineffective. Of course, the idol has to be nailed down so that it won't topple over. When the craftsmen finish their work, they pronounce the gods they created "good." If we remember the first chapters of Genesis, we remember that God pronounced his creation "good." What irony that the human creatures God has created should use the same evaluation, "It is good," for their false gods. The words represent a rejection of the Lord, who is the first and the last, and reveal a failure to seek him as they face difficulty. They do not turn to the Lord but remain hardened in their unbelief.

> [8] **"But you, O Israel, my servant,**
>   **Jacob, whom I have chosen,**
>   **you descendants of Abraham my friend,**
> [9] **I took you from the ends of the earth,**
>   **from its farthest corners I called you.**
>   **I said, 'You are my servant';**
>   **I have chosen you and have not rejected you.**
> [10] **So do not fear, for I am with you;**
>   **do not be dismayed, for I am your God.**
>   **I will strengthen you and help you;**
>   **I will uphold you with my righteous right hand.**

Isaiah shifts our attention away from the unbelieving world to God's people, "But you . . ." God's people also saw what the nations saw. They also noted the victories of the conqueror and, no doubt, were also filled with fear. But the Lord Jehovah desired to comfort his people and addressed them in the most tender way. God called his people, "Israel, my servant, Jacob, whom I have chosen, you descendants of Abraham my friend."

Each of these terms is important. When God calls his people "Israel" and "Jacob," he takes them back to their origins. God's people became known as Israel, the name God gave Jacob when he reissued his promises to Jacob at the Jabbok (Genesis 32:22-30). This special nation had become God's special servant because of God's choice. From the very beginning, God had special plans for this nation. The Messiah would come into the world through them. God describes the nation as the "descendants of Abraham my friend." That designation took these people back even further to the very father of the nation. Abraham was God's special and intimate friend. God chose Abraham and made many remarkable promises to his dear friend. The deep love God had for Abraham extended to all Abraham's descendants.

So no matter what these people saw in the world, they were to remember God's grace toward them. And it was grace. Personally, Abraham was no better than any other ancient man. He was great because God chose him. God made him the father of believers. These verses so clearly indicate that God actively made these people his own. "I took you. . . . I called you. I said . . . 'I have chosen you and have not rejected you.'" All this emphasizes God's grace, undeserved and free, toward sinful and fearful humans.

Verse 10 piles comfort upon comfort. It begins with words we so frequently hear in the Scriptures: "Do not fear." As God's people endured their captivity, they could easily despair. They might look around anxiously, wondering what peril or threat was next. God dispels their fear with the promise that he is with them and is their God, that is, he is next to them and pledges to remain with them as a powerful source of help. How different these words are from the words of encouragement that the nations spoke to one another in verse 6. There one human being encouraged another human being to be strong in the face of difficulty. But these words are spoken to humans by God. He can actually do something about their situation. This God promises to strengthen, help, and uphold his people. Notice how the comfort piles up.

The final words emphasize and underscore the comfort. God says he will do all this with his "righteous right hand." The right hand represents power and strength. God's powerful hand is righteous. *Righteous* means "right, correct, straight, appropriate, and proper." In righteousness God had determined to bring about the deliverance of all humanity from sin, death, and hell. He had promised to do so and would remain faithful to all those promises. God would remain righteous—right, true, straight—in carrying out the details of that promised deliverance. His people could depend on his righteousness to do what was necessary to fulfill all his promises. On the other hand, those who do not know the Lord can expect quite another thing from his righteous right hand. For them God's righteousness will bring judgment and punishment.

As events unfolded in the dark days of captivity, the generations after Isaiah could return to these words and find comfort. God had not deserted them. They would return from captivity, and God would fulfill all the promises he had made to his dear friend Abraham. They need not fear or be anxious about anything at all.

The terms of these verses, of course, apply to God's Old Testament people, but they also apply to God's people of all time. All believers are descendants of Abraham by virtue of their faith in the God of Abraham. When God directed Abraham to look up to the stars and count the great number of his descendants, God had more in mind than the little nation of Israel. He had all believers in mind, as the apostle Paul says so clearly, "Understand, then, that those who believe are children of Abraham" (Galatians 3:7).

With that in mind, any Christian can read these words and find rich comfort. Believers can turn to the Lord for comfort, knowing that the Lord stands behind these words. They are not the words of one human to another—a pep talk in the face of danger or difficulty. They are the words of the almighty Lord Jehovah—the first and the last—who desires to comfort his people in all their difficulties.

> [11]**"All who rage against you**
>   **will surely be ashamed and disgraced;**
>   **those who oppose you**
>   **will be as nothing and perish.**
> [12] **Though you search for your enemies,**
>   **you will not find them.**
>   **Those who wage war against you**
>   **will be as nothing at all.**
> [13] **For I am the LORD, your God,**
>   **who takes hold of your right hand**
>   **and says to you, Do not fear;**
>   **I will help you.**

When God's people worry about their enemies, God promises that the enemies will all disappear. The same righteousness that has saved God's faithful will destroy the unfaithful. They will become "as nothing and perish." Even if God's people look about anxiously for the next enemy to appear, no enemy appears on the horizon. They are zeros, less than nothing, ciphers. They simply do not exist.

On what ground does such comfort rest? It rests securely on the Lord Jehovah himself. We have seen this Lord described in the previous chapter: "He sits enthroned above the circle of the earth, and its people are like grasshoppers. He stretches out the heavens like a canopy, and spreads them out like a tent to live in" (verse 22). Affection for his people fills the heart of this powerful Lord. He has taken them by the hand and promised to help them. That is the foundation of all the comfort God proclaims in his Word. When he directs his prophets to comfort his people (40:1), he does not whisper empty words. He has the power to help. He stands behind the words of comfort with power, righteousness, and faithful love. All these things and more are tied to his name—Jehovah, the LORD, the God of free and faithful grace. His comfort is not just so many words.

> ¹⁴ **Do not be afraid, O worm Jacob,**
> **O little Israel,**
> **for I myself will help you," declares the LORD,**
> **your Redeemer, the Holy One of Israel.**

This verse is a part of the larger section, but it deserves a special comment because of three things. First, God's people are described with the words *worm* and *little*. Compared to the events and personalities of world history, God's people were little. Next to Cyrus and the great Persian Empire, they were insignificant. They were a little nation that could easily be consumed by the surrounding empires, as robins snatch worms from the ground. Earlier God described his people as "Israel" and "Jacob" and identified them as his servants. The people of God become God's servants by grace, because God has chosen them and uses them for his own purposes. Describing them as "worms" and "little" here provides a lesson in humility. Without God, Israel was weak and helpless. The encouragement not to fear could not be based on who these people were but solely on who God was and is.

That brings us to the second reason for singling out this verse. God is described as the "Redeemer" of Israel. We use that term so much that we sometimes do not understand its deep significance. In ancient Israel, a redeemer was someone who was responsible to help a relative. For example, if a person sold a piece of land because he had become poor, his nearest relative could redeem, or repurchase, the land. If someone had become so poor that he had to sell himself as a slave, he could be redeemed, or bought, from his bondage (see Leviticus 25).

The word *Redeemer* pictures God, the Lord Jehovah, as the kinsman-redeemer who would rescue his dear people, the descendants of his friend Abraham, from their helpless situation. God had redeemed his people from their bondage in Egypt. They could not have escaped by themselves, but he redeemed them. He would rescue them from their captivity in Babylon and bring them back to their homeland. Now he promises to redeem them from a greater bondage, the bondage of their souls to sin.

The third reason this verse draws special attention is the appearance of the term "Holy One of Israel." This name for God is a favorite of Isaiah. He uses it often throughout his prophecy. The name takes us back to the vision of the Lord in Isaiah chapter 6, in which the seraphim call to one another, "Holy, holy, holy is the LORD Almighty" (verse 3). The use of this special name for God throughout the prophecy provides one indication that one author composed both major sections, chapters 1 to 39 and chapters 40 to 66.

> ¹⁵ **"See, I will make you into a threshing sledge,**
>   **new and sharp, with many teeth.**
> **You will thresh the mountains and crush them,**
>   **and reduce the hills to chaff.**
> ¹⁶ **You will winnow them, the wind will pick them up,**
>   **and a gale will blow them away.**
> **But you will rejoice in the LORD**
>   **and glory in the Holy One of Israel.**

The Holy One of Israel provides comfort for his people of all time. But he is holy—separate, perfect, and different from all that is human. He is the opposite of all that is sinful, and he destroys all that is sinful as surely as any antibacterial drug destroys germs. God has chosen his people and sanctified them, that is, made them holy. They are washed by the blood of the Lamb, which cleanses them of every sin (1 John 1:7). Such cleansing is for all, but only those who believe receive its gracious blessings. Those who do not believe retain sin, and God destroys them as surely as drugs attack infection. An antibacterial drug that does not destroy bacteria ceases to be an antibacterial drug. A holy God who does not destroy sin ceases to be a holy God. At the same time, the antibacterial drug destroys bacteria in order to save the body. So a holy God has as his ultimate purpose the health and welfare of his people.

God will make his people the instrument of his judgment. God's people will become like a threshing sledge with sharp metal teeth. They will overcome all opposition since opposition to God's people is opposition to God himself. Even the mountains and hills will pose no difficulty. All who oppose God and his truth will become like so much chaff that the wind drives away. Those who strive against God, his people, and his truth will become nothing. Of course, at times it appears that just the opposite happens. Christians are hunted, ridiculed, persecuted, and appear like little worms doomed to be the prey of powerful unbelievers. But it is not so. It only appears so. The truth is different. Rejoice in the Lord. The holy God will see to it that all who oppose him and his people will come to nothing.

> [17] "The poor and needy search for water,
>   but there is none;
>   their tongues are parched with thirst.
>   But I the LORD will answer them;
>   I, the God of Israel, will not forsake them.
> [18] I will make rivers flow on barren heights,
>   and springs within the valleys.
>   I will turn the desert into pools of water,
>   and the parched ground into springs.

45

¹⁹ **I will put in the desert**
the cedar and the acacia, the myrtle and the olive.
I will set pines in the wasteland,
the fir and the cypress together,
²⁰ **so that people may see and know,**
may consider and understand,
that the hand of the LORD has done this,
that the Holy One of Israel has created it.

When God's people rejoice, it does not mean that they will never experience difficulty. These verses present God's people experiencing the difficulty of their captivity. The picture takes us over 150 years into the future. The Jerusalem of Isaiah's day had escaped the Assyrian army, which had laid siege to the city. God had delivered them by breaking the power of the Assyrian army; in one night the angel of the Lord killed 185,000 enemy soldiers (Isaiah 37:36,37). But the Babylonian captivity would come about 120 years later. In that captivity, God's people would be in a desperate condition—poor, needy, thirsty, lonely. They would find no relief.

But relief comes from God. Just as God had delivered his people in their bondage to Egypt centuries earlier, he would hear their prayers and deliver them from Babylon. The Lord would send them into captivity to train them and to purify them. In all ages, God sends difficulties to his people so that he might train them, purify them, and teach them to rely on him completely. He does not forsake his people, and he pledges the same in these words. In his own time, God will relieve his people.

God pictures the relief he sends to his people as a wonderful oasis in the desert. He turns the desert into pools of water and plants wonderful trees for the sake of his people. To underscore the richness of God's help, God mentions seven different trees here. For ancient people living in

Palestine, this picture was especially comforting. For anyone living in an arid climate, the promise of water and trees finds eager ears.

The section concludes with a statement of the reason God had not only sent difficulty but also provided deliverance. God acts so that others may see, know, and understand that he is in control, "that the hand of the LORD has done this." Note the appearance again of Isaiah's special name for God: "the Holy One of Israel."

> [21] **"Present your case," says the LORD.**
> **"Set forth your arguments," says Jacob's King.**
> [22] **"Bring in your idols to tell us**
> **what is going to happen.**
> **Tell us what the former things were,**
> **so that we may consider them**
> **and know their final outcome.**
> **Or declare to us the things to come,**
> [23] **tell us what the future holds,**
> **so we may know that you are gods.**
> **Do something, whether good or bad,**
> **so that we will be dismayed and filled with fear.**
> [24] **But you are less than nothing**
> **and your works are utterly worthless;**
> **he who chooses you is detestable.**

God had spent the middle verses of the chapter comforting his people in their difficulties. He has not forgotten the nations and their gods. He returns us to the debate that opened the chapter. There God had asked the nations to present their opinions on who called the conqueror on the stage of history. They had remained silent before God. Instead of speaking to God, they had vainly encouraged one another and created greater gods, overlaying them with gold and nailing them in place so they would not topple over. God renews his invitation for the nations to come and present their case before him. This time he adds, "Bring in your idols." They had turned away from the Lord to create idols (verses 5-7). Now, the Lord suggests that they should bring forth the idols to see if they are of any value.

He challenges the idols to speak. First, he asks the idols to tell what the former things were. Perhaps the words *former things* mean that the idols should tell what is about to happen in the immediate future—the next week or month, for example. On the other hand, perhaps they mean that the idols should provide some analysis of what has happened. In that way, someone might understand what past events will mean in the future, that is, how the past influences the future. In either case, the idols are silent. But God is not finished. If they cannot produce such an analysis of events and their impact on the future, or if they cannot predict tomorrow's events, perhaps these idols can predict the more distant future. God invites them to declare what the future holds. But the idols remain silent. God has one more challenge. If the idols cannot peer into the future, then God encourages them to do something—anything at all, whether good or bad. Yet the idols remain silent. It's as if a child had lined up a row of dolls or teddy bears and expected them to speak. By themselves, they would all remain silent no matter how vivid the child's imagination. These idols are as mute as a child's plaything.

What conclusion can be reached but the one God himself proclaims: You are less than nothing. They do not exist; they are not. A child may gain some pleasure out of silent toys, but all who trust in idols are detestable. Those who choose to rely on gods fashioned by the imagination of the human mind will be condemned. They oppose God's gracious invitation to come and learn the truth from him.

Instead, they have chosen to trust in what is not God and can never be God.

Remember that all who fashion God to fit their own expectations, inclinations, and desires create an idol, even if no image of wood or metal exists. As soon as any human abandons God's revealed truth and suggests that God does something different than what the Bible says, that person has invented an idol, a false god. God's Word is our only reliable source for information about who God is and what he wants us to believe. Everything else is "nothing," "utterly worthless," and "detestable."

> 25 "I have stirred up one from the north, and he comes—
> one from the rising sun who calls on my name.
> He treads on rulers as if they were mortar,
> as if he were a potter treading the clay.
> 26 Who told of this from the beginning, so we could know,
> or beforehand, so we could say, 'He was right'?
> No one told of this,
> no one foretold it,
> no one heard any words from you.
> 27 I was the first to tell Zion, 'Look, here they are!'
> I gave to Jerusalem a messenger of good tidings.

While the idols of the nations have remained silent, God cites his action in bringing a conqueror on the scene. This conqueror is one "who calls on my name." By virtue of his edict, Cyrus proclaimed the name of the Lord to all the world (see the edict as recorded in Ezra chapter 1 and *Ezra, Nehemiah, Esther,* in The People's Bible series, pages 10-12). No matter what Cyrus thought of the Lord, God had called forth Cyrus. The Lord uses the example of Cyrus to prove his superiority to all the idols. In verse 2 this conqueror comes "from the east." Here he comes "from the north." According to the compass, Persia was to the east of Palestine, but all invading armies came from the north into Palestine. The two directions should pose no serious difficulty for the reader.

Isaiah serves as God's recording secretary in this debate with the nations and the idols. In order to record the future events for the comfort of his people, God had opened the eyes of his prophet to see far into the future. God now asks if anyone but him had predicted these events. Only one answer can be given: "No one foretold it." Only God can predict the future with absolute reliability, and only God can claim to control not only the present but also the future. He is Lord of all history and controls all events for the benefit of his people.

Not only did the Lord predict what he would accomplish, he also recorded it for the sake of his people. He claims that his voice, that is, the voice of his messengers of good tidings, was the first to announce the good news to Zion. God does not operate in the dark and in secret. His Word announces his plans, his action, and his thoughts. Some of the words God reveals may be difficult at times. Peter said that some of Paul's words were hard to grasp (2 Peter 3:15,16), but the central message of all God's revelation remains always clear. It is as simple as "God so loved the world that he gave his one and only Son, that whoever believes in him shall not perish but have eternal life" (John 3:16). God has not hidden his message. It is an open book.

> [28] **"I look but there is no one—**
> **no one among them to give counsel,**
> **no one to give answer when I ask them.**
> [29] **See, they are all false!**
> **Their deeds amount to nothing;**
> **their images are but wind and confusion.**

Here God offers his summation of the entire debate. No one came to give God advice. No one answered his challenge. The idols remained silent before the challenge of God. What other conclusion could be reached than the one God reached: The idols all are false! The gods created by humans are nothing but wind and confusion, as different from the truth as water is from fire.

The silence of the idols reminds us of another challenge to the false gods of the people by Elijah, another prophet of God. Elijah challenged 450 prophets of Baal and 400 prophets of Asherah to come to Mount Carmel. On the mountain Elijah conducted a contest. The prophets of the idols were to call on their gods to come and set fire to the offering they had prepared for their idols. But in spite of the loud cries, bloodshed, and frantic activity of the false prophets, the idols did not answer. We read, "But there was no response, no one answered, no one paid attention" (1 Kings 18:29). When Elijah soaked his offering three times, he prayed to the Lord Jehovah. God sent fire down from heaven that consumed the offering, the altar, the soil, and even the water in the trench around the altar. On Mount Carmel, there was no question which God was true. In this case in Isaiah, there is no question either.

The Lord introduces his Servant

42 "Here is my servant, whom I uphold,
  my chosen one in whom I delight;
    I will put my Spirit on him
      and he will bring justice to the nations.
    [2] He will not shout or cry out,
      or raise his voice in the streets.
    [3] A bruised reed he will not break,
      and a smoldering wick he will not snuff out.
    In faithfulness he will bring forth justice;
    [4]   he will not falter or be discouraged
    till he establishes justice on earth.
      In his law the islands will put their hope."

Jesus anointed with the Holy Spirit at his baptism

"Here is my servant." With that announcement the Lord introduces readers of Isaiah to someone special and important. Of course, the Lord had many servants. They include Abraham (Genesis 26:24), Moses (Numbers 12:7), David (2 Samuel 3:18), and others such as Caleb (Numbers 14:24), Job (Job 1:8), Nebuchadnezzar (Jeremiah 27:6), and Zerubbabel (Haggai 2:23). In the Old Testament, David is the most frequently designated as the Lord's servant, and Moses is the second most frequently designated as such. God placed his prophet Isaiah on the list of his servants too (Isaiah 20:3). God even called the ancient nation of Israel "my servant" (41:8), although later Isaiah reminded the chosen people that as servants of God, they were blind and deaf (42:18,19). All these servants had a special purpose in God's plan of salvation. God chose each one for some special task. Although Job and Caleb did not have major roles, God designated them as his servants. For one thing, they were examples to his people. God called Nebuchadnezzar his servant, even though he was a Babylonian, because the king would carry out judgment upon God's unfaithful people.

At the beginning of this chapter, when God says, "Here is my servant," he makes an announcement of special importance. God announces this Servant boldly and dramatically. It is as if God had his arm stretched out and pointed to this one as his Servant, "Here he is!" No other servant of the Lord received such an introduction, and God's announcement signals something quite different and important about this Servant as compared to all the others. If we were to place all these servants together and look at them, God would direct our attention to this Servant. For example, if all these servants were placed on a table and spread out like rare coins, God would be pointing at one of them saying, "Here's my servant. This is the special one." In the verses that follow his announcement, God explains why this one is so valuable and important.

For one thing, God provides a contrast to reveal the importance of this Servant. The print on this page depends on contrast. We can read the words because the black letters stand out against the white paper. The Old Testament often provided contrasts in order to make a point. In this case, several contrasts become apparent as we study these verses. In the previous chapter, God pointed to the false gods, "See, they are all false! Their deeds amount to nothing; their images are but wind and confusion" (verse 29). What a contrast to the Servant that God points to in the first verse of this chapter! The works of the false gods are nothing; the gods themselves are nothing—but not this Servant and not his work. The Servant introduced here would carry out the Lord's work.

Now that God has our attention, he tells us why this Servant is especially important. Certainly God chose this Servant much as he had chosen other servants, including Abraham and the entire nation of Israel. Each of the prophets had also been chosen for their special role, and David had been selected from the sons of Jesse to be king. In one sense or another, it could be said that God upheld all his servants and delighted in them and the work he had given them to do. For example, David was a man after God's own heart (1 Samuel 13:14).

But this Servant is different. God endows this Servant with special gifts and importance. The last part of verse 1 gives this Servant a task no other servant had received. He would "bring justice to the nations." First, note that the target of his work would be "the nations." He would not only serve the single nation of Israel, but his work would also have value for the Gentiles. *Justice* in this verse means a judgment based on a legal decision. It is a term that defines the gospel, which is God's legal and judicial announcement that he has declared the entire world right, holy, and innocent. That's good news. All the world—the nations—stand before God's court convicted of sin, but because of the work of Jesus, God declares the world free of sin; he justifies the nations for Christ's sake. This judgment, or "justice" as translated by the NIV, exists because of the work of this Servant. Such a task would be impossible for any servant without the power of the Lord. So God said that he would put his Spirit on this Servant so that he could accomplish his task.

How would this Servant accomplish his task? He would not do it as Nebuchadnezzar or even David did. Both were powerful men who accomplished great things by force. Yet we note another contrast here. God announced in the previous chapter that he was stirring up one from the north to be a deliverer. That was Cyrus the Great. Cyrus would tread "on rulers as if they were mortar, as if he were a potter treading the clay" (41:25). But the Servant whom God draws our attention to in these verses would be meek, modest, and mild. "He will not shout or cry out, or raise his voice in the streets." Who was this Servant? Even Abraham rescued Lot by force (Genesis 14), and Moses sent the Levites out with swords drawn to restore order (Exodus 32:25-29). By now it should be clear that this Servant is the Messiah who would come. Zechariah described him as a king who would come into Jerusalem "righteous and having salvation, gentle and riding on a donkey" (Zechariah 9:9). We know him as Jesus Christ, and the remaining descriptions leave little doubt. If we have any questions, remember that Matthew quoted this passage to identify Jesus as the Servant and Messiah (Matthew 12:15-21).

Cyrus stomped his way to victory. His coming filled the islands (that is, the Mediterranean area) with fear, as Isaiah described in the previous chapter (41:5). This Servant would be gentle; the islands would hope in the words of this Servant. He would not prey upon the weak and snuff out all who stood in his way. God says, "A bruised reed he will not break, and a smoldering wick he will not snuff out." In the world of power, wealth, and ego, could such a Servant succeed? Remember that the Lord has put his Spirit upon this Servant. Much earlier, Isaiah had prophesied that this servant would be a "shoot" from the stump of Jesse and that "the Spirit of the Lord will rest on him" (11:1,2). The Spirit would give this Servant power to accomplish his tasks; he would succeed. Here God says, "He will not falter or be discouraged." He will accomplish his task of establishing justice on the earth. The word *justice* here returns us to the first verse, where we were told that this Servant "will bring justice to the nations." God's legal declaration of innocence would be established by this Servant, and God emphasizes again that its value is for all the earth, not just for Israel or Judah.

The news of this Servant's work would be of interest to those far beyond the borders of Israel and Judah. The islands, the distant coastlands of the Mediterranean world, would trust it. When God says that the islands would be interested in the law of this Servant, he reminds readers of the prophecy that the Servant would establish a new principle and publish it so that others could believe it and hope in it. *Law* here means more than the Old Testament ceremonial laws or even the Ten Commandments. It means all the revelation about this Servant—his Word, including the gospel.

God's people longed for the appearance of this Servant. When he came, God removed all doubt about his identity.

As Jesus came out of the water of the Jordan River, two important things happened. First, the Spirit of God descended on Jesus like a dove, and second, a voice said, "This is my Son, whom I love; with him I am well pleased." (Matthew 3:17). This incident is so similar to the first verse of this chapter that we cannot ignore it. At the transfiguration God again spoke: "This is my Son, whom I love; with him I am well pleased. Listen to him!" (Matthew 17:5). Through Isaiah, God announced, "Here is my servant," and sent his Spirit upon him: "I will put my Spirit on him." In effect God said, "This is the one." A brief review of the Savior's ministry will show us how Jesus fits the description so well. His gentleness and faithfulness are evident on every page of the New Testament. He did not falter even when crucified but accomplished the task his Father had given him. No wonder that the islands—yes, people throughout the world—trust in his words of grace and mercy.

As you might guess, not everyone thinks that this passage refers to Jesus. The ancient Jewish Targum suggested that this passage referred to the Messiah, but some do not see a reference to Jesus in this description at all. Some identify Cyrus as the servant. Others think that the servant is the nation of Israel. Yet remember that God describes a person who does things that no other servant has done or could do. When we lay out all the possibilities and examine them, only one person fits the description—Jesus Christ. As we look at each possibility, our examination will indicate which person God points to here. Jesus is so much more valuable and important than all the others God chose to be his servants. No other servant compares.

This is the first of four "servant" sections in Isaiah. The others are 49:1-7; 50:4-11; and 52:13–53:12. They form a central theme for the prophet and deserve our special attention. In these servant sections, God reveals more and more details about the Great Servant and his work. But we are not yet finished with what God tells us about this Servant in this passage.

> ⁵ **This is what God the LORD says—**
> **he who created the heavens and stretched them out,**
> **who spread out the earth and all that comes out of it,**
> **who gives breath to its people,**
> **and life to those who walk on it:**
> ⁶ **"I, the LORD, have called you in righteousness;**
> **I will take hold of your hand.**
> **I will keep you and will make you**
> **to be a covenant for the people**
> **and a light for the Gentiles,**
> ⁷ **to open eyes that are blind,**
> **to free captives from prison**
> **and to release from the dungeon those who sit**
> **in darkness.**

While all other gods are nothing, the God of the Scriptures is powerful and active. He has spoken about the Servant he had chosen. With a solemn introduction, he speaks again. Isaiah identifies God as "God the LORD." He is the true God, who reveals himself as the God of the covenant, Jehovah, the God of free and faithful grace. Not only does Isaiah identify God as the "LORD," but he also identifies him as the Creator and preserver of the earth. Often God claims the right to speak because he has created the world and everything in it. He guarantees a prediction because he is the Creator and preserver. So it is here. If anyone had a question about whether God could do what he promises to do in these verses, they were just to remember that he created the world. His power to create the world out of nothing, as described in Genesis, stands as a pledge for the promises in this section. It's not only God's work of creation that stands as a pledge but also his work of preservation. God has given everyone on earth life and breath. All creation continues because God's power still sustains it.

To whom is God speaking? It becomes clear that he speaks to the Servant he had identified in the first verse. What does this God say? The Lord explains in more detail what he meant by upholding his Servant and calling him. He also describes again the great task he has given this Servant. The section begins with an emphatic "I, the LORD." These thoughts flow directly from God; they are not the invention of any human mind.

The Lord tells us that his Servant was "called . . . in righteousness." The Lord had a special reason for choosing his Servant; it was in connection with righteousness. The righteousness of the Lord is the standard principle by which he acts. He demands that the entire human race be righteous, but at every step the human race—even his chosen people, Israel—has proven to be unrighteous. Even obedience to all the ceremonies of the Old Testament law has failed to produce a righteous people. God devised a plan to provide righteousness to all humanity. In accordance with his purposes of love and his plan to rescue his people Israel and all the world, he called this Servant. The apostle Paul wrote, "This righteousness from God comes through faith in Jesus Christ to all who believe" (Romans 3:22). God called this Servant, then, in order to carry out his righteous will for the deliverance of all humanity.

The task would be difficult, as the next verses clearly imply. But the Lord pledged to provide the necessary support and blessing. He took the Servant by the hand to provide strength and support. He also watched over his Servant, guarding and defending him in his work. The Lord promised, "I will keep you."

The next phrases are helpful to understand with absolute clarity that Jesus Christ must be this Servant. The Lord will make this Servant to be "a covenant for the people and a light for the Gentiles." The Lord tells us that the old covenant would be supplanted by a new one that this Servant would bring to pass. The Servant himself would be the covenant. The servant as "covenant" is God's promise that he would die (Genesis 15:12-18). To die, God was born as a human being in a Bethlehem manger. Christ died on Calvary's cross in fulfillment of this prophecy. We receive the benefits of his death in Christ's last will and testament—the Sacrament of the Altar (Matthew 26:28 KJV). God the Father promised all of this as he through the prophet Isaiah called the servant his "covenant."

As Luther writes:

> This testament of Christ is foreshadowed in all the promises of God from the beginning of the world; indeed, whatever value those ancient promises possessed was altogether derived from this new promise that was to come in Christ. Hence the words "compact," "covenant," and "testament of the Lord" occur so frequently in the Scriptures. Those words signified that God would one day die. "For where there is a testament, the death of the testator must of necessity occur" (Hebrews 9[:16]). Now God had made a testament; therefore it was necessary that he should die. But God could not die unless he became a man. Thus the incarnation and death of Christ are both comprehended most concisely in this one word, "testament." (LW 36:38)

The writer to the Hebrews speaks of Christ's new covenant:

> The blood of goats and bulls and the ashes of a heifer sprinkled on those who are ceremonially unclean sanctify them so that they are outwardly clean. How much more, then, will the blood of Christ, who through the eternal Spirit offered himself unblemished to God, cleanse our consciences from acts that lead to death, so that we may serve the living God!
>
> For this reason Christ is the mediator of a new covenant, that those who are called may receive the promised eternal inheritance—now that he has died as a ransom to set them free from the sins committed under the first covenant. (9:13-15)

What Jesus did for the Jews, God's people, he also did for the Gentiles. The Jews understood that God had made a covenant, or solemn contract, with them. Their history recorded the covenant with Abraham and the covenant at Sinai. For Jews, the Servant would be the solemn contract with them. His blood would seal the contract between God and his people. But the Gentiles had no background in the Jewish concept of covenant. They understood the difference between light and darkness. For them the work of the Servant would be a light. The work of this Servant, then, would benefit both Jews and Gentiles—yes, all people. Who else could this be but Jesus?

Isaiah's use of the word *people* here refers to the Jewish people. When used with its counterpart *Gentiles*, God tells us that the Servant would benefit Jews and Gentiles. One note should be added here. Some consider the Servant here to be the nation of Israel, but the Servant whom God introduced here could not be the Jewish people. If we accepted the opinion that the Servant should be identified as the Jewish nation in this verse, then the Jewish nation would be a covenant for themselves. It would make the verse meaningless to say that the Jewish people would be a covenant for the Jewish people.

But God has more for us to learn about this Servant. God has us look at the work of the Servant from another perspective. The Servant's work would open the eyes of the blind, free captives, and bring release to those in the dungeon of darkness. These phrases do not refer to physical bondage or physical blindness. They refer to spiritual realities. Of course, Jesus opened the eyes of the blind while he was on earth, but he did not remove blindness from the human experience. God speaks of a different kind of blindness. Because of sin all humanity remains blind to the truths of God. This Servant would provide the necessary insight to see the grace and mercy of God. Just as the blindness is spiritual, so the bondage is spiritual. All humans are slaves to sin and doomed to eternal punishment. This servant would bring release from sin's bondage and from the dungeon of judgment. Earlier Isaiah had written of the coming of this Servant: "The people walking in darkness have seen a great light; on those living in the land of the shadow of death a light has dawned" (9:2). The Lord's plan to deliver all the world is the great theme of Isaiah and of all Scripture.

Little doubt can remain that the one described in these verses is Jesus Christ. When we look at all the descriptions recorded for us here, we conclude that no one but Jesus could fulfill the prophecy. Over the centuries, believers have confessed that truth. In our own age, many want to cut Jesus out of the prophecies of Isaiah. They desire to go even further and cut him out of the entire Old Testament.

Reading this section without the prejudice of doubt and without the suspicion of unbelief, one can come to only one conclusion. This Servant is Jesus. The description eliminates all other servants, and the work of Jesus as well as the testimony of God the Father from heaven confirm it. "Here is my servant." This Servant has the approval of the Lord Jehovah. We do well to focus our attention on him and to listen to every word that comes from his mouth.

> [8] "I am the LORD; that is my name!
> I will not give my glory to another
> or my praise to idols.
> [9] See, the former things have taken place,
> and new things I declare;
> before they spring into being
> I announce them to you."

All the gods of humanity cannot compare to the Lord. No god in any culture anywhere on the face of the earth can match what the Lord has promised and carried out. Yet there are many opinions about God. Contemporary theology does not erect new images representing deities as ancient theologies once did, but contemporary theology still fashions God according to its own thought. Without the Scriptures, contemporary theology and all subsequent theologies build a god different from the Lord. But there is no other God. There is no other deliverance. Apart from Jesus Christ, all is darkness.

The Lord asserts his superiority. God connects his glory to the plan of salvation, the work of the Savior, the redemption of humanity from sin, death, and hell. He alone deserves the credit for such deliverance. No other god, whether represented by an ancient statue or explained in a book of theology, should receive the glory and praise for providing such great blessings. God is not one god among many. One religious experience is not as good as any other. The Lord does not provide an alternative way to heaven while Allah or Buddha provide other equally truthful ways to heaven. No! Only *one* God provides *one* way into his presence. Jesus is the only way to heaven, and God is jealous of his glory and praise. He will not allow any rival. Simply, no real rival exists.

God concludes his proclamation with a final proof of his ability to do what he has promised in these verses. He points us again to something: "See, the former things have taken place." What are they? The former things are all that God has done in the past. Among them would be the deliverance of his people from Egypt. He predicted that they would come out of Egypt, and it happened as he promised. Other events happened as God predicted they would. He promised that Abraham's descendants would become a great nation. That happened as he promised. He promised King Ahaz that the alliance against him and Judah would fail. It did. He promised to deliver Jerusalem from the Assyrians. He did so. All God's former promises and predictions assure believers that God does bring about the fulfillment of everything else he has revealed. God proclaims his ability to declare new things before they happen with the same reliability that he has made the old promises come to pass.

> [10] **Sing to the LORD a new song,**
>   **his praise from the ends of the earth,**
>   **you who go down to the sea, and all that is in it,**
>   **you islands, and all who live in them.**
> [11] **Let the desert and its towns raise their voices;**
>   **let the settlements where Kedar lives rejoice.**
>   **Let the people of Sela sing for joy;**
>   **let them shout from the mountaintops.**
> [12] **Let them give glory to the LORD**
>   **and proclaim his praise in the islands.**

> [13] **The LORD will march out like a mighty man,**
> **like a warrior he will stir up his zeal;**
> **with a shout he will raise the battle cry**
> **and will triumph over his enemies.**

Isaiah had heard the wonderful promises of the Lord and recorded them. With these verses the prophet encouraged all believers to sing in response to those promises. "Sing to the LORD a new song," Isaiah exhorts. The song is new because its content is new. The song overflows with joy over the redemption God promised and would bring to pass. It is not an old song celebrating the past victory of the Lord for his people, as is the Song of Moses (Exodus 15). This song proclaims wonderful new praise to the Lord for what his chosen Servant would accomplish.

God's prophet invites all the earth to sing this song: those who sail the sea, the inhabitants of the islands, and those in the towns in the desert around Judah. This song filled the air and could be heard to the very ends of the earth—as far and as wide as the human mind could imagine. In these two chapters, Isaiah mentions the islands, the countries bordering the eastern Mediterranean. At first the inhabitants of the islands were terrified at the approach of Cyrus. Then they were included as beneficiaries of the Servant's glorious work. Now they rejoice because of his work. God always wanted the entire world included in his redemption. The Lord Jesus died for all the world so that all the world could hear his gospel and rejoice in its blessings.

In verse 13, the picture changes. The song of praise flows from the mouths of grateful people because the Lord will march out like a warrior. In his righteousness God called the Servant and brought about forgiveness and deliverance from death and hell. The plan of God would mean that he would defeat his great enemy, Satan, and destroy Satan's greatest allies, sin and death. The redemption of humanity would be the great prize of his victory. According to the first promise of his coming (Genesis 3:15), this Servant would crush the head of the serpent and restore peace, holiness, and joy. Picturing the Lord as a mighty hero is another way of looking at his work of rescuing sinners and another cause for praise.

> [14] **"For a long time I have kept silent,**
> **I have been quiet and held myself back.**
> **But now, like a woman in childbirth,**
> **I cry out, I gasp and pant.**
> [15] **I will lay waste the mountains and hills**
> **and dry up all their vegetation;**
> **I will turn rivers into islands**
> **and dry up the pools.**
> [16] **I will lead the blind by ways they have not known,**
> **along unfamiliar paths I will guide them;**
> **I will turn the darkness into light before them**
> **and make the rough places smooth.**
> **These are the things I will do;**
> **I will not forsake them.**
> [17] **But those who trust in idols,**
> **who say to images, 'You are our gods,'**
> **will be turned back in utter shame.**

The Lord's plan required long preparation. When Isaiah wrote these words, a long history had already been recorded. God had created the world, called Abraham, delivered his people from Egypt, chosen David as king, and, most recently, destroyed the Assyrian army that had laid siege to Jerusalem. God had patiently endured the sins of his own people and withheld just punishment from the idolatrous nations of the world. God's plan was to provide an opportunity for all humans to reach out for him. That was their time of grace. The apostle Paul addressed the Greeks at a meeting of the Areopagus in Athens with similar thoughts:

From one man he [God] made every nation of men, that they should inhabit the whole earth; and he determined the times set for them and the exact places where they should live. God did this so that men would seek him and perhaps reach out for him and find him, though he is not far from each of us. "For in him we live and move and have our being." . . .

Therefore since we are God's offspring, we should not think that the divine being is like gold or silver or stone—an image made by man's design and skill. In the past God overlooked such ignorance, but now he commands all people everywhere to repent. For he has set a day when he will judge the world with justice by the man he has appointed. (Acts 17:26-31)

The Lord compares himself to a pregnant woman about to give birth. From the beginning, the Lord planned to bring the Savior into the world and to bring judgment upon all those who rejected his plan. The Lord was like a pregnant woman ready to deliver the child she nurtured for nine months. "When the time had fully come" (Galatians 4:4), God sent his only begotten Son into the world. Isaiah saw the coming of the Savior and the judgment of the world at the same time without the benefit of chronology. Both Christmas and final judgment day appear together for Isaiah. In our day, we know the Messiah has already come. Now we wait for him to return in judgment. God has set a day for the coming judgment; we only wait for it to come, like a pregnant mother awaits the coming of her child. The idea of an expectant mother fits both parts of God's plan. Peter's comments are helpful:

> The present heavens and earth are reserved
> for fire, being kept for the day of judgment
> and destruction of ungodly men.
>
> But do not forget this one thing, dear friends:
> With the Lord a day is like a thousand years,
> and a thousand years are like a day. The Lord
> is not slow in keeping his promise, as some
> understand slowness. He is patient with you,
> not wanting anyone to perish, but everyone to
> come to repentance. (2 Peter 3:7-9)

When God described these events for Isaiah and Isaiah's readers, he described the two comings of the Servant as a single coming. God says that when he comes, he will bring destruction to the earth. The mountains and hills will be laid waste. But something else will also happen. The blind will find paths on which to walk. These are the spiritually blind who by themselves cannot find a way. God will find a way to bring them safely to himself. God will guide them. God will turn the darkness into light. God does all this. He will cause the spiritually blind to see and walk. In these words, God showed his prophet the first coming of the Servant, the gathering of believers, and the second coming of the Servant, the final day of judgment, all in one picture. On the one hand, God will bring judgment to the earth, but, on the other, he will lead and guide his own. He pledged, "I will not forsake them."

For the ancient readers of Isaiah's prophecy, God included one more event in this picture—the return of God's people from captivity in Babylon. The language of this section recalls the exodus from Egypt when God made the Red Sea dry up so his people could leave Egypt. The return from Babylon would be a similar deliverance. Both of these deliverances from bondage are Old Testament pictures that point us to God's greater deliverance from the bondage of sin and hell. God had delivered his people from Egypt, he would deliver them from Babylon, and he would deliver them from the bondage of sin by the coming of this Servant, Jesus Christ. God does not forsake his people.

Believers have found great comfort in such promises. God has brought us, who were by nature spiritually dead and blind, to faith. He has called, gathered, and enlightened us by the power of his gospel. As comforting as such thoughts are for believers, we know there are two sides to God's truth, "Whoever believes and is baptized will be saved, but whoever does not believe will be condemned" (Mark 16:16). God issued the same warning to the people of Isaiah's time: "But those who trust in idols . . . will be turned back in utter shame." Again and again in Isaiah's prophecy, we see the folly of the human obsession to fashion a god who thinks and acts as we do. The gods and theologies that humans create are absolutely worthless. On the day of judgment, all the gods fashioned by the human mind will be worthless. Isaiah wrote earlier, "In that day men will throw away to the rodents and bats their idols of silver and idols of gold, which they made to worship" (2:20).

> [18] **"Hear, you deaf;**
> **look, you blind, and see!**
> [19] **Who is blind but my servant,**
> **and deaf like the messenger I send?**
> **Who is blind like the one committed to me,**
> **blind like the servant of the LORD?**
> [20] **You have seen many things, but have paid no attention;**
> **your ears are open, but you hear nothing."**
> [21] **It pleased the LORD**
> **for the sake of his righteousness**
> **to make his law great and glorious.**

²² **But this is a people plundered and looted,**
    all of them trapped in pits
    or hidden away in prisons.
They have become plunder,
    with no one to rescue them;
they have been made loot,
    with no one to say, "Send them back."
²³ **Which of you will listen to this**
    or pay close attention in time to come?
²⁴ **Who handed Jacob over to become loot,**
    and Israel to the plunderers?
Was it not the LORD,
    against whom we have sinned?
For they would not follow his ways;
    they did not obey his law.
²⁵ **So he poured out on them his burning anger,**
    the violence of war.
It enveloped them in flames, yet they did not understand;
    it consumed them, but they did not take it to heart.

The Lord continues to speak, now asking, "Who is blind but my servant?" We may be surprised at the appearance of the word *servant* here. Can this be the same Servant we read about earlier? If we look at what God says about this servant, however, we will discover that this servant is much different from the one described in the first part of the chapter. These verses describe this servant as deaf and blind. Yet he is also God's messenger and "the servant of the LORD."

Here we find one clue to this servant's identity: this servant has seen and heard many things yet has actually paid no attention to any of them. Isaiah wrote that the Lord had made his law great and glorious. The Lord did that for the sake of his righteousness. In other words, God's righteous will to save the world caused him to proclaim the truth in words, "his law." So the Lord had provided this servant with words to hear and actions to see. Who knew of the creation? Who knew how God chose Abraham? Who could know the deliverance of God's people from Egypt? Who witnessed all the great acts of God for the sake of his people? Who would have seen and heard all the promises of God to bring redemption and salvation to the world through Abraham's descendants? Who heard the promises of God's prophets? Who could know all this and still be deaf and blind? Is there one person who had heard and seen such wonders? It appears to be a collective personality. Isaiah identifies the servant in verse 22: "But this is a people plundered and looted." Who else could this servant be than the very people of God, Israel? Certainly God considered his Old Testament people his servants. God chose them to carry out his purposes. Surely they were God's messengers; they possessed the truth of God. We still read and study the message God entrusted to them.

But what a contrast to the Servant described in the first verses! The people of Judah had seen and heard so much. But none of it penetrated their hearts. Throughout the first portion of his prophecy, Isaiah threatened them with God's judgment. When God called Isaiah, he told him that his task was to harden the people of Judah in their unbelief. God instructed Isaiah to say to Judah, "'Be ever hearing, but never understanding; be ever seeing, but never perceiving.' Make the heart of this people calloused" (6:9,10). So it had happened. And yet through Isaiah's ministry, God pleaded with his people. Here too this indictment was a shrill and sharp call for them to repent. Isaiah even included himself with the sinful nation: "Was it not the Lord, against whom *we* have sinned?" Sin infects all people, even believers. Isaiah acknowledged his sin and repented; others also repented. The majority did not. They went on their way undisturbed by the prophet's warnings. They walked straight toward God's judgment in blind ignorance.

71

Through his prophet Isaiah, God still called to them, but they were blind and deaf.

What is God to do with people who refuse to listen to his prophets, who do not follow his ways or obey his law? The last verse of the chapter gives a clear and unmistakable answer: "So he poured out on them his burning anger." The violence of war was one of the ways God poured out his judgment. God's blind and deaf people would feel the fury of the Babylonian conquerors. Their city would be burned in flames because they had not turned to the Lord and repented of their sins. Sadly, in the midst of that great judgment, they still would not understand that their troubles came from God as a result of their sins.

Unbelief always has the same end. The Jewish leaders who rejected the Savior, and all who agreed with them, did not understand the wonderful truths and blessings they saw with their own eyes. The miracles and sermons of Jesus did nothing for them. They remained blind and deaf. Even after the raising of Lazarus (John 11), the Jewish leaders did not believe. They sought to kill Jesus and Lazarus. Just as their forefathers had remained blind and deaf, so did they. Just as their forefathers felt the fury of conquerors, so did they. The Romans destroyed Jerusalem as surely as the Babylonians had six centuries earlier.

These are the "former things" for us to note (verse 9). God has brought judgment upon all who rejected his gracious invitation. God presents an invitation before all people as they read his Word. The Bible is still the most widely bought book in the world. Yet so many do not follow God's ways or believe his Word. They will eat, drink, and be merry all the way to their own judgment. Like all unbelievers before them, they are blind to the truths of God and deaf to his call to repent. Believers, on the other hand, are like Isaiah. By God's grace we are among them. We know that we have sinned and deserve God's judgment as surely as everyone else. Yet God has opened our ears to hear his gospel and cleared our vision so that we might see Jesus, the Servant of God, who has released us from sin, death, and hell.

Only the Lord, the Redeemer, delivers his people by grace

43 But now, this is what the LORD says—
he who created you, O Jacob,
he who formed you, O Israel:
"Fear not, for I have redeemed you;
I have summoned you by name; you are mine.
2 When you pass through the waters,
I will be with you;
and when you pass through the rivers,
they will not sweep over you.
When you walk through the fire,
you will not be burned;
the flames will not set you ablaze.
3 For I am the LORD, your God,
the Holy One of Israel, your Savior;
I give Egypt for your ransom,
Cush and Seba in your stead.
4 Since you are precious and honored in my sight,
and because I love you,
I will give men in exchange for you,
and people in exchange for your life.
5 Do not be afraid, for I am with you;
I will bring your children from the east
and gather you from the west.
6 I will say to the north, 'Give them up!'
and to the south, 'Do not hold them back.'
Bring my sons from afar
and my daughters from the ends of the earth—
7 everyone who is called by my name,
whom I created for my glory,
whom I formed and made."

The chapter begins with an unexpected thought. The last verse of the previous chapter announced God's burning wrath upon his people. They did not obey his law; they were blind and deaf to all that God had done for them. Because of their sins, God had sent "the violence of war" upon them. But they remained blind and deaf. We might have expected that Isaiah would continue with a fierce announcement of judgment. In spite of all God did for his people, they deserved God's judgment. God would have been justified in abandoning such ungrateful and stubborn people to their own sins. The phrase "But now," however, introduces something unexpected. We read tender words of faithful love from the Lord, the God of free and faithful grace.

Isaiah introduces these unexpected words of love and grace by telling his readers that this message comes from the Lord. The words are not a prophet's wishful thinking. Remember that Isaiah has included himself among the blind, deaf people of God. He wrote, "Was it not the LORD, against whom *we* have sinned?" (42:24). By nature Isaiah and all humans of all time are spiritually blind, dead, and enemies of God. All deserve the fearsome judgment of God, because all have sinned. We expect the announcement of God's judgment upon sin. Like Isaiah, we all hope for an escape from God's judgment. All our wishes do not make it so. But the Lord himself, that is, the God of free and faithful love, announces the unexpected. He claims the authority to make such a gracious announcement because he has created and formed his people.

"Fear not!" The Lord says, "Fear not, sinner. Fear not, my people. Instead of punishment and judgment I will give you deliverance." The unexpected announcement to set aside fear comes for three reasons; all three of them trace the comfort back to the Lord himself. First, the Lord says, "I have redeemed you." While God's people were blind and deaf, in bondage to their own sinful nature, and headed toward certain judgment, the Lord had bought them out of their predicament. He had redeemed them. This was true when Israel was in Egypt. It would be true again when they are taken as prisoners of war and led as captives to Babylon. It remains true for every sinner. God's people are encouraged to dispel their fears because God has rescued them from themselves and the consequences of their own sins and failures. The verb *redeem* implies that God's people are helplessly trapped and unable to gain their own release. But God says, "Fear not, for I have redeemed you." What an unexpected word of comfort and grace. Second, God called his people by name. He singled them out from all the nations of the earth and called them. God chose them to be his. Third, these people were God's own possession. He claimed them: "You are mine."

These sweet words of comfort apply first of all to God's faithful people in the days of Isaiah. Centuries before Isaiah, the Lord had redeemed his people from their bondage in Egypt. God had claimed those people as his special possession. But they had become blind to the Lord's gracious activity for them and deaf to his loving call. Isaiah announced that God would send the Babylonians to destroy Jerusalem and take them captive to Babylon. That event would take place over a century later. From that bondage, the Lord would also redeem his people. He would purchase their release from Babylon just as a redeemer would buy his Israelite kinsman from bondage (Leviticus 25:47-49). Among the thousands in Judah who had abandoned the Lord, there were still faithful believers who treasured these words of comfort. In the troubled days ahead, these words sustained them. God himself said, "Fear not, for I have redeemed you." But they also treasured these words for the promise of a deeper and more significant redemption. They looked for a greater spiritual redemption far superior to the release from Babylon.

When we read these words thousands of years later, we too find comfort in them. The Lord has redeemed us too but from that greater bondage. By our sins, we were slaves of sin and in bondage to death and punishment. The Lord redeemed us from sin, death, and hell. He bought us with the price of the blood of Christ on Calvary. God called us by name when he washed us in the water of Baptism. All believers belong to the Lord; they are his possession. The Lord says "Fear not" to believers today as clearly as he did to believers in Isaiah's day. Like them, we live in the midst of a generation that has abandoned the Lord. But God has redeemed us and claimed us to be his. "Fear not."

Armed with these promises, God's ancient people faced the troubles of life. The Lord does not promise that his own faithful believers would escape all difficulty and pass through life without trouble. They would "pass through the waters" and "walk through the fire." When the people of Israel left Egypt, they did indeed pass through the waters. By God's power, Moses made a way through the Red Sea. That deliverance stood in the background of these promises. Just as the Lord had provided such deliverance in the past, he would provide an even greater deliverance in the future. God cites two dangers—water and fire. They symbolize all the dangers his people would experience (see Psalm 66:12). As God's people endure the dangers, God himself—God continues to speak—pledges protection. We have noted the deliverance God provided at the Red Sea. After the Babylonians had taken Judah captive, Nebuchadnezzar sent three men who remained faithful to the Lord into a fiery furnace (Daniel 3). They were not burned because the Lord protected them. Daniel trusted the Lord for protection as he entered the lions' den (Daniel 6). God assures his people that even their great trials will somehow work out for the best (Romans 8:28). The reason is clear: the Lord has redeemed them and they are his possession.

God reveals the past, the future for Judah, and the future for all believers in a single composite picture that stretches from creation to the final deliverance on the Last Day. Between creation and the Last Day, God assures his people of his gracious protection. Consider how many times the pronoun *I* appears in this chapter. The chapter records the words of the Lord, and he claims that he and he alone is responsible for the protection and deliverance his people have received and would receive in the future. Everything depends upon him: "I am the LORD." When we have finished the chapter, we should have no doubts about the source of all the promises.

The end of verse 3 takes us to a specific historical event, the release of Judah from Babylon. Cyrus of Persia conquered Babylon and established a new empire. He issued the edict that freed the Jews and allowed them to return to Palestine. God foretold these events in the days of Isaiah before Babylon became a power in the region and before Persia overcame Babylon. As a ransom to Cyrus for releasing Judah, God promised to give Egypt, Cush, and Seba. In other words, God restructured the ancient world for the sake of his ancient people and his plan of salvation. It is as though God compensated the Persians for liberating Israel. Although Cyrus died before the Persians conquered these nations, nevertheless, the Persian king planned the campaign against Egypt, and his son Cambyses carried it out.

This prophecy was specific, and it also underscored the principle of redemption. The second part of Isaiah's prophecy uses the word *redeem* frequently, and the work of redemption receives prominence. According to the Law of Moses (Leviticus 25,27), a price had to be paid in order to redeem someone or something. In this case God paid a price to redeem his people from their captivity in Babylon. While Cyrus never understood the principle involved, God gave him Egypt for releasing his people. Egypt, Cush, and Seba were the ransom.

The principle of redemption has been applied to more than just Judah's release from Babylon. *Redemption* has come to be a familiar term to all Christians. We regularly confess that God has redeemed us. He paid the ransom necessary to secure our release from our spiritual bondage to sin, death, and judgment. This redemption did not come cheaply. God paid a dear price when he offered his Son, Jesus Christ, in exchange for sinful humanity. The apostle Peter wrote, "You know that it was not with perishable things such as silver or gold that you were redeemed from the empty way of life handed down to you from your forefathers, but with the precious blood of Christ, a lamb without blemish or defect" (1 Peter 1:18,19). Luther paraphrased Peter in his explanation to the Second Article in the Small Catechism, "Jesus Christ . . . has redeemed me, a lost and condemned creature, purchased and won me from all sins, from death, and from the power of the devil, not with gold or silver but with his holy, precious blood and with his innocent suffering and death." Isaiah will return to the idea of redemption again and again in this second part of his prophecy. For now, he turns to another question: Why does God release his people? God himself gives the answer: "Since you are precious and honored in my sight, and because I love you." God's undeserved love for sinners remains the only reason God does anything for any human. "God so loved the world that he gave his one and only Son" (John 3:16).

Such undeserved love also prompts God to repeat his encouragement to his people, "Do not be afraid, for I am with you." The redemption that he pictures stretches out far beyond the release from Babylon. That becomes clear when God tells us that he will bring his people from the four corners of the compass. God's people will come not only from Babylon but from wherever they have been dispersed throughout the world. On the day of Pentecost, we note such a gathering as Jews from all over the Mediterranean world came to Jerusalem to worship (Acts 2). That day they heard the gospel, and God gathered them into his New Testament church. But a greater gathering is yet to be. It will occur on the Last Day, when God will bring all his people into the heaven he has prepared for them, no matter where they have been scattered. In this passage God mentions "my sons . . . and my daughters" to indicate that *all* will be gathered together. Then God identifies those who would be gathered together: "everyone who is called by my name," that is, all believers. The apostle John saw this great multitude assembled before the throne of the Lamb. It was "a great multitude that no one could count, from every nation, tribe, people and language (Revelation 7:9).

> [8] **Lead out those who have eyes but are blind,**
> **who have ears but are deaf.**
> [9] **All the nations gather together**
> **and the peoples assemble.**
> **Which of them foretold this**
> **and proclaimed to us the former things?**

> Let them bring in their witnesses to prove they were right,
>   so that others may hear and say, "It is true."
> [10] "You are my witnesses," declares the LORD,
>   "and my servant whom I have chosen,
> so that you may know and believe me
>   and understand that I am he.
> Before me no god was formed,
>   nor will there be one after me.
> [11] I, even I, am the LORD,
>   and apart from me there is no savior.
> [12] I have revealed and saved and proclaimed—
>   I, and not some foreign god among you.
> You are my witnesses," declares the LORD, "that I am God.
> [13]   Yes, and from ancient days I am he.
> No one can deliver out of my hand.
>   When I act, who can reverse it?"

The Lord had promised to redeem his people from their Babylonian captivity, giving Egypt, Cush, and Seba as a ransom price for his people. The release from Babylon pointed still further ahead to another redemption when God would gather his people—all of them, sons and daughters—"from the ends of the earth." Isaiah wrote these words around 700 B.C. Cyrus signed the edict releasing Jews from captivity and allowing them to return to Judea in 538 B.C.—about 160 years after Isaiah's ministry.

Some scholars stumble at these dates. They wonder how Isaiah could have predicted the future with such accuracy so far in advance. One approach concludes that someone closer to the rise of Cyrus wrote these verses. In other words, they claim that Isaiah did not write either these verses or any of the second part of the prophecy. But such a claim makes the writer of this second half of Isaiah a deceiver and a fraud. Consider verse 9, "Which of them foretold this and proclaimed to us the former things?" The writer of this portion of Isaiah portrayed God as the foreteller of the future. The writer hung God's superiority on his ability to predict events *in advance* of their occurrence. The writer claims that these words were written *before* the events took place. If this writer did not pen these words until *after* Cyrus appeared and after the Jews returned to Jerusalem, then these words represent a grand hoax and a revision of history. Such a writer or later editors would have attached these words to an earlier record written by Isaiah. What other conclusion can one reach but that someone—intentionally, perhaps even with the best of intentions, or unintentionally—chose to deceive the reader. Perhaps one could temper such an accusation and suggest that inserting these words into the writing of Isaiah after the return to Judea represents an interpretation of history—a kind of wishful thinking. But the prophet does not present his case in that way.

Why must we stumble here or at other places where God's prophet so clearly tells his readers of events to come long before they occur? Why stumble when Isaiah reports, "The virgin will be with child and will give birth to a son, and will call him Immanuel" (7:14). Why should we shake our heads when Isaiah points to the coming of the Messiah with these words: "A shoot will come up from the stump of Jesse; from his roots a Branch will bear fruit" (11:1). We cling to the words of Isaiah that assure us of God's help and protection, "Fear not, for I have redeemed you; I have called you by name; you are mine" (43:1). What makes Isaiah's predictions any less than the Word of God? In fact, Isaiah implies an interesting question, "If God cannot predict the future, is he any better than any other god?" We could rephrase the question, "If God cannot predict the future, what makes our theology any different than the theology of Islam, Buddhism, or Mormonism?" Some, of course, will suggest that no difference exists, because all religions seek to penetrate the mysterious theological truth of one supreme being. They claim, then, that one opinion about the supreme being is as good as another; it's only a different perspective. So the nations still fashion gods just as the ancients did, even though they build no gold or silver idols.

When we read Isaiah, we find comfort in the words that come from a God who desires to tell us what he has on his mind and in his heart. Isaiah received his message from the Lord by inspiration. The Lord chose to reveal his mind and heart through Isaiah. Believers take the words of God's prophet at face value. They come from a God who controls history. He desires not only to redeem his people but to comfort them with the knowledge of how he redeemed them and what he has in store for them in the future. We read Isaiah with an eye to the future, when God will gather us and all believers to himself. That's a future Isaiah predicted. God blotted out all our transgressions—another promise of God through his prophet. We do not stumble at such wonderful promises. They are all part of the revelation God has made to us, all his sons and daughters, who are called by his name (43:7). It is not too much to believe that God told his Old Testament people about Cyrus and the coming Messiah before they appeared. These prophecies are not just the words of a human prophet speculating about theology and world history. They are the words of God transmitted through the human medium of his prophet. This we believe by the power of God's Holy Spirit.

God challenged his people and all the nations to try to prove that he could not predict the future. He issued the same challenge in chapter 41: "Present your case. . . . Bring in your idols to tell us what is going to happen" (verses 21,22). In these verses God calls two groups to present their case as though they were in a court. On one side are the nations, and on the other side, his people Israel. The nations cannot respond any more than they could in chapter 41. They have no witnesses to prove their case. No one can come from the nations to support a claim that another god foretold events before they occurred.

God refers to his people as his witnesses, but witnesses "who have eyes but are blind, who have ears but are deaf." In the previous chapter, God called his people his blind and deaf servant (42:18,19). They did have eyes, but they did not see; they could make no sense of what they saw. When Jesus concluded his preaching in parables, he often said, "He who has ears, let him hear" (Matthew 13:9). Those who rejected him heard the words but refused to let the message penetrate their understanding. Likewise here, the people did witness great deliverance by the hand of the Lord, but they were blind to what it meant. They did not believe.

God's Old Testament people had witnessed the deliverance from Egypt—an event that shaped God's Old Testament in many profound ways. In Isaiah's own day, when God's people had been threatened by the alliance between Israel and Aram (chapter 7), God promised deliverance through Isaiah, and it came. Much later, when the Assyrians laid siege to Jerusalem, God's people saw the 185,000 Assyrian soldiers lying dead at the gate of Jerusalem. Isaiah had foretold the deliverance of Jerusalem before it happened (chapter 37). Even though many continued to worship idols and were therefore blind and deaf to the Lord, they saw these events. They could be God's witnesses in court, even though they were spiritually blind and deaf. They still had ears and eyes. A witness testifies only to what he has seen and heard.

Just as the events related by a witness support the conclusion of a prosecutor or defense attorney, so the events related by God's witnesses support his conclusion. The Lord concludes: "I, even I, am the LORD, apart from me there is no savior. I have revealed and saved and proclaimed—I, and not some foreign god among you." Even the unbelief of God's blind and deaf witnesses could not alter this conclusion. The events spoke for themselves, and God's people had no choice but to tell the truth of what they had seen and heard.

The Lord concludes with neither a confident boast nor a hopeful assertion. What he says remains true, based on the evidence of his past activity on behalf of his people. "I, even I, am the LORD." Muslims make a similar assertion: "There is no God but Allah, and Muhammad is his prophet." But the God of the prophet Isaiah here sets himself against Allah and against every other god—"Apart from me there is no savior." The word *savior* means "one who sets free, aids, helps, or rescues." God delivers and rescues. He delivered his people from Egypt. He would deliver them from Babylon. He promised to deliver the entire world from the bondage of sin and death. The Lord—that is, Jehovah, the God who made the promises to Abraham, Isaac, and Jacob—asserts his superiority above all other concepts of god or formulations of theology. No other god can save. No other god saved the Old Testament people from the Egyptians, the Assyrians, or the Babylonians. No other god provides rescue from sin, death, and hell. All theological speculation apart from the Lord, as revealed in the Scripture, does not lead to rescue and help. Only the Lord, the God of free and faithful grace, offers redemption and salvation.

All information about the Lord and his activity in human history flows from the Lord himself. He has "revealed and saved and proclaimed." His actions would remain a dark mystery unless he explained them. The human mind cannot penetrate the truth of God without the aid of God (1 Corinthians 2:6-16). God revealed his plan before the event was to occur. He then carried out the plan. Once God accomplished his plan, he caused news of it to be heard—he proclaimed it. Such was God's pattern in the long history of Israel and Judah. His pattern has not changed. Isaiah served as God's prophet to reveal a great salvation to come, and in chapter 43 Isaiah speaks of two great deliverances: one from Babylon through Cyrus and another greater spiritual deliverance from sin and death through the Lord's servant, the Messiah. In time God brought about both. He saved. Subsequent writers proclaimed the activity of God. Nehemiah and Ezra, among others, proclaimed the first deliverance. Matthew, Mark, Luke, and John, among others, proclaimed the second. Is there any god like the Lord? And so the section concludes, "When I act, who can reverse it?"

> [14] **This is what the LORD says—**
>   **your Redeemer, the Holy One of Israel:**
>   **"For your sake I will send to Babylon**
>   **and bring down as fugitives all the Babylonians,**
>   **in the ships in which they took pride.**
> [15] **I am the LORD, your Holy One,**
>   **Israel's Creator, your King."**
>
> [16] **This is what the LORD says—**
>   **he who made a way through the sea,**
>   **a path through the mighty waters,**
> [17] **who drew out the chariots and horses,**
>   **the army and reinforcements together,**
>   **and they lay there, never to rise again,**
>   **extinguished, snuffed out like a wick:**
> [18] **"Forget the former things;**
>   **do not dwell on the past.**

¹⁹ See, I am doing a new thing!
      Now it springs up; do you not perceive it?
   I am making a way in the desert
      and streams in the wasteland.
²⁰ The wild animals honor me,
      the jackals and the owls,
   because I provide water in the desert
      and streams in the wasteland,
   to give drink to my people, my chosen,
²¹   the people I formed for myself
      that they may proclaim my praise.

God has made his argument. He is the only savior of his people. As the Redeemer, he has more to say and points his faithful people ahead to the future. The Lord promises deliverance from Babylon. That deliverance lay in the future. Babylon was a rich, powerful, and glorious city. Its merchants conducted world trade and brought their commodities up the Euphrates River in ships. The ancient historian Herodotus described the ancient freighters that brought cargo to Babylon. Commerce was alive and well in ancient Babylon. But all that would come to an end. The Lord would overthrow Babylon.

We should note that the Lord would do this "for your sake," that is, for the sake of his faithful people. He intends to do everything so that all things benefit his own people. Because he and he alone is the Redeemer, the Creator, the King, the Holy One of Israel, his promises will come to pass. The Lord piles up his names here as a monument to his greatness. The Lord acts. No one else does. All action flows from the Lord. We begin to see a definition of grace emerge. God acts for the sake of his people. In the remaining verses, we will discover more about grace and the redemption God provided.

The Lord would break the power of the Babylonians and make these once powerful Gentiles fugitives. Their ships, which once carried precious cargo, in the future would transport them as fugitives. The Lord would dispatch the necessary forces to make this happen. Not only would God break the power of the Babylonians, but God would also release his people from captivity. They would find a way through the desert so they could travel back to Jerusalem.

This deliverance follows the pattern of the deliverance God provided for his people under Moses. Back then, as verse 16 reminds us, God "made a way through the sea" and destroyed Pharaoh's army in the sea. Pharaoh's soldiers were "extinguished, snuffed out like a wick." This past deliverance from Egypt was cause for celebration each year in the Passover. It was a staggering miracle that deserved to be remembered annually.

God suggests, however, that the people should forget this great deliverance. That does not mean that they were to forget all about it; it simply means that they were not to dwell on this past deliverance. God had a new and better one in store for his people. He says, "See, I am doing a new thing!" As God described this new thing, it might have reminded God's Old Testament people of the journey through the wilderness under Moses. Then God fed his people in the wilderness; he provided water for them, sometimes miraculously. The same things are mentioned here.

How is God's promised deliverance new and different from the exodus and journey to the Promised Land? The deliverance from Babylon becomes greater because it is a key event in God's plan of salvation. More than the deliverance from Egypt, the release from Babylon paves the way for the fulfillment of all God's promises of a spiritual deliverance. Leaving Babylon behind, the people came back to Palestine to rebuild the temple, resettle in Jerusalem, and resettle in the villages and towns of Palestine. They resettled

Galilee, inhabited towns like Bethlehem and Capernaum, and made Jerusalem the center of their worship once again. A great Redeemer would come from Bethlehem, begin his work in Galilee, and enter Jerusalem riding on a donkey. The people remained in the land until the coming of Jesus. One deliverance paved the way for the greater. No wonder, then, that they were to forget the deliverance from Egypt. It was a great deliverance, but an even greater one awaited. It was all part of God's plan for his people.

For this greater deliverance, the people were to proclaim the praise of God. He had formed them for the purpose of praise. God would refresh his people; they would praise him. So many centuries later, we have been delivered from sin, death, and divine punishment so that we might praise God. Peter wrote, "You are a chosen people, a royal priesthood, a holy nation, a people belonging to God, that you may declare the praises of him who called you out of darkness into his wonderful light" (1 Peter 2:9). Paul reminds us that "whatever you do, do it all for the glory of God" (1 Corinthians 10:31). Like the Old Testament believers, New Testament believers have no other ultimate purpose than to give glory to God.

> [22] **"Yet you have not called upon me, O Jacob,**
>   **you have not wearied yourselves for me, O Israel.**
> [23] **You have not brought me sheep for burnt offerings,**
>   **nor honored me with your sacrifices.**
> **I have not burdened you with grain offerings**
>   **nor wearied you with demands for incense.**
> [24] **You have not bought any fragrant calamus for me,**
>   **or lavished on me the fat of your sacrifices.**
> **But you have burdened me with your sins**
>   **and wearied me with your offenses.**

Why would God provide such a wonderful deliverance? It was by grace and grace alone. God explains grace carefully here, and his explanation deserves our attention. Grace does not depend on human effort. God reminds his people that they did not call him. He called them. God's action is the reason they are his people. God chose Abram before he was circumcised, changed his name to Abraham, and promised to bring blessings upon the entire earth through him.

When the people became a nation while in captivity in Egypt, they offered God no sacrifices. Only after God sent Moses did they sacrifice lambs and swab their blood on their doorposts. God's deliverance was freely offered without sacrifices. The intricate system of burnt offerings, grain offerings, and incense were all instituted after the deliverance from Egypt. God's people had not earned God's deliverance because they had fulfilled his regulations. God never instituted a religion that rewarded people on the basis of their performance. God freely offered deliverance after deliverance to his people, in spite of their failure to comply with his laws. The laws of God did not serve as a gate that controlled his blessings or that could be opened by people if they did as God demanded. God's laws served as a mirror to show the people their sins and as a guide for them to know what was pleasing to God. The sacrifices and worship could not earn blessings from God. All the ceremonial laws only gave the people a guide so their faith could show itself by actions.

God did not institute the sacrifices or outline the worship practices of his people to make them his slaves. The laws were not made so that the people could work hard in order to curry the goodwill of God. The blessings were freely given and the laws were given so that the people could express their joy and appreciation for the gifts and blessings of God. But the sins of the people caused God to exert himself on their behalf. The NIV translation of the phrase "you have burdened me with your sins" could be better translated as "you have forced me into labor with your sins." God became the servant of his sinful and rebellious people.

How was God forced into labor because of the sins of the people? Consider the plan God carried out to bring about redemption for Israel and Judah and also for all the world. Consider how the Lord of all became a human and was born in Bethlehem to a lowly descendant of David. Consider the sweat of Jesus in the Garden of Gethsemane. Consider the labor of carrying a cross through the streets of Jerusalem. The sins of the world caused God's labor. God had to rescue humanity from sin and death because there was no one else who could do it. No God offered forgiveness by grace except the Lord. No theology but the theology of the cross offers forgiveness.

> ²⁵ **"I, even I, am he who blots out**
> **your transgressions, for my own sake,**
> **and remembers your sins no more.**

God alone blots out the transgressions and sins of his people. No human can remove one single stain. Not one prayer, not one sacrifice, not one act of religious devotion can remove sins. Nor can all the prayers, sacrifices, and worship earn what God freely offers for his own sake. What could possibly motivate the Lord of the universe to blot out and forget sin? Nothing in any human. Only God's grace alone. This verse trumpets that truth. The words "for my own sake" are the notes of God's trumpet song of grace. Sins are removed because God chooses to forgive them. No sins are forgiven because a sinner performs some action—a penance to remove the sin. Sins are forgotten not because any sinner can undo the sin or make up for it with a series of good deeds. Even a lifetime of good effort and wonderful intentions cannot cause God to forgive. He forgives because he forgives. He forgives because he loves. He blots out sins freely by grace. He does not wait for any human to be good first so that he can reward the sinner with forgiveness. He forgives *for his own sake.*

> ²⁶ **Review the past for me,**
> **let us argue the matter together;**
> **state the case for your innocence.**
> ²⁷ **Your first father sinned;**
> **your spokesmen rebelled against me.**
> ²⁸ **So I will disgrace the dignitaries of your temple,**
> **and I will consign Jacob to destruction**
> **and Israel to scorn.**

Perhaps some might think that God blotted out the sins of his people because they would sometime in the future be his servants. Could anyone be forgiven in view of their future good life? Such a thought makes God's forgiveness dependent on future human actions or thoughts. The sinner would then still earn forgiveness. All this thought does is place the human effort *after* the awarding of grace rather than *before.* God cited the example of the first father of his people. Some think this first father is Adam; others, Abraham; but most consider him to be Israel or Jacob. Certainly Jacob fits very well because the people are called by his name so frequently in this section (40:27; 41:8; 42:24; 43:1,15,22).

Consider Jacob. He deceived his father in order to gain the birthright, fled in fear from his angry brother, stole away from his uncle Laban with what he had earned while with his uncle, and favored Joseph over his other children. He was not always the model of virtue and faith. Had God given him what he deserved, Jacob would have been cast aside with all the other sinners of the world. Yet God, by grace, chose him.

Later, when the Israelites left Egypt, they did not remain faithful in the wilderness. At the foot of Mount Sinai, they built a golden calf. Those who were called to serve God rebelled against him repeatedly. Sin made Israel and Judah a hopeless case deserving judgment. The entire nation did not deserve the forgiveness of God because they were so faithful or because they would be faithful in the future. Their history proved just the opposite. Again and again they incurred the wrath of God and managed to find a way to make themselves subject to his judgment.

Because of their repeated sin and frequent rebellion, God would eventually bring his judgment. Even those who were called upon to serve in the temple had rejected the grace of God. Isaiah called them "the dignitaries of your temple." They would be disgraced. The coming Babylonians would carry out God's judgment. The temple vessels themselves would be desecrated and carried off to Babylon. Because of the sins of God's people, they would be consigned to destruction. Isaiah in this verse identifies God's people and recalls all that God did to make the nation his special people.

When God prepared such a wonderful new redemption and offered it freely without any merit on the part of his people, what was he to do when his free offer was rejected? God had no choice but to bring judgment. Instead of turning to the Lord, apart from whom there is no savior (verse 11), most of the people turned to false gods. They would be sadly disappointed. No other god could provide redemption and deliverance. Yet God offered it freely by grace. When anyone rejects the Lord and his grace, he or she chooses to abandon the blessings of God. Such rejection can only bring judgment. If someone gave you a map through a minefield but you chose to ignore the map and walk through the field without its information, the tragic results would be your own fault. So it will be for all who choose to ignore the one and only redemption from sin and death God provided in Jesus Christ.

The Lord will pour out his Spirit and cause his people to flourish once again

44 "But now listen, O Jacob, my servant,
    Israel, whom I have chosen.
  ² This is what the LORD says—
    he who made you, who formed you in the womb,
    and who will help you:
  Do not be afraid, O Jacob, my servant,
    Jeshurun, whom I have chosen.
  ³ For I will pour water on the thirsty land,
    and streams on the dry ground;
  I will pour out my Spirit on your offspring,
    and my blessing on your descendants.
  ⁴ They will spring up like grass in a meadow,
    like poplar trees by flowing streams.
  ⁵ One will say, 'I belong to the LORD';
    another will call himself by the name of Jacob;
  still another will write on his hand, 'The LORD's,'
    and will take the name Israel.

The last words of the previous chapter announced judgment upon God's people. God said he would "consign Jacob to destruction and Israel to scorn." The sins of the people were the reason for these sharp words of judgment. They deserved nothing else than such judgment. The first words of this chapter announce a contrast, "But now listen, . . ." The people deserved judgment, but God remains always more ready to extend grace than to inflict punishment. Jacob was still his servant, and God had chosen these people. They were his. More important, he had promised great things for all the world through the people he had chosen as his own.

Because God had chosen them, he assures them, "Do not be afraid." His grace would provide blessings. God calls his people by an unusual name, Jeshurun. The name is only used on three other occasions—all from Deuteronomy—when Moses rehearsed the covenant of God with a new generation of Israelites (32:15; 33:5,26). The old generation had died in the wilderness because of their rebellion and sin. A new generation had taken their place and were ready to advance into the Promised Land. On the threshold of that momentous event which God had promised, Moses referred to the people as Jeshurun three times. The meaning of the name is not clear, but most consider it to mean "my upright, or righteous, one." It's as if it were God's pet name for his people and provides an important contrast to the people who rebelled against God in the wilderness during the days of Moses and those who turned away from him in Judah during the days of Isaiah.

One generation had died in the wilderness to be replaced by another through whom God would fulfill his promises. Centuries later another unfaithful generation would be swept away. God would send the Babylonians against his unfaithful people. The armies of Nebuchadnezzar would destroy Jerusalem and carry the population of Jerusalem and the cities of Judah away captive. Isaiah predicted the disaster long before it occurred. God's people had reason to fear. The faithful perhaps would fear that they would be destroyed in exile, assimilated into the population of the Babylonian Empire. The promise that the kingdom of David would be established forever seemed to be swallowed up in the catastrophe of the Babylonian captivity. What hope did they have that God would bring about the redemption he had promised? The sinful human heart grows fearful even when God issues his promises. It needs constant reassurance. The Lord therefore assures his people, "Do not be afraid."

God's choice serves as the foundation of all his blessings. One generation of unfaithful, rebellious sinners would experience the judgment of God, but the Lord would not forget his chosen people. A new generation would arise. On that new generation, God would pour out his Spirit like one pours water on dry ground. The picture emphasizes the grace of God. The people could not come to life on their own any more than a seed can germinate and grow without water. A desert will not bloom by itself, but it will turn green and blossom when the rain comes. So God's people had no spiritual life without the power of God's Spirit. They were dead and lifeless until his grace would awaken them to spiritual life. A time would come when God's faithful would once again blossom and grow "like grass in a meadow, like poplar trees by flowing streams." God provides this blessing by grace for his unfaithful people.

The Lord has in mind the return of a faithful remnant from the Babylonian captivity. Another generation would return to rebuild Jerusalem and the cities of Judah. God would use them to fulfill the other greater promises of redemption, victory, and glory, all of which are centered on the Messiah, Jesus Christ. In other places in the Old Testament Scriptures, including in Isaiah's prophecy, God promised that he would pour out his Spirit upon all humanity.

But here God promises that his people would once again confess their faith in him. He does not see only scattered individuals professing their faith in him, but many. Some would say, "I belong to the LORD;" others would call themselves by the name of Jacob, the forefather of the nation; still others would write that they belong to the

Lord. The translation of the NIV suggests that they would write *on* their hands "The LORD's," but most likely this means they would write "The LORD's" *with* their hands. By spoken and written confession, a new generation would once again pledge faithfulness to the Lord. God's Holy Spirit would work such a miraculous change of heart.

> ⁶ "This is what the LORD says—
>   Israel's King and Redeemer, the LORD Almighty:
> I am the first and I am the last;
>   apart from me there is no God.
> ⁷ Who then is like me? Let him proclaim it.
>   Let him declare and lay out before me
> what has happened since I established my ancient people,
>   and what is yet to come—
>   yes, let him foretell what will come.
> ⁸ Do not tremble, do not be afraid.
>   Did I not proclaim this and foretell it long ago?
> You are my witnesses. Is there any God besides me?
>   No, there is no other Rock; I know not one."

The Lord based his promise to "Jeshurun" on what he had done for his people. He made them and formed them. The Lord's activity toward his people has the tender care of a mother who has carried her child "in the womb" (verse 2). With such care and tenderness invested in his people, God would also help his people. God's activity in shaping his people is a significant thought in this section of the book. Later in this chapter, God's activity in the making and forming of his people will be placed in contrast to the way the idolaters formed and shaped their gods. But before God ridicules the foolishness of idolatry, he asserts his superiority. He has done more than make and shape his people, and he draws the attention of his people to all that he has done and would do.

With a solemn introduction, "This is what the LORD

says," God gives himself a series of significant names that help us understand what he had done for his people. He is "Israel's King." He has administered the affairs of his people efficiently. No single human king who ever ruled over God's people was a perfect king. They all had faults, some of them serious faults. The Lord is the perfect, wise ruler of his people. He controls all the affairs of his people in a way that is best for them. He is also their "Redeemer." The word for *redeem* used here is a special word found repeatedly in the second part of Isaiah's prophecy. Altogether, it appears 24 times in chapters 40 through 66 and only once in the first 39 chapters. The word emphasizes the activity of God. He and he alone must redeem his people after they have made themselves slaves by their own sin and rebellion. God would pay the price necessary to buy back his helpless people from the consequences of their own folly. Of course, the word points us ultimately to the payment God's own Son made in order to secure the release of all humanity from sin, death, and hell.

He is also "LORD Almighty." LORD is the special name God revealed. He is Jehovah, the God of free and faithful grace, that is, the God of the covenant. He is the I AM who appeared to Moses. Additionally, he is all powerful in that he controls the hosts of heaven. The idea that he governs the hosts of heaven finds expression in the word *almighty.* The KJV rendered it as "LORD of hosts." The term, which the NIV translates as "LORD Almighty," emphasizes God's superiority, which God again underscores by the next words, "I am the first and I am the last." Before the Israelites became a nation, before Abraham, before Adam, God is God. He existed before the first words of Scripture: "In the beginning . . ." (Genesis 1:1). God did not emerge from the history of the created world. He is independent of creation because he called everything into existence by his powerful word. These phrases encourage us to look ahead to the end of history too. When the last human is born, God will still be God. When the created world ceases to be, he will remain the first and last, Alpha and Omega, the beginning and the end. These terms stand in sharp contrast to the idols created by human hands.

There is no God like the God of the Scriptures. The Lord says it so clearly, "Apart from me there is no God." No one should have any doubt of that truth, but the sinful heart still resists that truth. To quell all doubts, God issues a challenge to those who trust in other gods and who have made idols. He challenges the false gods and those who believe in them to match his ability, specifically his power to care for his people in the past and to predict what will happen to them in the future. The God of the Scriptures is a God of action. He does things for the benefit of his people. Even more impressive, God foretells his actions before they take place. Can any god created by human thought claim to do that? No, such gods remain silent and mute.

God acts because of his faithful love for his people. They receive all the benefits of his action. When God claims superiority over the false gods, it is not only because he is a jealous God unwilling to share his glory with another. His superiority assures his faithful people that he can take care of them. God encourages his people not to fear and tremble as they face the difficulties of the Babylonian captivity or any other catastrophe or problem. When the flood of troubles roars as a mighty stream toward his people, God assures his people that he is the rock that remains. The waters may swirl fiercely around it, but the rock provides safety in the midst of life's surging troubles.

For the Jews, such comfort was necessary as they

faced captivity. Surely, believers through the ages have not faced exactly the same difficulties as the Jews did in captivity. Nevertheless, God continues to be the rock who provides safety, no matter what roaring streams of trouble rush toward us and future generations of God's people. There is no other rock. We need to hear the encouragement too: "Do not tremble, do not be afraid." Our confidence and hope are built on our King, the Lord Almighty, the Redeemer, the first and the last. He is our rock. Apart from him no safety or redemption exists because apart from him there is no god.

> ⁹ **All who make idols are nothing,**
> **and the things they treasure are worthless.**
> **Those who would speak up for them are blind;**
> **they are ignorant, to their own shame.**
> ¹⁰ **Who shapes a god and casts an idol,**
> **which can profit him nothing?**
> ¹¹ **He and his kind will be put to shame;**
> **craftsmen are nothing but men.**
> **Let them all come together and take their stand;**
> **they will be brought down to terror and infamy.**

God is the rock amid the storms of life. The contrast cannot be put more bluntly than the first line of verse 9, "All who make idols are nothing." The word for *nothing* takes us back to the creation of the world, before God shaped the "formless and empty" earth and while darkness still spread over the face of the deep (Genesis 1:2). The idol worshipers belonged to the world before God's creative activity. They are nothing, and all they treasure has no value. God created the world and everything in it. What have these idol makers done? The contrast is striking. How can the work of craftsmen, as great as they may be, compare to the glory of God's creation? The craftsmen themselves are a creation of God, wonderfully made to live, breath, and move.

We apply these words about idol worship and the creation of idols first to all who worship idols and create them. Billions of people who bow down to idols still live in this world. For those who still worship images, these words are a scathing indictment. The point here is that those who make and worship idols are nothing in comparison to God. Those who worship idols are blind and ignorant, and all they value is worthless. Those are strong words, but without the Redeemer nothing of value exists. The apostle Paul came to that startling conclusion: "I consider everything a loss compared to the surpassing greatness of knowing Christ Jesus my Lord, for whose sake I have lost all things. I consider them rubbish, that I may gain Christ" (Philippians 3:8).

Most modern religious thought has abandoned the worship of idols, but it still fashions gods. Anytime a theology grows in the mind of a scholar or group of scholars and it abandons the truth that God revealed in the Scriptures, that theology becomes nothing but an idol, a creation of the human mind. It is as ridiculous for a craftsman to fashion a god from wood, stone, or metal as it is for any human to fashion concepts of God apart from the Scriptures. Those who fashion such a god are nothing, and what they treasure has no value. Outside the God of the Scriptures, there is no god, and that includes not only the idols but also all concepts about God that depart from the Scriptures.

Luther identified idolatry as all religion that hopes to earn something from God by human effort, in other words, all religion based on works. He was correct. That is the sum and substance of all false religion. The God of the Bible is a God of grace, who redeems helpless sinners not because they are good but only because of his undeserved love for those helpless sinners. Any theologian who proclaims that God must first see good deeds or even good intentions before he responds crafts an idol. Any theologian who suggests that humans must somehow cooperate with God before he will love them creates a god as surely as ancient craftsmen fashioned their idols. God is a God of grace. "It is by grace you have been saved, through faith—and this not from yourselves, it is the gift of God—not by works, so that no one can boast" (Ephesians 2:8,9).

[12] The blacksmith takes a tool
    and works with it in the coals;
he shapes an idol with hammers,
    he forges it with the might of his arm.
He gets hungry and loses his strength;
    he drinks no water and grows faint.
[13] The carpenter measures with a line
    and makes an outline with a marker;
he roughs it out with chisels
    and marks it with compasses.
He shapes it in the form of man,
    of man in all his glory,
    that it may dwell in a shrine.
[14] He cut down cedars,
    or perhaps took a cypress or oak.
He let it grow among the trees of the forest,
    or planted a pine, and the rain made it grow.
[15] It is man's fuel for burning;
    some of it he takes and warms himself,
    he kindles a fire and bakes bread.
But he also fashions a god and worships it;
    he makes an idol and bows down to it.
[16] Half of the wood he burns in the fire;
    over it he prepares his meal,
    he roasts his meat and eats his fill.
He also warms himself and says,
    "Ah! I am warm; I see the fire."
[17] From the rest he makes a god, his idol;
    he bows down to it and worships.
He prays to it and says,
    "Save me; you are my god."

In verses 9 to 11, we learned that those who worship a god that is different from the one in the Bible are nothing. The lesson continues in these verses with another important point. Those who worship idols are foolish. How could Isaiah make the point more clearly? Blacksmiths and carpenters are human and work to the point of exhaustion in order to make an idol that takes "the form of man." The human mind cannot create the divine. Water cannot go uphill by itself. Certain rules apply. The human mind cannot conceive of what lies beyond its experience and knowledge. How can a human mind—bound by space, time, matter, and energy—conceive of God, who lies outside all those categories and is an infinite, all-powerful spirit? We know about God only because he has told us what to think about him. Paul made the point so clearly in 1 Corinthians when he quoted from a later chapter in Isaiah, "No eye has seen, no ear has heard, no mind has conceived what God has prepared for those who love him" (2:9; Isaiah 64:4)

Foolish indeed is the one who creates a god from the same wood he uses to cook his food and then bows down and says, "Save me; you are my god." Foolish indeed are those who make a god according to their own thoughts and imaginations. How are ancient worshipers of idols essentially different from modern worshipers of gods fashioned from the concepts and principles in their own minds? Can either expect such a god to rescue them? Such gods are worthless mind games that are absolutely useless in the face of human suffering, human evil, the raw brute force of nature, and death. All theologies not based on the Scriptures only whistle in the dark.

> ¹⁸ **They know nothing, they understand nothing;**
> **their eyes are plastered over so they cannot see,**
> **and their minds closed so they cannot understand.**

¹⁹ **No one stops to think,**
    no one has the knowledge or understanding to say,
  "Half of it I used for fuel;
    I even baked bread over its coals,
    I roasted meat and I ate.
  Shall I make a detestable thing from what is left?
    Shall I bow down to a block of wood?"
²⁰ **He feeds on ashes, a deluded heart misleads him;**
    he cannot save himself, or say,
    "Is not this thing in my right hand a lie?"

Such a contrast! The Lord is a rock in the storms and floods of trouble. His faithful people cling to him and find safety. Yet so many do not trust the Lord Almighty. Instead, they manufacture their own gods to help them in the midst of life's troubles. In this section God tells his people that all who worship idols are worthless. Gods created by the human mind are nothing by comparison to the Lord's great, surpassing power and grace. Something strangely backward occurs when humans do not listen to the God who made them and instead tell God what he is and what he means to say. Those who manufacture gods are incredibly foolish.

One more lesson remains from this section. Not only are the worshipers of false gods foolish, but they are blind to the foolishness of idolatry. God identifies the reason for their blindness: "Their eyes are plastered over so they cannot see, and their minds closed so they cannot understand." If anyone doubts the blindness of unbelief, ask anyone who has tried to share the truth of God's grace with an unbeliever. The unbeliever will persist in his or her unbelief. It happens in foreign mission fields, where people prefer to worship false gods and resist the message of Christ. It has been thus through the ages. The early Christian martyrs lost their lives and property because of this blind unbelief. Every time the gospel is rejected, we encounter such blindness.

One insight catches our attention. Those who refuse to believe feed "on ashes." Their hearts and minds are not nourished on anything but worthless ashes, the speculation of the human mind. Those who worship idols do not nourish their hearts and minds on what God has said. If they don't read the words of God, how can they come to any conclusion but to reject the God of the Bible? Unbelief holds to the delusions of the human spirit and mind and rejects the God of redemption and grace. What value are all the speculations of all the philosophers and theologians in the face of death and sin? No one stops to think that human answers are lies. Just as an idolater does not stop to think how foolish it is to worship wood, stone, or metal.

> ²¹ **"Remember these things, O Jacob,**
> **for you are my servant, O Israel.**
> **I have made you, you are my servant;**
> **O Israel, I will not forget you.**
> ²² **I have swept away your offenses like a cloud,**
> **your sins like the morning mist.**
> **Return to me,**
> **for I have redeemed you."**
>
> ²³ **Sing for joy, O heavens, for the Lord has done this;**
> **shout aloud, O earth beneath.**
> **Burst into song, you mountains,**
> **you forests and all your trees,**
> **for the Lord has redeemed Jacob,**
> **he displays his glory in Israel.**

"Remember these things." God encouraged his people to think about the foolishness and the blindness of worshiping idols. In Isaiah's day, the encouragement was as necessary as it is in any age. Yet the people of Isaiah's day generally did not remember either the great blessings God had given them or the folly of worshiping other gods. Because of the idolatry of his people, God would send the Babylonians to carry the Jews away captive.

Yet the Lord promised to do for his people what no block of wood could do. He has made them; they have not made him. He is not an idol fashioned by the human mind and heart. A block of wood cannot think, but the Lord can. He will not forget his people or the promises he has made to them. Their captivity in Babylon might suggest that God had forgotten all about them, but he had not. His promises would stand, and he would fulfill them. A block of wood cannot forget or remember because it is inanimate and mindless. Not so God. He pledges not to forget.

God can do one more thing even greater than to call and remember his people. He will sweep away their sins. The most crucial issue in the lives of men and women is their sin. God does what no idol can do; he forgives. Here God speaks as though he has already done it. "I have swept away your offenses." In the days of Isaiah, it was as good as done. The picture comforted believers in Isaiah's age and in ours. Just as the sun chases away the morning mist, so God forgives sins. This forgiveness is free, but it is not cheap. God says, "I have redeemed you." The price of the forgiveness of sins was the death of God's own Son, Jesus Christ.

Notice that God invites his people to repent, or to turn to him, but not so that they can receive forgiveness. Their repentance does not move God to forgive. No work can remove sin. No religion can remove sin. No therapist can remove guilt and sins. No worship can remove sins. God freely forgives sin by grace. God redeems. Redemption and forgiveness are tied together. God has redeemed humanity and forgiven sins before any sinner turns to God. Through Isaiah, God extends an invitation for his people to return. God desires them to believe what he has already done— pictured here in the words of prophecy as already having been accomplished. Your sins are forgiven. You are redeemed. Believe it. Turn to God and receive what he freely and graciously offers.

Such a message of forgiveness is what the human heart so desperately needs and what only God so freely and completely offers. When the human heart trusts that God has forgiven sins for the sake of Christ, joy enters the heart. The section concludes with a passage so typical of Isaiah. The prophet invites the heavens, earth, mountains, forests, and trees to rejoice. In the word *redeem,* we find the reason for the joy. It is well to note that the word *redeem* receives special attention in these verses. It occurs again in the next verse. Of all the things that separate the God of the Bible from other theologies, redemption is at the top of the list. Just as all the Bible tells us of Christ, so God's central and most distinctive activity is redemption. It is his glory, his shining achievement. He has done what no other god—no other theology—has done or can do. No other god can rescue human beings from sin (Acts 4:12). Only the theology of the cross can save. Rejoice! Rejoice, believers!

The Lord chooses Cyrus to deliver Judah from captivity

²⁴ "This is what the LORD says—
your Redeemer, who formed you in the womb:

I am the LORD,
who has made all things,
who alone stretched out the heavens,
who spread out the earth by myself,

²⁵ who foils the signs of false prophets
and makes fools of diviners,
who overthrows the learning of the wise
and turns it into nonsense,

²⁶ who carries out the words of his servants
  and fulfills the predictions of his messengers,

who says of Jerusalem, 'It shall be inhabited,'
  of the towns of Judah, 'They shall be built,'
  and of their ruins, 'I will restore them,'
²⁷ who says to the watery deep, 'Be dry,
  and I will dry up your streams,'
²⁸ who says of Cyrus, 'He is my shepherd
  and will accomplish all that I please;
  he will say of Jerusalem, "Let it be rebuilt,"
  and of the temple, "Let its foundations be laid."'

Verse 24 begins another section of the prophecy with the announcement "This is what the LORD says." The section begins with a carefully constructed bridge to the previous section. The Lord identifies himself as "your Redeemer," an idea that occurred in the previous verses (verses 6,22,23). Verse 24 also recalls the opening verses of the chapter, "This is what the LORD says—he who made you, who formed you in the womb" (verse 2). The same Lord who spoke about forgiveness and redemption continues to speak the words in this new section, "I am the LORD." The first person also is part of the bridge. The sections shows the artistry of a skilled wordsmith.

Why is such a thought important? The Lord will reveal some very specific prophecies. For the first time he will mention Cyrus by name. He had referred to him in chapter 41 as the one whom he had stirred up from the north and east (verses 2,25) but had not named him. Now the Lord reveals his name—a specific prophecy that causes some to question whether Isaiah could possibly have written these words. But the Lord who had spoken earlier speaks here too. He stands behind his promises to forgive sin as well as his promise to call forth a ruler named Cyrus. Since he is the Lord Almighty, we do not question whether or not he can predict the future. We simply trust that it is as he says.

He identifies himself as the "LORD"—that is, Jehovah, the Savior-God—and then continues by listing all that he has done and will do. The NIV translates the nine different actions of God as relative clauses beginning with "who" and emphasizes them by the margins. The emphasis falls on the action of this "LORD." He made all things. He stretched out the heavens without anyone's help. He spread out the earth. Who was there to help him? This thought too is part of the bridge. We have just read of the craftsmen who have made their gods out of wood. Now we have a contrast. God made the heavens and the earth out of nothing. He did it without the help of anyone. Again the Lord claims to be supreme. No human effort can reach him; no human speculation can comprehend him. Humans are his creation; God does not exist because any human mind created him.

The Lord identifies himself with another series of actions. God supports the truth. He foils the signs of the false prophets. He gave Moses signs to demonstrate the superiority of the Lord who had sent him. After Moses' staff turned into a serpent, it swallowed the staffs of the Egyptian magicians, which they had also turned into serpents (Exodus 7:8-12). God also overthrows the learning of the wise, which is contrary to his grace and mercy. This grouping concludes by asserting that the Lord supports the words of his prophets. When Moses spoke, God did as his messenger had predicted. So it happened with Elijah and the other prophets too. This God not only acts, but he also communicates the truth. He therefore subverts and undercuts the false teachers and supports his own messengers.

Finally, the Lord not only acts but also speaks. His

words are first for Jerusalem and the desolate towns of Judah. The Lord promises to restore Jerusalem. He assures his people that they will return from the captivity and that Jerusalem and the Judean countryside will again ring with the sound of people. City walls broken and battered by the Babylonian armies will be rebuilt. God even promises to remove obstacles that would prevent the people from returning to Jerusalem and the cities of Judea. He will dry up the streams. The picture recalls the exodus from Egypt, when God dried up the Red Sea so his people could pass through safely.

One final promise: Cyrus would be the one who would make the rebuilding of Jerusalem and Judea possible. He would serve as a shepherd of the Jewish exiles and make it possible for them to return from captivity. The use of the word *shepherd* only means that Cyrus would be the leader that God would use to return his captive people to their homeland. The Jewish historian Josephus claimed that Cyrus read these words of Isaiah and was so impressed that he desired to fulfill the prophecy. Whether Cyrus ever read Isaiah's prophecy is an open question. We don't have any more to go on than the reference by Josephus. But, ultimately, it doesn't matter. God chose Cyrus to be the instrument for his people's return to Judea.

From the first reference to this foreign conqueror in chapter 41, the prophecy has become more and more specific and more and more concrete. The process will continue because we have another great hero to learn about as we go along—the Servant of the Lord, the Messiah. The prophecies about him also will grow more and more specific and concrete through the remaining portion of Isaiah's prophecy. For the time being, Isaiah will concentrate on Cyrus and the return from Babylon.

45 "This is what the LORD says to his anointed,
to Cyrus, whose right hand I take hold of
to subdue nations before him
and to strip kings of their armor,
to open doors before him
so that gates will not be shut:
² I will go before you
and will level the mountains;
I will break down gates of bronze
and cut through bars of iron.
³ I will give you the treasures of darkness,
riches stored in secret places,
so that you may know that I am the LORD,
the God of Israel, who summons you by name.

God named Cyrus for the first time in the last verse of chapter 44. God called Cyrus his shepherd who would rebuild Jerusalem and the temple. Of course, Cyrus did not build Jerusalem and the temple himself, but he signed the edict that allowed a remnant of the Jewish people to return to Palestine and rebuild. Cyrus further ordered the return of the gold and silver articles that Nebuchadnezzar had taken from the house of God. In addition, he paid for the rebuilding of the temple from the royal treasury (Ezra 6:3-5). Isaiah's prediction, made over a century before the events unfolded, is astonishing; it still raises many questions and causes doubts for many. Yet Isaiah wove the specific reference to Cyrus into the very fabric of the prophecy. Without it, the prophecy becomes a ragged and torn tapestry. The references to Cyrus complete the prophecy and give it a wonderful artistic richness. Cyrus becomes a significant motif that carries us to the announcement of a greater hero—the Servant of the Lord, the Messiah. The Persian king, for all his faults and imperfections, becomes a type of the perfect and complete Servant of the Lord. The Messiah would release God's people from the captivity of sin, death, and hell—a much more significant deliverance than Cyrus could ever imagine.

Chapter 45 begins with another assertion that the Lord, Israel's Savior-God, stands behind the words of Isaiah and behind the success of Cyrus. We may be surprised that God's prophet calls Cyrus, a foreign king, the Lord's anointed. Yet God raised up Cyrus for a specific purpose. Just as God anointed prophets, kings, and priests for specific functions among his people, so God anointed Cyrus. Although Cyrus was not from among God's people, nevertheless, he had a specific role to fill in God's plan. The Lord promised to "go before," or lead, this Persian king and grant him success against his enemies. Babylon's mighty gates would open before him. The Lord would remove obstacles and even give him "the treasures of darkness." Ancient kings often hoarded the spoils of war in secret places. When Cyrus was victorious, God allowed him to reap the financial benefits of his victories.

Verse 3 concludes with the first of three reasons for God's action. The Lord granted Cyrus victories and success so that he would know that it was the Lord who stood behind him. The writer of 2 Chronicles concluded his account with the words of Cyrus: "The LORD, the God of heaven, has given me all the kingdoms of the earth and he has appointed me to build a temple for him at Jerusalem in Judah. Anyone of his people among you—may the LORD his God be with him, and let him go up" (36:23). The book of Ezra also begins with a record of the edict of Cyrus in which the Persian king asserts the very same thought.

We must not read too much into the decree of Cyrus. He did have some rudimentary knowledge of the true God, but we have no evidence that he actually became a convert.

Cyrus also acknowledged the Babylonian god Marduk, in a proclamation to the Babylonians. Later Isaiah will say that Cyrus did not acknowledge the Lord, and yet the Lord used him to accomplish his purposes, just as he used the decree of Caesar Augustus to bring Mary and Joseph to Bethlehem. The Lord controls all things, including the events and personalities of history.

> [4] **For the sake of Jacob my servant,**
>   **of Israel my chosen,**
> **I summon you by name**
>   **and bestow on you a title of honor,**
>   **though you do not acknowledge me.**
> [5] **I am the LORD, and there is no other;**
>   **apart from me there is no God.**
> **I will strengthen you,**
>   **though you have not acknowledged me,**
> [6] **so that from the rising of the sun**
>   **to the place of its setting**
> **men may know there is none besides me.**
>   **I am the LORD, and there is no other.**
> [7] **I form the light and create darkness,**
>   **I bring prosperity and create disaster;**
>   **I, the LORD, do all these things.**

The Lord clearly identifies the second reason for his action: "For the sake of Jacob my servant, of Israel my chosen." Notice that God's people still are precious in the eyes of the Lord. He calls them "my servant" and "my chosen," special names that reveal their close relationship with the Lord. He has not forgotten them. He has remained faithful to the covenant he once made with Abraham, and he intends to fulfill all the promises he made concerning his people.

The rise of Cyrus would not only demonstrate to Cyrus that the Lord had called him by name, but the Persian king's position in history would benefit God's people. The Jews would return to Palestine and rebuild their nation. Another more significant chapter would be written a little over five hundred years after the Jews returned to rebuild Jerusalem and the cities of Judah. When God's time finally arrived, "God sent his Son, born of a woman, born under law, to redeem those under law, that we might receive the full rights of sons" (Galatians 4:4,5). God planned the redemption of his people and carried it out. The return to Palestine was just one step in God's plan. It set the stage for the greater fulfillment in Christ.

God promises in these words that this important first step would be carried out by a foreign king—a Persian who did not acknowledge the Lord. Perhaps we might wonder how God could carry out his plan by using a foreign ruler. But that need not cause us difficulty. God rules all things. The choice of Cyrus demonstrates God's absolute authority over all things. In addition, it underscores one of the themes of this portion of Isaiah: the superiority of the Lord over all other gods.

The absolute superiority of the Lord weaves its way through this section of Isaiah and finds expression here. "I am the LORD, and there is no other; apart from me there is no God." In so many ways this strand of thought finds expression frequently in the chapters we have read so far. The Lord asked in chapter 40, "To whom will you compare me?" (verse 25). He announced that all other gods were false: "See, they are all false!" (41:29). He proclaimed that he was jealous of his praise and glory: "I am the LORD; that is my name! I will not give my glory to another or my praise to idols" (42:8). The Lord again asserted his superiority in the next chapter: "I, even I, am the LORD, and apart from me there is no savior. I have revealed and saved and proclaimed—I, and not some foreign god among you"

113

(43:11,12). In the previous chapter, "the LORD Almighty" had said, "I am the first and I am the last; apart from me there is no God" (44:6).

Why does this thought receive such emphasis? The answer lies in the importance of the Lord's work. Only the Lord blots out sins. Only the Lord is the Redeemer. No other religious idea, no other god, no other theology offers what the Lord offers: forgiveness, life, and salvation. We look beyond Cyrus to this greater work of God. No other God so carefully planned the redemption of his people and all the world. The Lord's superiority rests on his plan to send a Redeemer more important than Cyrus. The second part of Isaiah's prophecy (chapters 40–66) deals with this important activity of the Lord. The assertions of God's superiority in these chapters find expression in Peter's words to the Sanhedrin (the Jewish high council): "Salvation is found in no one else, for there is no other name [that is, the name of Jesus Christ] under heaven given to men by which we must be saved" (Acts 4:12). All gods are not the same. All theologies do not lead to the same heaven. All thoughts about God are not only different viewpoints or different interpretations of the same God. The God of the Scriptures asserts that only he forgives sins and only he has provided the ransom price necessary to redeem sinners.

Only the God of the Scriptures claims to have raised Cyrus to power in order to accomplish God's own purpose. We noted that the reason the Lord had raised Cyrus to prominence was, first, so that Cyrus would know God is the Lord Jehovah and, second, so that God could rescue his people. The Lord offers a third reason: so that all humanity may know that there is no other God than the Lord. These reasons expand outward like ripples from a stone's splash in a pond. God's action was carried out for the benefit of

Cyrus, then a larger ripple included Judah, God's people, and finally, the largest ripple included all humanity "from the rising of the sun to the place of its setting." The action of God in sending Cyrus was not limited to reestablishing the national identity of God's people in Palestine. Cyrus set the stage for the coming of the Messiah, whose coming was for all the world. That's what Jesus told Nicodemus, "God so loved the *world* . . ." (John 3:16).

Verse 7 seems to present some problems when God proclaims, "I bring prosperity and create disaster." In his wisdom God does allow disaster to overtake even his own. Job serves as a primary example. He lost his possessions, his family, and his health. On the other hand, God granted Abraham great wealth. He brings disaster upon so many and at the same time brings prosperity to many others. Such a pattern has persisted through the centuries. Christians are killed for their faithful witness. Unbelievers often prosper. The Lord asserts that he does all these things. We may be puzzled by his dealings in our world and in our own lives, but whether he brings prosperity or creates disaster, he always has the best interests of his people in mind. So he has promised, "In all things God works for the good of those who love him" (Romans 8:28).

> 8 **"You heavens above, rain down righteousness;**
> **let the clouds shower it down.**
> **Let the earth open wide,**
> **let salvation spring up,**
> **let righteousness grow with it;**
> **I, the LORD, have created it.**

The greatest of all blessings transcends prosperity and disaster. God provides the rich blessings of his grace in Christ for all the earth. His blessings come down from above to a thirsty and dry earth. The picture is appropriate. Righteousness does not come from the earth. On earth "there is no one righteous, not even one" (Romans 3:10). But a righteousness comes from God (Romans 3:21). It comes from above, and, in this picture, God commands the clouds to pour it down upon the earth, which desperately needs it. Without the righteousness God alone provides, there is no salvation. In spiritual terms, the picture means that by nature humanity does not have what is necessary for salvation. We are dead in trespasses and sin (Ephesians 2:1). God must give what is necessary—his righteousness. He declares all the world righteous; it rains from above. Only this gift of God's grace—like the rain—can cause faith. Once we receive God's gift—righteousness—like the parched earth when we believe, faith then brings forth a rightness of life that conforms to God's standard. So salvation and righteousness grow together.

Who is responsible for all this? The Lord. It is as much his gift to humanity as rain is a gift to a dry and lifeless land.

> 9 **"Woe to him who quarrels with his Maker,**
> **to him who is but a potsherd among the potsherds on**
> **the ground.**
> **Does the clay say to the potter,**
> **'What are you making?'**
> **Does your work say,**
> **'He has no hands'?**
> 10 **Woe to him who says to his father,**
> **'What have you begotten?'**
> **or to his mother,**
> **'What have you brought to birth?'**

God's action did not come without complaint and question from his people. Consider those who saw Jerusalem and the temple destroyed—what anguish they endured as they saw foreign armies destroy so much of what they loved. Consider the exiles. Foreign soldiers forced them to march across the desert to Babylon and then detained them there. God's people must have frequently asked what God was doing. Those who returned to Palestine 70 years later might also have wondered what God was doing when their enemies made life difficult and prevented them from rebuilding their land. After it was all done, God's people might have wondered why God did it all. Why did he rip them from their homeland only to return them several generations later? Why all this suffering and pain?

Complaining about God's handling of history or about the way he manages our own individual lives is like the pot complaining to the potter who shaped it. If the Lord wants his people to be potsherds lying broken on the ground, that's what they will be. The potter exercises complete control and can make what he wishes with the clay he works with his hands.

So it is with us. If the Lord chooses to make us broken clay pots, that is what he has chosen to make of us. He decides, and we are to have complete confidence in the ability of the Lord to make us serve his purposes. No matter how he has made us, no matter what calling he has given us, no matter whether we are broken or whole, we are his. It is foolish to complain and wish we were something different. Whatever God has made of us, we have one purpose—to glorify him.

Our suffering, our bearing the cross, is reflective of Christ's bearing the cross for us because as Isaiah notes, he is our suffering servant. Just as Christ overcame suffering, sickness, pain, sorrows, and sin, so by faith in him we will too. His victory is ours in faith. Heavenly glory will be ours after the sorrows of life here.

> ¹¹ "This is what the LORD says—
>   the Holy One of Israel, and its Maker:
>   Concerning things to come,
>   do you question me about my children,
>   or give me orders about the work of my hands?
> ¹² It is I who made the earth
>   and created mankind upon it.
>   My own hands stretched out the heavens;
>   I marshaled their starry hosts.
> ¹³ I will raise up Cyrus in my righteousness:
>   I will make all his ways straight.
>   He will rebuild my city
>   and set my exiles free,
>   but not for a price or reward,
>   says the LORD Almighty."

The Lord asserts his sovereignty. He decides what to do with his children, with all humanity, with Cyrus, and with all he has created. He is the Creator and the Holy One of Israel, and he will do whatever he thinks best. So often humans question why God does what he does. But the Lord responds here by saying that he can do whatever he wants because he has created the earth, mankind on the earth, and the heavens and all the starry universe. He and he alone decides what to do.

God made Cyrus part of his plan. The Lord determined to raise up Cyrus, bless him with success, and use him to set his people free and rebuild Jerusalem. All that Cyrus did was done by the will of God. Cyrus did not bribe the Lord to achieve all his successes. God's people did not pay Cyrus a fee in order to return to Palestine. Nor did the Lord have to pay Cyrus to do what the Lord wanted him to do. The Lord does not operate on a "pay for what you get" policy. So often we think that nothing happens unless you pay wages or offer some kind of bribe or incentive. God is independent of such things. He doesn't need payment. In addition, he is the sovereign Lord, who can do whatever he wants. The entire history of Cyrus and God's people occurred as predicted because the Lord caused it to happen. It happened without payment because God determined to do it. He was and is the Lord Almighty, who can do whatever he chooses.

> ¹⁴**This is what the LORD says:**
>
> **"The products of Egypt and the merchandise of Cush,**
>   **and those tall Sabeans—**
> **they will come over to you**
>   **and will be yours;**
> **they will trudge behind you,**
>   **coming over to you in chains.**
> **They will bow down before you**
>   **and plead with you, saying,**
> **'Surely God is with you, and there is no other;**
>   **there is no other god.'"**

God's people could have expected that the Persian conquest of Babylon would mean nothing more than a change in masters. But God promises the unexpected. Because of the edict of Cyrus, God would return his people to Judah to rebuild their nation. By their return, God would continue to prepare for the eventual coming of the Great Servant of the Lord, the Messiah. The future was secure because God stood behind every promise. This is another promise of a bright future for God's people. Isaiah had foretold that the Babylonians would invade Judea, raze Jerusalem and the temple, and cart off the Jewish population to Babylon as captives. That future was dark and painful. This verse announces a reversal of their situation.

Nations from the continent of Africa would "come over to you." Egypt had held Israel captive for many years in order to build her treasure cities (Exodus 1:11). An astonishing reversal would take place in the future. The rich products and merchandise not only of Egypt but also of Cush and the Sabeans would be at the disposal of God's people. The Egyptians, who once had been the taskmasters of Israel, would "trudge behind" God's people and would come over to them "in chains."

How could such a change take place? It happened because these nations came to know the Lord God of Israel. They were led to faith so that they could confess, "Surely God is with you, and there is no other; there is no other god." God tells his Old Testament people that foreign nations will come to believe and submit to the truth. This did not mean that at some time in the future all nations would be united into a worldly empire with Jerusalem and God's people at the center. Instead, God pictures the results of Pentecost when people from all over the world came to believe in Jesus. That conversion continues today in Christian mission fields. The proclamation of the gospel by missionaries in Africa and in other parts of the world results in some who believe. They will be gathered together in the assembly of believers; they will "come over." They will confess their faith in the one true God. Those converts are pictured in chains. In this case the chains represent their voluntary submission to the Lord and to the truth possessed by his people. In the dark days of captivity, such a promise was sure to bring hope to the faithful among God's people. With this promise, God points them to the future and stamps this promise with his approval, "This is what the LORD says."

> **15 Truly you are a God who hides himself,**
> **O God and Savior of Israel.**
> **16 All the makers of idols will be put to shame and disgraced;**
> **they will go off into disgrace together.**

¹⁷ But Israel will be saved by the LORD
with an everlasting salvation;
you will never be put to shame or disgraced,
to ages everlasting.

After these wonderful truths, Isaiah interjects a confession of his own faith. He confesses his faith in the God and Savior of Israel. First, Isaiah confesses his faith in "God who hides himself." We don't often think of God as one who hides himself from us, but there are several ways to understand what the prophet wrote.

First, God is hidden from the naturally sinful human mind. By nature, humans may understand that God created the world. Paul reminds us that "God's invisible qualities—his eternal power and divine nature—have been clearly seen, being understood from what has been made" (Romans 1:20). All humans marvel at the beauty of the created world to the point that, as the psalmist says, only fools believe there is no God (Psalms 14 and 53). Such knowledge of God, however, is too vague to save anyone. God hides behind the mountains and the stars. When we examine nature, we marvel at God's greatness and begin to understand something of the powerful God who has left his imprint on the world in which we live. From that perspective, God is hidden in nature, because nature teaches us nothing at all about God's grace and mercy and not a syllable about Christ and his cross.

God has taken steps to reveal more about himself. He has given us a clear record of his love for humanity in the Scriptures. As John wrote, "These are written that you may believe that Jesus is the Christ, the Son of God, and that by believing you may have life in his name" (John 20:31). But nothing remains hidden about the record of Scripture. The Bible proclaims Christ from beginning to end. Yet all this knowledge is hidden from the natural sinful minds of all men and women.

Paul calls the gospel a mystery—"secret wisdom, a wisdom that has been hidden" (1 Corinthians 2:7). Left to ourselves, we could not understand what God has done for our eternal deliverance from sin, death, and hell. By our sinful nature, we think of the gospel as foolishness, and even in our age of mass communication, humans consider the pure, simple gospel only so much foolishness. It is hidden from so many people, even when believers witness eloquently about the Lord. Paul wrote, "The man without the Spirit does not accept the things that come from the Spirit of God, for they are foolishness to him, and he cannot understand them" (1 Corinthians 2:14).

Only God can make this secret message of life and forgiveness in Christ clear to the sinful human mind. By the work of the Holy Spirit through the gospel message, God lifts the veils from our eyes. He enlightens our dark understanding by the gospel. His power changes us. But God is hidden here too. God hides behind the words of Scripture and the elements of the sacraments—water, wine, and bread. Who would think that the God who stretched out the heavens, raised the mountains, and placed the stars in their places would connect with humans through Word and sacrament? Who would imagine that God would change hearts by such common things? Yet the Holy Spirit uses these simple things—the gospel in Word and sacrament—to work in the hearts of humans and to create faith there.

God remains hidden in another way too. As we explore how God hides himself in this way, we must keep in mind some important truths. Once we come to faith in the Lord, we treasure his Word because we know that God has revealed himself to us through that Word. Outside of the Scriptures, we have no other communication from God, no other reliable information. We depend on the reliability of the Scriptures, trusting that God has inspired the writers of both the New and Old Testaments to give us accurate information about himself. The Scriptures are verbally inspired and absolutely reliable and true in all they proclaim. There is nothing hidden about the Scriptures. They are an open book and absolutely clear about the work of God in creating, redeeming, and sanctifying the world. We even confess those truths every Sunday in the creeds we use in worship. A child can understand these important truths.

But as clear as the Scriptures are, God remains a hidden God. His being lies beyond our ability to understand. How can we grasp the concept of a God who is eternal—without beginning or end? We can say that God is eternal, but that does not mean we really understand what it is to be eternal. Everything any human knows has a beginning and an end. Even the words we speak and write are defined by space and time. God exists beyond our plane of existence and experience—far above all we are and know, far beyond what any human can know. He is hidden because we cannot grasp all he is. So much of him lies beyond our human intellects, perceptions, and emotions. He is so great and majestic that all the most eloquent and beautiful words of every language cannot communicate him fully. Certainly he communicates clearly in his Word, but that tells us only what we need to know. Scripture does not reveal all there is to know. The apostle John reminded his readers of that when he wrote: "Jesus did many other miraculous signs in the presence of his disciples, which are not recorded in this book. But these are written that you may believe that Jesus is the Christ, the Son of God, and that by believing you may have life in his name" (John 20:30,31).

Consider a couple examples. How is God to describe the glory of heaven to us? We have never been there, and it is so beautiful and glorious that we cannot comprehend it. Yet God has told us that it lies beyond death for all believers. He has described it in many places in the Scriptures, but when we arrive in our Father's house, it will be more glorious and wonderful than we could ever have imagined here on earth. Consider Moses, a prophet of God who talked with God as no other human did. When Moses asked God to show him his glory, God said, "You cannot see my face, for no one may see me and live" (Exodus 33:20). Then God limited what Moses could see. He put Moses in a cleft in a rock, covered him with his hand, and then allowed Moses to see his back. God said, "But my face must not be seen" (verse 23). Clearly, there is much about God that we cannot know or understand. So much about him remains hidden, yet he has so carefully and clearly revealed to us what we need to know.

This idea takes us back to the vision of God that Isaiah saw when he was called to be God's prophet. The seraphs called to one another "Holy, holy, holy is the LORD Almighty; the whole earth is full of his glory" (Isaiah 6:3). God is separate and distinct from all we know and are. He is holy. He is sinless; we are not. He is almighty; we are not. He is a spirit; we are flesh and blood. He lives in a world far beyond and far above our world. All too often even believers think of God as a buddy like themselves, someone we can understand. But we dare not make God so small that he fits our minds. He is too great for that. He loves us; he is our friend; he came to live among us; he promises to take us to live in the place he has prepared for us. But he is so much more. Isaiah cried, "Woe to me! . . . I am ruined!" (6:5). Sinful humans are such puny, frail creatures next to the inexpressible majesty of God. So the great depth of God remains hidden behind the words he has revealed to us. The words we have from God tell us what he wants us to know, but so much about God remains hidden from our minds.

Yet there is another way that God is hidden. Isaiah wrote down the words of the Lord promising that Cyrus would set the exiles free and that Egypt, Cush, and the Sabeans would convert and confess that the God of Israel is the only true God. What a marvelous change would take place. God would control the affairs of men to make this a reality. How did he do that? God's ways are hidden as he carries out his plan for the world. What forces brought about the rise of Cyrus? Why Persia? How could Egypt change so? We scratch our heads when confronted by these questions and a thousand others. Our questions may extend to any era of human history. Why did events happen as they did? What forces brought Hitler and others to power? How does that all fit into God's great and good plan? In response to these questions, God remains hidden. He does not reveal these things to us.

We ask similar questions about our own lives. Why did things happen as they did? Why the suffering? Why the success of some and the failure of others? What will happen tomorrow? God remains hidden. He chooses not to answer such questions. If we look in the Scriptures, we will not find the answers to these questions either. God does not call us to understand everything. He calls us to faith. He tells us that he loves us to the point of sending his Son to shed his blood for us. Then he says, "Trust me. Believe! Even when you don't understand and even when nothing seems to make sense, trust and believe." God is a hidden God in the sense that he does not tell us everything we might like to

125

know. He does not tell us how he takes care of the larger history of our own nation or the world. He does not tell us exactly what he will do to take care of us as we face trial, persecution, and crisis. He does not tell us when he will return to judge the world. He has hidden all that information from us. We are to trust and believe whether we understand or not. Most of the time we don't understand; we simply trust.

So Isaiah confesses that God is a hidden God and he trusts in that God. Those who did not trust in God made idols. They sought to make God into something they could see and understand with their human intellect and senses. But those who made God so small that he could fit into their own minds will be disgraced when confronted with the Lord God Almighty. Their theological concepts will only bring them disgrace. On the other hand, those who trust in the Lord will be rescued from their sins and from death. The Lord will save them with an everlasting deliverance. What God has in store for those who believe lies beyond earth's time and space. It extends forever—beyond every here and now; it will be spectacular glory and unimaginable joy. The glory of God's people is not limited by the fortunes of war or the cycles of political power. God's people are not to be like the other nations of the world. Their glory will be eternal. So Isaiah believed and confessed seven hundred years before Christ. So we confess so many centuries after Christ's appearance.

> [18] **For this is what the LORD says—**
> **he who created the heavens,**
> **he is God;**
> **he who fashioned and made the earth,**
> **he founded it;**

> he did not create it to be empty,
>   but formed it to be inhabited—
> he says:
> "I am the LORD,
>   and there is no other.
> ¹⁹ I have not spoken in secret,
>   from somewhere in a land of darkness;
> I have not said to Jacob's descendants,
>   'Seek me in vain.'
> I, the LORD, speak the truth;
>   I declare what is right.

The hidden God now speaks. He is identified as "the LORD," that is, Jehovah, the God of free and faithful grace. God further identifies himself as the Creator of heaven and earth. Interestingly, he indicates that his creation was made to be inhabited. He did not spend the energy necessary to create the world just to make it a work of art and leave it empty. He made it to be the home of human beings.

The God who created the earth for men and women now speaks and again asserts that there is no other God. He says, "I have not spoken in secret." What this great God has chosen to reveal to humanity is clear. He has hidden nothing of his grace. He has not kept the gospel hidden "somewhere in the land of darkness." Even if the unbelieving world does not understand the gospel, its message is not hidden. The message of God, from the time of the first sin to the last letter of the New Testament, has been about Christ, the One who would crush Satan's head and who would return to call us from our graves. All that is related to the gospel has not been spoken in secret. The Bible still ranks among the most widely available books in the world. God's revelation had a purpose as surely as his creation. If God created the world to be inhabited, he revealed the truth to be believed. So he invites all to abandon their false gods and believe in him.

20 "Gather together and come;
   assemble, you fugitives from the nations.
   Ignorant are those who carry about idols of wood,
   who pray to gods that cannot save.
21 Declare what is to be, present it—
   let them take counsel together.
   Who foretold this long ago,
   who declared it from the distant past?
   Was it not I, the LORD?
   And there is no God apart from me,
   a righteous God and a Savior;
   there is none but me.

The Lord once again calls the nations together to state their case. They drag along their idols of wood and pray to gods that cannot save them. Every concept of God that anyone proposes and proclaims outside of the revealed truth of God in the Scriptures becomes an idol, a false god. No god but the Lord can foretell the future. The announcement that Cyrus would come to release God's people proves the Lord's sovereignty and power. It testifies that God will act to rescue his people. Once more God asserts that there is no God but him.

22 "Turn to me and be saved,
   all you ends of the earth;
   for I am God, and there is no other.
23 By myself I have sworn,
   my mouth has uttered in all integrity
   a word that will not be revoked:
   Before me every knee will bow;
   by me every tongue will swear.
24 They will say of me, 'In the LORD alone
   are righteousness and strength.'"
   All who have raged against him
   will come to him and be put to shame.
25 But in the LORD all the descendants of Israel
   will be found righteous and will exult.

The message of the one true God is a message of invitation and grace. He announces judgment upon all who reject the salvation only he can provide and the forgiveness only he can give. Yet his primary message is an invitation to believe. He invites here, "Turn to me and be saved." We cannot save ourselves. God must do it; so when sinners turn to God and believe, they are saved by God. This invitation remains extended to all the earth. It is not limited to God's Old Testament people of Israel or Judah.

The Lord God has proclaimed, "I, even I, am he who blots out your transgressions, for my own sake, and remembers your sins no more" (43:25). Only the God of the Bible has paid the price to obtain forgiveness for all the world. No other religion announces the sacrifice of God's own Son for the forgiveness of sins. No other God can say, "The blood of Jesus, his Son, purifies us from all sin" (1 John 1:7). God takes an oath here to verify that message. He cannot swear by anyone higher than himself, for there is no one higher. Therefore he swears by himself that what he proclaimed is true and will not be revoked. God's promises of deliverance and redemption stand forever and are intended for all the ends of the earth—for Isaiah, for me, for you, and for the generations after us.

One little phrase is repeated in the last two verses of the chapter: "in the LORD." Those who believe and trust in the Lord find righteousness and strength in him. They do not find these things in themselves but "in the LORD alone." This phrase is repeated in the next verse too and is again tied to the idea of righteousness. The Lord has declared all the world righteous in his sight because of the work of Jesus. That simply means that the Lord has removed all sin and declared that every human who ever lived or who will ever live is free from the consequences of sin. This grand gift for the whole world becomes the personal possession of everyone who believes. It is found "in the LORD" and nowhere else. What shall God do when thousands refuse to accept his gifts? Those who do not believe refuse to have their sins covered by the righteousness of Christ. All who do not believe and come to him will be put to shame. But all who believe and receive the righteousness God has himself prepared for sinners "will be found righteous and will exult." They are justified by grace. They rejoice in that justification. Hallelujah! May we be among them.

God addresses the rebellious and stubborn-hearted house of Israel

46 Bel bows down, Nebo stoops low;
       their idols are borne by beasts of burden.
   The images that are carried about are burdensome,
       a burden for the weary.
 ² They stoop and bow down together;
       unable to rescue the burden,
       they themselves go off into captivity.

The Lord had issued a gracious invitation at the end of the previous chapter, "Turn to me and be saved, all you ends of the earth" (verse 22). The Lord promised righteousness and joy to all believers—the spiritual descendants of Israel (verse 25). But the Lord also threatened judgment upon those who have raged against him. The first two verses of this chapter turn our attention to Babylon and the judgment God has in store for the Babylonians at the hand of Cyrus. The next three chapters will explore the judgment the Lord will send on Babylon, but at the same time, we find God addressing those among his people who persist in their stubborn rebellion against him and all the blessings of his grace and mercy. God does not play favorites. He will bring judgment to all who oppose his love and mercy, whether they are Jews or Gentiles.

First, we read about the gods of the Babylonians. Bel and Nebo were two of the most important gods of the Babylonian Empire. Consider how Nebo is included in the name of the great Babylonian king Nebuchadnezzar. Nebo, or Nabu, was considered the god of learning, writing, astronomy, and all science. He was the son of Bel, who some suggest was the chief god of the Babylonians and was also known by the name Marduk. Often ancient civilizations tied their gods to their success. Four men carried images of their gods on their shoulders in great, glorious processions celebrating victory.

Isaiah does not picture these gods of the Babylonians in any kind of festive procession. Instead, beasts of burden carry them as spoils of war. Perhaps they have been tied securely so that they do not fall to the ground. One can easily imagine the idols swaying and lurching with each step the beasts take. The once revered gods of Babylon are carted off into captivity, unable to stop the ignoble procession.

Why has this happened? There can be only one answer: Babylon has been defeated. God has swept up her once proud and glorious empire and discarded it in the wastebasket of history. Babylon is nothing any longer. Its gods are carried away by the new conqueror; they can offer no rescue. The idols carry no one. Instead, they must be carried themselves—a burden to the animals who haul them away. They cannot even ease the burden of the animals who bear them away. All this provides a vivid contrast with what the Lord says to the house of Jacob in the following verses.

> ³ **"Listen to me, O house of Jacob,**
> **all you who remain of the house of Israel,**
> **you whom I have upheld since you were conceived,**
> **and have carried since your birth.**

⁴ **Even to your old age and gray hairs
I am he, I am he who will sustain you.
I have made you and I will carry you;
I will sustain you and I will rescue you.**

The captured gods of the Babylonians presented a pathetic picture of impotence. By comparison and contrast, the Lord has carried his people. From the beginning of their history, the Lord had carried them. The terms *Jacob* and *Israel* stretch back to the age of the patriarchs. A quick review of the history of the people of Israel recalls all that God had done for them—the exodus from Egypt, the water and manna in the wilderness, the victories of the judges and the kings, and most recent the miraculous deliverance from the Assyrian forces at the very gate of Jerusalem (Isaiah 36,37). God had carried his people in spite of their often rebellious ways. He had made them what they were.

God had not yet finished with them. The Lord promised to carry them long into their old age. He would not change; he would remain the same Lord of grace. He promised to persist in his faithful and loving care of his people. In English we often use a pronoun to identify the subject. In Hebrew the subject is normally included in the verb; pronouns, then, are used more rarely. But when a Hebrew writer wants to emphasize the subject of a verb, he will use a pronoun. In the last part of verse 4, the pronoun *I* appears six times. These pronouns underscore the action of the Lord. We might demonstrate the emphasis by translating the verse, "Even to your old age and gray hairs, *indeed, I* am he; *I myself* will bear you as a burden. *I* have made you *myself,* and *I myself* will carry you. *I myself* will bear you, and *I myself* bring you to safety." All these promises depend on the action of the Lord. Only his gracious action has sustained his people in the past, and only his action will sustain them in the future.

These promises are addressed to the "house of Jacob." When Isaiah wrote these words, the house of Jacob was not what it once had been. The ten tribes of the Northern Kingdom of Israel had been swallowed up in the Assyrian advance. Samaria, its capital, lay in ruins. God had checked the Assyrian advance by destroying 185,000 soldiers and had preserved Jerusalem from destruction. The Jewish countryside had nevertheless been ravaged by the Assyrians. The Lord here addresses those "who remain of the house of Israel." Those who remained were both the faithful believers and the rebellious unbelievers.

God had a purpose for speaking these words to both groups among his people. First, the words of Isaiah served to confirm the unbelieving Jews in their unbelief. When the Lord had called Isaiah to be his prophet, he had charged him with a difficult task, "Make the heart of this people calloused; make their ears dull and close their eyes" (6:10). These unbelieving Jews would hear the beautiful promises of God's grace but would not listen. They would remain in their unbelief. As a matter of fact, the clear promises would only confirm their unbelief, much as the most dramatic miracle of Jesus—the raising of Lazarus—led the Jews to resolve to kill Jesus (John 11:45-53). The harsh rebukes of Isaiah would not penetrate the hard unbelief of the people of his day any more than the harsh rebukes of Jesus changed the hearts of those who did not believe in him. The unbelieving and rebellious audience of the prophet's message would consider God's prophet and all who believed his message to be foolish.

But there was another audience among those who remained of the house of Israel. Mixed among these unbelievers were those still faithful to God. Their hearts needed the sweet promises of the Lord. Isaiah predicted that the Babylonians would lead Judah away captive. The faithful would be led away captive as well as the unbelievers. Neither God nor the Babylonians would distinguish between believers and unbelievers as Jerusalem was sacked and the population deported. The faithful were to find strength and courage from the promises of God, and they did. Here the Lord promises to continue to sustain, carry, and rescue them as he had in the past. No matter how difficult the captivity or heartrending the situation, God would make everything work out according to his plan. He is a "God who hides himself" (45:15)—often difficult to understand—but he is also always a gracious, compassionate, and loving God who cares for his own. God's faithful people always need the strength and encouragement God's promises offer.

We are another audience for the prophet's words. As we read the words addressed to the "house of Jacob," we find strength and courage to face our own brand of life's trials. We are of the house of Jacob by faith in Jacob's great descendant, Jesus. We may not have to witness the destruction of our nation and a deportation to a foreign country as did these ancient Jews, but we do face our own trials and difficulties. The apostle Paul encouraged the early Christians, reminding them, "We must go through many hardships to enter the kingdom of God" (Acts 14:22). In the midst of whatever hardships we face, God's promise applies to us too. No matter what we have experienced in life, God has carried us and upheld us. He promises us no less than he promised the believers of Isaiah's day, "Even to your old age and gray hairs I am he, I am he who will sustain you."

⁵ "To whom will you compare me or count me equal?
    To whom will you liken me that we may be compared?
⁶ Some pour out gold from their bags
    and weigh out silver on the scales;
  they hire a goldsmith to make it into a god,
    and they bow down and worship it.
⁷ They lift it to their shoulders and carry it;
    they set it up in its place, and there it stands.
    From that spot it cannot move.
  Though one cries out to it, it does not answer;
    it cannot save him from his troubles.

The contrast between the Lord and the gods of Babylon is clear. The Lord carried his people; Bel and Nebo could not even carry themselves. They had to be carried. For the fourth time, we have looked in on the manufacture of idols (40:19; 41:7; 44:9-20). Each time God unmistakably emphasized the folly of idol worship. Luther suggests that superstition is the mistress of money, and that, while many are all too willing to pay for expensive idols, Christ and the gospel go poor (LW, Volume 17, page 141). Some do pour gold from their bags to create expensive idols. But all their gold creates is something that has to be carried. The idols cannot speak, cannot act, and cannot rescue. They just stand there mute—perhaps beautiful and shining—but nonetheless powerless, unfeeling, unthinking, and silent. Even though thousands and perhaps millions bow down in worship or pray to them, nothing happens. How can such inanimate, lifeless *things* save any person?

⁸ "Remember this, fix it in mind,
    take it to heart, you rebels.
⁹ Remember the former things, those of long ago;
    I am God, and there is no other;
    I am God, and there is none like me.
¹⁰ I make known the end from the beginning,
    from ancient times, what is still to come.

> I say: My purpose will stand,
>   and I will do all that I please.
> ¹¹ From the east I summon a bird of prey;
>   from a far-off land, a man to fulfill my purpose.
> What I have said, that will I bring about;
>   what I have planned, that will I do.

You rebels, pay attention. The Lord addressed those among his people who had rejected the gift of his grace. They were to listen to these words. The lesson remains the same one repeated from earlier passages: "I am God, and there is no other." Some think that these words were for those among the Jews who had adopted the worship of idols in the Babylonian captivity. They might just as well have applied to those who worshiped idols at any time in the history of God's Old Testament people. The people of Isaiah's day, almost two hundred years before the captivity, had their flirtations with idols. So perverse is the human heart that it rejects the living God and substitutes a lifeless piece of gold.

We have noted that one of the things that makes the Lord different from all other concepts of god is that he removes sin by the sacrifice of his own Son (see 43:25; 44:22). God here claims another activity that makes him different from every other concept of god. He can predict the future. He says, "I make known the end from the beginning." This is not the first time that God has claimed to predict the future in this portion of Isaiah (see 41:25-27; 42:9; 44:7,8; 45:21). He had also predicted the coming of Cyrus, mentioning him specifically by name (44:28; 45:1,13). In addition, the Lord has predicted the coming of another Servant (42:1-7). That Servant—greater than Cyrus—would be the great Immanuel (7:14) and the Branch from the stump of Jesse (11:1-9). Later in the prophecy of Isaiah, God reveals a great deal about the coming of this Great Servant (see chapter 53, for example).

God's ability to predict the future proves his superiority. In God's mind, what has been planned is the same thing that he announces before it happens and what eventually does happen. God predicted he would call "a bird of prey." That's Cyrus. He predicted it, and it happened just as he said. The argument of the Lord depends on the prediction and its fulfillment.

Yet so many scholars question the references to Cyrus. They assert that Isaiah, who lived almost two centuries before the rise of the Persians, could not have known of Cyrus. These scholars suggest that another writer, much later than the time of Isaiah, penned these words. Such a writer would have a much clearer view of history and the rise of Cyrus. Yet this approach makes the later writer a fraud and a deceiver. He claims to be Isaiah or at least includes his words under the name of Isaiah. If he were a contemporary of Cyrus and claimed to write the words of Isaiah, he has chosen to "help out" God by claiming to write a prediction that was, in fact, only a record of an historical event. It would be like adding a diagram of a computer to Leonardo da Vinci's sketchbook and then claiming, or allowing others to believe, that he had preconceived the idea. No matter how noble the intention, such an addition would make these words a deception. If someone had added these words after Cyrus appeared, doesn't that distort God's claim: "I make known the end from the beginning, from ancient times, what is still to come"?

If we say that Isaiah did not write the words regarding Cyrus and that someone later on inserted these words, that person, whoever he or she may be, becomes a liar. Besides, the later writer manufactures God as surely as the idol worshipers. God becomes a creation of the writer's mind, no matter how noble the intent. That's exactly what Isaiah warns against so strongly here. How foolish to manufacture

God, either by creating an idol or by conceiving some godly concept that is not found in the Scriptures. Don't make God what you want him to be. Let God be God. He says that he predicts the future. Why does anyone say that God can't do that? Perhaps because God can predict the future, he is too great to be accepted on his own terms. The sinful human mind must remanufacture him as smaller and easier to understand and accept. For many, God must conform to human concepts of time, probability, and experience.

> ¹² **Listen to me, you stubborn-hearted,**
>   **you who are far from righteousness.**
> ¹³ **I am bringing my righteousness near,**
>   **it is not far away;**
>   **and my salvation will not be delayed.**
> **I will grant salvation to Zion,**
>   **my splendor to Israel.**

The Lord addresses the same people he addressed earlier when he called them rebels. Here he calls them *stubborn-hearted*. They are unbelievers who do not accept the Lord's ability to predict the future. But God's prediction becomes more than the revelation of future events. It foretells more than the rise of Cyrus. The magnificent future God predicts includes all he will do to redeem the world from sin, death, and hell. God ties that deliverance to the words *righteousness* and *salvation*. The central revelation of God's Word is that he would declare the world righteous and free of iniquity, transgression, and sin because of the work of the Great Servant. That Servant would be bruised and crushed for the sins of the world.

As far as God was concerned, this righteousness was near. In the mind of God, the saving work of Christ was as good as done. By his grace God grants salvation—rescue— to his people. God performs all the action again. No human effort can bring righteousness near. God must prepare it, and he must bring it to those who are dead in sin (Ephesians 2:1). It comes to all humanity by grace.

In these two short verses, we discover the great gift of God's grace. God has done everything to prepare the gift. It is finished. God requires no human effort to complete it. God has wrapped this precious gift and offered it by grace to all the world. It is described here as "salvation" and "splendor." Those who receive the gift from God with the hand of faith possess it. They are God's Israel. But there are some "stubborn-hearted" who do not believe and who refuse the offer of God. What a tragedy that they have rejected God's best and most precious gift—tragic because those who reject God's gift do not have righteousness, salvation, or splendor! Those among the house of Jacob who resist the grace of God have hardened their hearts to the Lord of free and faithful grace. Their judgment looms enormous; it grows larger as we consider all the blessings God has provided for them and all the truth he has revealed to them. Yet they refuse!

God announces that proud Babylon will fall

47 "Go down, sit in the dust,
    Virgin Daughter of Babylon;
  sit on the ground without a throne,
    Daughter of the Babylonians.
  No more will you be called
    tender or delicate.
  [2] Take millstones and grind flour;
    take off your veil.
  Lift up your skirts, bare your legs,
    and wade through the streams.
  [3] Your nakedness will be exposed
    and your shame uncovered.
  I will take vengeance;
    I will spare no one."

Under Nebuchadnezzar, Babylon rose to great power. With the help of his wife Amytis, the Babylonian king rebuilt and embellished the city of Babylon. He rebuilt the temples of Marduk and Nabu (called Bel and Nebo in chapter 46) and built a massive gate called the Ishtar Gate, from which a procession way stretched into the city. The procession way was lined by walls decorated with enameled bricks showing lions, dragons, and bulls—all symbols of Babylonian gods. The Babylonian king built the famous hanging gardens for his wife to remind her of her homeland. Some of Nebuchadnezzar's architectural works were classified among the seven wonders of the ancient world. Babylon was a beautiful city, marked by the best the ancient world could offer. When Isaiah wrote these words, all this glory was still in the future, but something else was also in the future—Babylon's fall. This chapter poetically commemorates Babylon's downfall. It is a dirge, but instead of expressing grief, it taunts the victim.

God describes the city as the "Virgin Daughter of Babylon." The city was beautiful, and like a virgin daughter, it had not yet been conquered by an enemy or ravaged by warfare. But the grandeur of Babylon would come to an end. The city was the beautiful queen of all that the Babylonian armies controlled, but God commands her, "Go down, sit in the dust." Proud Babylon would descend from the throne and take her place in the dust and dirt of ruin. Down she would come! Considering all the beauty of the city, it is no wonder some called her "tender" and "delicate." Babylon was luxury. Her citizens were pampered by Nebuchadnezzar's success on the battlefield and in his architectural achievements. But God says, "No more will you be called tender or delicate."

From the pampered life of a queen, the city would be reduced to the status of a common slave girl. She would "take millstones and grind flour." Normally, slave girls were the ones who ground flour (two stones were worked against each other by hand to produce flour). The veil mentioned here was made from finely woven cloth and identified a woman of high station. Babylon would have to take off the veil and assume the role of a slave girl who did not wear any kind of veil. The description of Babylon's slave-girl status continues. Pampered women covered their legs, but slave girls had to tie up their skirts to do the work. Babylon's fate is even worse than that. Babylon is pictured as a prisoner of war, wading through streams and absolutely disgraced, walking naked and exposed. She could no longer hide her sins and her shame. How different she would be from a virgin daughter, a queen on her throne.

Remember that none of this had happened yet. When Isaiah wrote these words, Nebuchadnezzar had not even been born. At the time of Isaiah, Assyria dominated the Middle East, and God had delivered his people from the Assyrians by a miracle (chapters 36, 37). Because of the sins of God's people, Isaiah's mission was to announce the future captivity of the Jews in Babylon. But Babylon itself would also fall. God revealed these events to his prophet long before they occurred. In the next chapter, the Lord reveals why he foretold these events. Over a century after Isaiah wrote these words, the Babylonians led the Jews away to Babylon as their captives. Seventy years later Cyrus of Persia would bring proud Babylon down to the dust so that the Jews could return home. It happened as recorded by God's inspired prophet.

The Lord stands behind the announcement of Babylon's destruction. "I will take vengeance." No one other than the Lord, the Savior-God of Israel, would bring all this to pass. His judgment would be thorough; no one would be spared.

No one could oppose him. No man would meet God in order to talk him out of his judgment. No one could object, oppose, offer advice, or even plead for mercy. God would carry out the judgment just as he had foretold it through his prophet Isaiah.

> **⁴ Our Redeemer—the Lᴏʀᴅ Almighty is his name—
> is the Holy One of Israel.**

This short verse offers praise to the Lord for his deliverance. The Lord is the Redeemer of his people, that is, he would purchase the release of his people—buy them back from Babylon and from their own sins, rebellion, and guilt. The Lord is "our Redeemer," and the Lord's action as the Redeemer of his people appears first in the sentence and first in the minds of God's people.

Isaiah provides two more names for God here. He is the "Lᴏʀᴅ Almighty." The prophet uses the name for God that takes us back to his faithfulness to all his promises; he is Jehovah, the God of free and faithful grace. The same Jehovah promised deliverance to Abraham and appeared to Moses. All his actions on behalf of sinful, wayward, and helpless humanity reside in that name. Isaiah adds "Almighty" to the name Jehovah. He is the Lord of hosts. The NIV translates that phrase as "Lᴏʀᴅ Almighty." The words mean that Jehovah holds the sovereign power that controls the hosts of heaven, the stars, and the angel hosts, or armies. Finally, Isaiah uses his favorite name for God— "the Holy One of Israel." The Lord is separate from all the rebellion and sin of his people. He is holy and transcends everything human and everything Jewish. Yet this holy God steps into the history of Israel in order to bring about the redemption of all the world.

In these names for God, we have a brief summary of God's activity. He is the "Redeemer," a term that shows us the loving heart of God and his desire to rescue his people. He is the "LORD Almighty," a term that implies both his unflinching faithfulness to all his promises and the ability to carry them out. His love for his people remains constant, and his power has no limit. He is "the Holy One of Israel." He exists far above everything earthly, yet this great God has graciously connected his name to a human nation. Neither that nation nor any other nation could become holy, but the Lord will make Israel and all the world holy and righteous by his righteous decree. In Christ Jesus, God pronounced the whole world of sinners holy, righteous, and not guilty.

This little verse reminds us that we are dealing with more than the downfall of Babylon. God connects his great plan for the redemption of all the world to the collapse of Babylon and the return of the Jews to Palestine. The Servant of the Lord and his cross link the holy God and the sinful, rebellious race of humanity.

> 5 **"Sit in silence, go into darkness,**
> **Daughter of the Babylonians;**
> **no more will you be called**
> **queen of kingdoms.**
> 6 **I was angry with my people**
> **and desecrated my inheritance;**
> **I gave them into your hand,**
> **and you showed them no mercy.**
> **Even on the aged**
> **you laid a very heavy yoke.**
> 7 **You said, 'I will continue forever—**
> **the eternal queen!'**
> **But you did not consider these things**
> **or reflect on what might happen.**

The prophet's taunt returns to the fall of Babylon. As in the first verse of the chapter, the Babylonians are given two commands from God. They cannot resist because God has determined their fall. They will sit in the dark silence of bondage. These words imply grief and anguish, a situation in stark contrast to the joy and pleasure they had enjoyed as a powerful and prosperous kingdom. The once exalted position of Babylon as "queen of kingdoms" will disappear.

Why does God bring this destruction upon Babylon? God answers the question, and as he does, he reveals why he has allowed his own people to be taken captive by the Babylonians. The captivity in Babylon came from God's hands because his people had turned away from him. The first part of Isaiah's prophecy had clearly identified the rebellion of Judah. God's people had become his "obstinate children" (30:1). They had chosen to abandon the Lord. Isaiah described them as a people who wanted "illusions" (30:10) not truth and who said to God's messengers, "Stop confronting us with the Holy One of Israel!" (30:11). Because of their rebellion, God threatened judgment and then carried it out through the Babylonians. God says here, "I gave them into your hand."

The Babylonians were only tools in the hands of God to refine and purify his people. Of course these foreigners did not understand God's truth or his great plan for the redemption of the world. The Babylonians were like every other powerful nation in the world's history. They were conquerors. They showed no mercy to the people God had given into their power. Their ruthless attitude extended even to the aged. They had no compassion for those who were the weakest among the conquered Jews. In addition, Babylon was arrogant. Babylon proudly claimed, "I will continue forever—the eternal queen!"

The people of Babylon did not think beyond their rise to power. They did not consider that their fate would be no different than that of all the other empires of the ancient world. The rise to power and the dominance it brings are only temporary. Babylon was so arrogant that it thought there would be no end to its power, dominance, and luxury. No one could tell them differently. They could learn the truth only by the descent into the dust and dirt, which God announced in the first verse.

> 8 "Now then, listen, you wanton creature,
>   lounging in your security
> and saying to yourself,
>   'I am, and there is none besides me.
> I will never be a widow
>   or suffer the loss of children.'
> 9 Both of these will overtake you
>   in a moment, on a single day:
>   loss of children and widowhood.
> They will come upon you in full measure,
>   in spite of your many sorceries
>   and all your potent spells.
> 10 You have trusted in your wickedness
>   and have said, 'No one sees me.'
> Your wisdom and knowledge mislead you
>   when you say to yourself,
>   'I am, and there is none besides me.'
> 11 Disaster will come upon you,
>   and you will not know how to conjure it away.
> A calamity will fall upon you
>   that you cannot ward off with a ransom;
> a catastrophe you cannot foresee
>   will suddenly come upon you.

The Lord continues his address to proud Babylon. The city appeared secure, at least by all human observation and thought. In that security its people found the time to lounge in luxury and wanton pleasure. The security and luxury spawned arrogance. In this instance, Babylon's arrogant claim sounds like a claim the Lord makes for himself.

The Lord says, "I am the LORD, and there is no other; apart from me there is no God" (45:5; see also 45:6,14,18,21; 46:9). The arrogance of Babylon was an affront to the Lord himself, as the city boasted, "I am, and there is none besides me."

Babylon, pictured as a wanton woman, felt secure. She believed that she was so secure that she would never suffer the difficulties that would naturally fall upon a woman. Loss of children and widowhood were the two most devastating catastrophes that could happen to an ancient woman. As quickly as these words come out of the mouth of this woman Babylon, the Lord announces that both these disasters would occur "on a single day." The destruction of Babylon would come certainly and suddenly.

The Lord allows no doubt about the reason for her destruction. He characterizes Babylon as a wicked and worldly city. First, God mentions that her "sorceries" and "potent spells" will not avert the city's destruction. Babylon was the birthplace of astrology and the home of magic and the black arts. The signs of the zodiac trace their history through Babylon. Herodotus, an ancient Greek historian, claimed that the horoscope comes from Babylon. Astrology, even today, claims to predict the events of human history through the movements of the planets and stars. Babylonians believed that the stars controlled human history. In truth, God controls history and calls out the stars by name. God said, "Lift your eyes and look to the heavens: Who created all these? He who brings out the starry host one by one, and calls them each by name" (40:26). The belief that the position of the stars controls human history defied the Lord of hosts (translated as the "LORD Almighty" by the NIV) as surely as Babylon's creed: "I am, and there is none beside me." The Babylonians trusted in magic and astrology. But neither magic nor astrology could help them. Both were foolish, worthless visions—impotent dreams of the human mind. What's even worse, such beliefs perverted the truth of the Lord of hosts.

The wickedness of Babylon had grown to the point that its citizens were no longer worried about the consequences of their sins. Babylon trusted in its ability to hide its own evil. Babylon said, "No one sees me." Such a statement also defies God, who knows all things and sees all things. Those who commit evil suppress their guilty consciences with this idea: "No one sees me." The words deny the presence of a holy God, who reigns above all that is human. Those who say "No one sees me" picture God as blind and impotent. Such a god becomes no more threatening than the idols of wood, stone, and metal. Such a god cannot punish sin or exercise any kind of control on human history. He cannot reach out any more than a statue could extend its arms. How different this god is from the God of the Bible, whom Jesus says knows when a sparrow falls and even knows how many hairs are on each human head (Matthew 10:29,30).

The Babylonians had even found some apparent justification for their pride. "Your wisdom and knowledge mislead you." The skill and knowledge of the Babylonians in the ancient world was great. Science also traces its roots through Babylon. The technical skill of the Babylonians allowed them to build their capital city into one of the wonders of the ancient world. Such knowledge and wisdom led the citizens of Babylon to assert their pride: "I am, and there is none besides me." Note again, the creed of Babylon directly opposes the assertions of the Lord Jehovah. The arrogance of this worldly city could result in only one outcome—disaster at the hands of God.

The judgment of God would not be turned away. With

all their spells, magic, and wisdom, the Babylonians could not conjure it away. No spell or ritual can ward off God's judgment. So often those who defy the true God and abandon him believe that they can appease an angry God by doing the right thing. Pagan civilizations all over the world believed, and still believe, that if they offered the right sacrifice, the gods would send rain for their crops, provide protection, give them some great blessing, or simply smile on their personal history. The underlying principle remains simply that God will do something good for me if I do what he wants. But such an idea perverts God's grace and provides only an illusion. The Lord cannot be appeased by human effort, human sacrifice, or any human ransom. Grace, and grace alone, motivate God's actions, "for [his] own sake" (43:25), which he freely offers without charge or payment. The hope that the Babylonians might "conjure" the catastrophe away by their spells or that they could ward it off with a ransom perverts God's truth and becomes another example of their arrogance. Their religion did not offer anything but a religion of rewards and punishment, a religion of law. They considered their human effort to be of value to the Lord. But he is not swayed by any human effort or work.

The arrogance of Babylon sets the city against God. The city becomes a symbol of all who oppose God. Centuries later when God's people were captive in Babylon, some would return to these promises and find hope. For the Jews, the most immediate application of these words was the fall of historical Babylon. Ancient Babylon would fall. Jews would leave their captivity and, under the protection of Cyrus, rebuild their land. The promises of God's prophet Isaiah encouraged the faithful to trust in the Lord and gave them strength to endure the hardships of their daily lives as captives in Babylon. God's promises always provide the strength to endure life's troubles. That applies to us as surely as it did to the Jews in Babylon, even though we experience different hardships and difficulties than they did.

This prophetic vision certainly sees the fall of ancient Babylon at the hand of Cyrus, but Babylon has become a symbol for all who oppose God. Consider the picture God paints here for us. Babylon defied God, lived in luxury and security, committed sin, and then claimed, "No one sees me." Her religion had no time for the Redeemer, the Lord Almighty, the Holy One of Israel of verse 4. Instead, such religion became only a collection of superstitions—magic and astrology. The Babylonians based their religious beliefs on earning blessings from the gods by doing the right thing. It was not a religion of grace but a religion of law. As we read of the fall of Babylon, we perhaps should stretch our vision beyond that historical ancient city. The fall of all God's enemies also enters the picture. One strand of thought in this picture stretches all the way to the end of time, when God will bring about the destruction of all who defy him.

It should not surprise us that God inspired later writers to use the picture of Babylon as a picture of God's ultimate judgment upon all his enemies. The apostle John recorded the announcement of an angel of heaven, "Fallen! Fallen is Babylon the Great!" (Revelation 18:2). John's vision is not a retelling of the fall of ancient Babylon but a foretelling of the destruction of all God's enemies. In John's vision after the announcement of Babylon's fall, another voice from heaven cried out, "Come out of her, my people, so that you will not share in her sins" (verse 4). Just as the Jews left Babylon to return to their homeland, so, at the end of time, God will bring his faithful people home to heaven. God's faithful will be separated from the evil world and brought safely home. All who opposed God will experience the swift, certain destruction of God's judgment.

> [12] "Keep on, then, with your magic spells
> and with your many sorceries,
> which you have labored at since childhood.
> Perhaps you will succeed,
> perhaps you will cause terror.
> [13] All the counsel you have received has only worn you out!
> Let your astrologers come forward,
> those stargazers who make predictions month by month,
> let them save you from what is coming upon you.
> [14] Surely they are like stubble;
> the fire will burn them up.
> They cannot even save themselves
> from the power of the flame.
> Here are no coals to warm anyone;
> here is no fire to sit by.
> [15] That is all they can do for you—
> these you have labored with
> and trafficked with since childhood.
> Each of them goes on in his error;
> there is not one that can save you.

The tone of God's message changes with these words. Babylon is hopelessly trapped in her own superstitions—her "magic spells" and "sorceries." God becomes exasperated by the city's persistence in its arrogance. What action should God take? In poetic irony, God gives them up to their own delusions, "Keep on, then, . . ." They have no interest in the path of truth but persist in their superstitions. So God taunts them: "Perhaps you will succeed, perhaps you will cause terror." Of course, they will not. But the Babylonians don't believe that. They think that their efforts will bring them safety and deliverance. God reminds them of the inevitable result of turning away from him: "All the counsel you have received has only worn you out!"

So it has always been. Those who abandon the God of

grace and the redemption he so freely offers work hard at their superstitions, spend great sums of money on amulets and good luck charms, and even offer expensive gifts to their gods hoping to buy their blessings. Great temples and shrines have been built the world over by those who believe they can bribe gods by their works and their gifts. All such efforts only wear out those who do not believe that God forgives freely for Christ's sake. What is God to do? God finally throws up his hands and says, "All right! Believe what you want. It won't do you any good."

When Isaiah mentions "those stargazers who make predictions month by month," he refers to astrology. Babylon had not simply dabbled in astrology; they had labored at it "since childhood." It was a persistent feature of Babylonian life. A special cast of astrologers predicted good or evil fortune based on the path of the sun and the planets through the 12 divisions of the zodiac. Some suggest that this special group of prognosticators were supported by the government treasury. Ultimately, their predictions were worthless. God's judgment is certain. Astrologers with their horoscopes will experience the Lord's judgment as surely as all those who do not believe. They will be like stubble in the fire. This fire does not bring comfort. It is not like a warm, cheerful campfire that we sit around, roasting marshmallows and telling stories. No one sits by this fire; it burns hot with judgment.

God's closing words add one final note to this taunt of Babylonian hopes. Each of the astrologers wanders off, each one to his own way. No hope remains. Not one of them can save the Babylonians. Salvation comes only from God, and the Babylonians had rejected the Lord and chosen astrology and a religion of works instead. From that source no one can find any hope or real comfort.

The Lord rebukes and encourages his people

48 "Listen to this, O house of Jacob,
    you who are called by the name of Israel
    and come from the line of Judah,
you who take oaths in the name of the LORD
    and invoke the God of Israel—
    but not in truth or righteousness—

Chapter 47 announced the fall of Babylon with the command "Go down, sit in the dust, Virgin Daughter of Babylon" (verse 1). Although God's people had not yet been carried away captive to Babylon, Isaiah already saw Babylon's fall. In these first nine chapters of the second part of Isaiah, God's prophet foretold the rise of Cyrus, who would make it possible for the Jews to leave their Babylonian captivity and return to their homeland.

The announcement of Babylon's fall was of vital importance to the house of Jacob, God's people. Of course, Babylon's fall would significantly change the ancient political and military world; it would simply alter the course of history. But God had a far more important result in mind. The fall of Babylon would usher in a series of events that would eventually bring the Messiah into the world. His coming would accomplish a much more significant deliverance—not from political bondage but from bondage to death and sin. The spiritual deliverance accomplished by the Messiah would have eternal consequences for the house of Jacob as well as for all nations. In this chapter, God therefore turns to his people and encourages them, "Listen to this."

God announces both law and gospel. The first portion of the chapter scolds the house of Jacob for the hardness of their hearts. The second portion of the chapter tenderly invites his faithful people to leave Babylon and trust in the Lord's promises.

The Lord rebuked his people with harsh language. By

his grace, the Lord had called them to be his people. He gave them the name of their forefather, Israel—a name that reminded them of God's choice and his faithfulness to them over the centuries. They had even used the special name of God—Jehovah, or Lord—to make oaths and had kept his name in their memory, acknowledging him as the God of Israel. Neither the Lord nor all he had done for them was unknown to these people. Yet they had used the name of the Lord without "truth or righteousness."

Some suggest that the house of Jacob had adopted an outward and insincere worship of the Lord. They certainly had, but it was not just a matter of sincerity or insincerity. Their concepts of God were defective. By using the word *righteousness* here, God rebukes his people for their false religion. To have righteous worship means that their concepts of God and theology conform to or flow from God's own righteousness. But that was not the case with these people. Their theology was false because it had missed what was essential. It was not true because it did not conform to God's righteousness.

What does that mean? God ties his righteousness to Christ, as Paul wrote, "Righteousness from God comes through faith in Jesus Christ to all who believe" (Romans 3:22). The great fault of their religion and their concepts of God was that it did not have the Messiah at its center. As a result, it was not true. Members of the house of Jacob had the words and forms right. Many of these were very sincere and devout in their religious practices, but their religious expressions flowed from hearts that adopted essentially a religion different than the one God had revealed. Consider the apostle Paul before his conversion. He was a Pharisee, zealous and devout. Like the people the Lord rebukes in the following verses, he had taken "oaths in the name of the LORD and invoke[d] the God of Israel." Yet all his religious fervor was "not in truth or righteousness." He did not have its essence— Christ. Paul later even commented on his attitude before his conversion. He wrote that he was "circumcised on the eighth day, of the people of Israel, of the tribe of Benjamin, a Hebrew of Hebrews; in regard to the law, a Pharisee; as for zeal, persecuting the church; as for legalistic righteousness, faultless" (Philippians 3:5,6). Only after he came to faith did he have the truth. Then he worshiped God in truth and righteousness.

In our world today, many measure the truth of religion by the sincerity of its adherents. But the truth of religion, at least from the Bible's perspective, depends on whether or not it conforms to the revelation of God. Many are devout and zealous, as Paul was before his conversion. Some spend many years in sincere devotion to their religious principles; others offer large sums of money to build temples and churches or to carry out their religious mission. But their religion without Christ can only be like that of the house of Jacob, "not in truth or righteousness."

True religion is not some vague spirituality that depends on sincere and heartfelt dedication. True religion conforms to the patterns God has revealed—his righteousness. When the Lord returns to judge the world, he will judge men and women not by their sincerity but by their faith in the truth of the Scriptures, by their faith in the Bible's essence— Christ. Hypocrisy always remains a problem for all religious systems, including the true faith, but we miss the point if we think that God scolds his people only for their insincerity and hypocrisy. He rebukes them because they have abandoned his truth and righteousness and adopted essentially false religious concepts.

² you who call yourselves citizens of the holy city
      and rely on the God of Israel—
      the LORD Almighty is his name:
³ I foretold the former things long ago,
      my mouth announced them and I made them known;
      then suddenly I acted, and they came to pass.
⁴ For I knew how stubborn you were;
      the sinews of your neck were iron,
      your forehead was bronze.
⁵ Therefore I told you these things long ago;
      before they happened I announced them to you
   so that you could not say,
      'My idols did them;
      my wooden image and metal god ordained them.'
⁶ You have heard these things; look at them all.
      Will you not admit them?

The Lord asserts his ability to foretell the future. The history of God's Old Testament people is a history of prophecy. God foretold the coming of the Messiah to Adam and Eve. He told Noah to prepare for the coming flood. He called Abraham and told him that his descendants would be as numerous as the stars of heaven and sand on the seashore. He sent Moses to deliver his people from Egypt. These and other things God had foretold long before they occurred. When the time came, all of them came to pass. These were the "former things."

Why had God foretold these things? God's answer is a brutal rebuke to the people who had heard of all God's activity. God says that they were stubborn and describes them as having necks of iron and foreheads of bronze. That's a graphic way to say that they were stiff-necked. Remember Stephen's address to those who were about to stone him: "You stiff-necked people, with uncircumcised hearts and ears! You are just like your fathers: You always resist the Holy Spirit!" (Acts 7:51). God knew that the stubborn unbelief of his people would resist him. He knew that if he did not foretell these events, the people would claim that their false gods had accomplished them. God announced these former things in advance so that he and he alone could claim to be responsible. How perverse the people actually were! Even when they came out of Egypt, the people made a golden calf and said, "These are your gods, O Israel, who brought you up out of Egypt" (Exodus 32:4). Iron necks and bronze foreheads aptly describe their persistent unbelief.

Yet they had to admit that the Lord had done just as he foretold, didn't they? A fair reading of the record of God could lead to only one conclusion. He and he alone did it all. God asks his people, "Will you not admit them?" As clearly as Israel's history had recorded God's ability to foretell future events and to bring them to pass, it also recorded the stubborn unbelief of the house of Jacob.

> **"From now on I will tell you of new things,**
> **of hidden things unknown to you.**
> ⁷ **They are created now, and not long ago;**
> **you have not heard of them before today.**
> **So you cannot say,**
> **'Yes, I knew of them.'**
> ⁸ **You have neither heard nor understood;**
> **from of old your ear has not been open.**
> **Well do I know how treacherous you are;**
> **you were called a rebel from birth.**
> ⁹ **For my own name's sake I delay my wrath;**
> **for the sake of my praise I hold it back from you,**
> **so as not to cut you off.**
> ¹⁰ **See, I have refined you, though not as silver;**
> **I have tested you in the furnace of affliction.**
> ¹¹ **For my own sake, for my own sake, I do this.**
> **How can I let myself be defamed?**
> **I will not yield my glory to another.**

The Lord shifts his attention in the second part of verse 6 to "new things, of hidden things unknown to you." This thought has been a motif of these chapters. Earlier God had proclaimed, "See, the former things have taken place, and new things I declare; before they spring into being I announce them to you" (42:9). Israel's history had recorded the wonderful acts of God's grace on behalf of his people— his calling of Abraham, the Exodus, the conquest of the Promised Land, repeated deliverance from their enemies. All these events had taken place in the past. But the Lord had also advised his people to "forget the former things; do not dwell on the past" (43:18). God's people were not to concentrate on the past, because God was doing "a new thing" (43:19). The new would be greater than the old, so God encouraged his people to look forward.

The new things centered on the coming of Cyrus. He would deliver the Israelites from bondage. Cyrus was the Lord's servant to bring about the fall of Babylon, but there was a greater Servant still to come. The coming of Cyrus anticipated the coming of the great and glorious Servant— the Messiah. Where else in all of Scripture do we read of the coming of Cyrus? Up until the time of Isaiah, the Lord had chosen not to reveal the details of how he would deliver his people from Babylon. Now he revealed this event. Isaiah had the wonderful responsibility to record these new things in his prophecy.

Just as God had a reason for revealing the former things before they occurred, so he had a reason for hiding the details of Cyrus until the time of Isaiah. God says that he hid these events from his people so that they could not say, "Yes, I knew of them." Isaiah's prophecy was new and fresh. It wasn't the same old story. God knew his rebellious people—yes, all people—very well. The natural human heart is treacherous and rebellious. Sinful humans grow tired of the same old thing. We listen to the news, among other reasons, because it changes every day. We are not interested in yesterday's news. God did not tell his people about Cyrus earlier because, at the time of Isaiah, the people would have treated this information as old, stale news they already knew.

God tells his people that they were rebels from the very beginning. Jacob illustrates the rebellious human heart. Consider how he deceived his father (Genesis 27). So God says here that his people were rebels "from birth." All the blessings God's people had received had come by grace. But the history of Israel was not only a record of God's merciful actions; it also recorded the shameful sins and failures of his people. Time and time again, they worshiped false gods. No sooner had they left Egypt than they set to work shaping their own god from gold and silver. They deserved the wrath and punishment of a holy and just God. But God had chosen this rebellious and stubborn people to carry out his plan of saving the entire world. So he did not destroy them. He delayed his wrath.

Note the reason: "for my own name's sake." God repeats that thought four times in these verses. He leaves no doubt about the reason for his actions. God does not withhold his judgment and wrath because the people had some commendable quality or even some potential value in themselves. God does this he says, "for my own name's sake," "for the sake of my praise," and then in verse 11, he says, "For my own sake, for my own sake." All is grace from beginning to end. These words thunder against all self-righteousness, as Luther noted. On the one hand, God's people were iron-necked and with bronze foreheads, stubborn, rebels from birth, and treacherous. On the other hand, God is gracious and loving in withholding his wrath and persistent in carrying out his plan to save the entire world through the Messiah.

The coming Babylonian captivity would not annihilate the house of Jacob or the line of Judah. In spite of their unbelief and their stubbornness, God would refine them. A remnant would return. That was God's plan. The furnace of affliction would refine God's people as heat refines precious metals, but God was not looking for silver. The Lord brought back a remnant to Palestine in order to complete his plan of salvation. Such a plan involved more than silver and gold. God's plan was to purchase all the world from sin, death, and eternal punishment with the holy precious blood of Jesus Christ. No human deserves such love. No human can do enough to cause God to take such action. All God's blessings come by grace, and grace alone.

The repetition of "for my own sake" underscores the grace of God and his faithfulness to all his promises. If God had allowed his people to be destroyed and obliterated off the face of the earth, all his promises would be null and void. God would then be viewed as powerless to save his people. If he could not save his own people, how could he save the world? If he did not mean what he said in the past, all he said about the future becomes meaningless. God asks, "How can I let myself be defamed?" God's greatness resides in his promise to bring about spiritual deliverance and to forgive. His plan called for the coming of the Messiah through the family tree of Judah. God remained faithful to his plan. He withheld his wrath and refined his people rather than annihilate them as they so richly deserved. Sadly, the people remained addicted to idolatry. We measure the greatness of God in the astounding fact that he carried out his plan through these rebellious and treacherous people. It is no small wonder that God continues to carry out his plan in this world through us, who are no better than the house of Jacob. We are by nature sinful, dead in sin, but we are changed by the grace of God and empowered by it to serve the Lord, our Savior-God.

> [12] **"Listen to me, O Jacob,**
> **Israel, whom I have called:**
> **I am he;**
> **I am the first and I am the last.**
> [13] **My own hand laid the foundations of the earth,**
> **and my right hand spread out the heavens;**
> **when I summon them,**
> **they all stand up together.**

In these next verses, the tone of harsh rebuke fades away and turns into a tender, loving invitation: "Listen." The Lord pleads with his people to listen to him because all his words are words of grace and mercy, life and deliverance. The Lord has called these people to be his. He is not one of their idols that they created from gold, silver, or wood. He is the God of the covenant. Before all things, he was. When all things have ceased to be, he remains. He is eternal. Consider this. We might have difficulty remembering the names of the Babylonian gods or the gods of the Egyptians. They have all disappeared except in the pages of history. Only a few are curious about them. But the God of the Bible still endures. He is Jehovah, the first and the last. Because he is the eternal God who transcends all history and all time, God's people need to listen to him.

In addition, he is not some powerless deity that can do nothing. God had the power to create the earth. He laid the foundations of the world in which we live and stretched out the vast universe. All the created world listens to him. All natural forces stand at attention, waiting for God to call upon them and use them in his service. If the forces of nature stand at attention and await the command of God, shouldn't God's people do so as well? "Listen," the Lord pleads.

> ¹⁴ **"Come together, all of you, and listen:**
> **Which of the idols has foretold these things?**
> **The LORD's chosen ally**
> **will carry out his purpose against Babylon;**
> **his arm will be against the Babylonians.**
> ¹⁵ **I, even I, have spoken;**
> **yes, I have called him.**
> **I will bring him,**
> **and he will succeed in his mission.**
> ¹⁶**"Come near me and listen to this:**
>
> **"From the first announcement I have not spoken in secret;**
> **at the time it happens, I am there."**
>
> **And now the Sovereign LORD has sent me,**
> **with his Spirit.**

Not only should God's people listen because he is the eternal and powerful Lord of all, but they should listen to him also because he can foretell the future. The Lord asks, "Which of the idols has foretold these things?" Of course, none of them has the ability to foretell the future. None of them actually exists except in the imagination of misguided human minds. God's challenge to these empty gods to foretell the future has been part of the argument of these first nine chapters in the second part of Isaiah.

The Lord can foretell the future. He foretold the former things, and they came to pass as he said they would. He used the pen of Isaiah to foretell "new things"—a great and glorious future for his people. From chapters 40 to 48, the subject of Isaiah's prophecy has been the deliverance of God's people from Babylon. The house of Jacob and the line of Judah will be carried away captive, but the Lord will send his servant Cyrus to destroy Babylon and make it possible for the people of Judah to return home and rebuild their land.

This prophetic promise stands on the Lord's ability to make it happen as he promised. Over the centuries, God's people have accepted Isaiah's words as God's revelation and therefore true. Over those same centuries, others have shaken their heads in disbelief and rejected both Isaiah's words and God's ability to foretell the future. Listen to God's claim: "I, even I, have spoken; yes, I have called him. I will bring him, and he will succeed in his mission." What do these words mean if they were written after Cyrus conquered Babylon? What does the prophecy of Isaiah mean if the words were written after Cyrus appeared? It becomes an artistic fabrication—a lie. God then becomes a fabrication of some ancient religious writer—an invention no better than the gods of gold, silver, and wood fashioned by ancient peoples.

From God's perspective, and from the perspective of his prophet, the deliverance promised has already become a reality. The last part of verse 16 presents a curious insertion. The Lord had just been speaking. He will resume speaking again in verse 17. But who speaks these words: "And now the Sovereign Lord has sent me, with his Spirit"? The Lord would not send himself. Could these be the words of Cyrus, God's chosen deliverer? Could it be someone else?

God certainly did designate Cyrus as his servant, even calling Cyrus "his anointed" (45:1). But Isaiah had also introduced another Servant of the Lord, who would provide an even greater deliverance—that Servant whom God identified as one in whom he would delight and on whom he would put his Spirit (42:1). The best explanation for these words asserts that they are spoken by the greater Servant of the

Lord, the Messiah, and they announce that the deliverance God has so long promised is certain. The Great Servant has been sent and endowed with the Spirit. It's as good as done. Only waiting remains, waiting for the fullness of time when the Messiah will come to redeem the world.

This interpretation makes sense for three reasons. First, the Lord endows his Great Servant with the Spirit. Cyrus is indeed powerful and a great deliverer who freed God's people from captivity, but the Lord does not say that he endowed the Persian king with his Spirit. Already in the first part of Isaiah's prophecy, the Messiah was described as receiving the Spirit: "The Spirit of the LORD will rest on him" (11:2). The reference in chapter 11 must refer to the Messiah; God identified him as the "shoot" that will come from the "stump of Jesse." We do not read that Cyrus received a similar power from the Lord. Second, the deliverance God gave his people through Cyrus was a demonstration of his power. More than that, the deliverance from Babylon assured God's people that God could provide a still greater deliverance from sin, death, and hell. The work of Cyrus, as important as it was to the Jews in Babylon, was a preliminary event to the coming of God's great Savior (see this progression illustrated in 41:25–42:9). Third, these words recall the introduction of the Servant of the Lord in chapter 42 and anticipate the message of the next chapters. Chapter 49 will take the idea of the Servant of the Lord a step forward. After chapter 48, we no longer hear about Cyrus or Babylon. Isaiah will concentrate on the greater deliverance. Isaiah has begun to weave the tapestry that will reveal the Great Servant of the Lord. He began in chapter 42. This verse continues to weave a strand of the tapestry leading us to the next chapters.

> [17] **This is what the LORD says—**
>> **your Redeemer, the Holy One of Israel:**
> **"I am the LORD your God,**
>> **who teaches you what is best for you,**
>> **who directs you in the way you should go.**
> [18] **If only you had paid attention to my commands,**
>> **your peace would have been like a river,**
>> **your righteousness like the waves of the sea.**
> [19] **Your descendants would have been like the sand,**
>> **your children like its numberless grains;**
> **their name would never be cut off**
>> **nor destroyed from before me."**

With the announcement that the words come from the "LORD"—that is, Jehovah, the Savior-God—God's people are given another reason to listen to him. He is the God of free and faithful grace. The Lord once more chooses to identify himself as the Redeemer and the Holy One of Israel. Both names are important. "Holy One of Israel" identifies God as the one who transcends all human history and all human thought. He is holy—without sin, surely—but also separate and different. He tied himself to Israel by promise. God continued to desire to be associated with the nation that had been treacherous and rebellious. He remained constant in love and faithfulness. He is also their Redeemer. The rebellious people of Israel and Judah had necks of iron and foreheads of bronze. They could only bring themselves to spiritual disaster. Like all humans, they were addicted to sin and unable to escape its lure. Only the Lord could deliver them. He is the One who would buy them back from their own addiction and its consequences. He is the Redeemer. The prophecy of Isaiah will turn its attention to the work of the Great Servant in redeeming not only Israel and Judah but all the world. Such a God deserves our attention. God pleads for his people to listen to what he says.

Imagine Jehovah speaking these words as a father to his wayward child. "I am the LORD your God," he says. As a loving father, he knows what is best for his child, and he has provided the direction every child needs. But, like that rebellious child, the people had not given God their full attention. The Lord stood ready to grant them wonderful blessings, but they had not done what he had asked. As a loving father, the Lord had noted their sins and rebellion and watched as they squandered the blessings he was so eager and ready to give. The situation may remind us of the parent of a child addicted to alcohol or drugs. God had tried to correct his people who were addicted to sin. He had assured them of his love, threatened punishment when they turned away from him, and then watched as the people went their own way. Parents of addicts watch as their dear children squander their money, their talents, and even their lives. So God had watched his people waste his blessings.

But all was not lost. God is still the Redeemer. He promised to buy his dear children back from their own sins and folly. He would not desert them.

> [20] **Leave Babylon,**
> **flee from the Babylonians!**
> **Announce this with shouts of joy**
> **and proclaim it.**
> **Send it out to the ends of the earth;**
> **say, "The LORD has redeemed his servant Jacob."**
> [21] **They did not thirst when he led them through the deserts;**
> **he made water flow for them from the rock;**
> **he split the rock**
> **and water gushed out.**

By their addiction to sin and idolatry, God's people would not only squander their heritage, but they would see their own country destroyed. The Babylonians would torch the temple, raze Jerusalem, and lead the people away from their homes as prisoners of war. That was the just consequence for their sin. But God would reverse the fortunes of his people. In place of the tears, sorrow, and shame of captivity, God would fill their hearts with gladness and put ecstatic shouts of joy on their lips. Joy dominates this verse because the Lord will deliver his people from their captivity and bring them back to their homes and Jerusalem.

God compares the deliverance promised in these verses with the deliverance of his people from Egypt. In that great exodus, God cared for his people through miracles. He provided water for them in the desert, even making it gush out of a rock (see Exodus 17:6 and Numbers 20:11). God promises to provide for his people in the new exodus with the same power and care. There would be joy and confidence when the LORD redeemed his people. The redemption is finished. It is done as God promised it would be.

These verses provide an appropriate conclusion to the first section of the second half of Isaiah's prophecy. They point God's people to the promised release from captivity and to the greater redemption that lies beyond. Three events seem to be blended into this one picture. First, God had promised that he would send Cyrus to punish Babylon for their arrogant idolatry. The historic Babylon would fall, and God would bring his people out of captivity, back to their homeland. Second, another redemption would come after the people returned to their homes. A greater Servant would come to redeem God's people from the bondage of sin, death, and hell. Babylon, a picture of the unbelieving and arrogant world, would fall, but God's people would be delivered. Third, at the end of time, the Great Servant of the Lord would return a second time to destroy all the Babylons—all the powers of evil—permanently. Then God's people would be released from all sin and death for all time. The apostle John repeats God's exhortation to leave Babylon in Revelation: "Come out of her, my people, so that you will not share in her sins" (18:4).

²² **"There is no peace," says the LORD, "for the wicked."**

But not all will be delivered! This somber verse announces the consequences of unbelief. Those who do not listen to the Lord have no redemption and no peace.

This verse marks the end of this section. Isaiah repeats it at the end of the next section also (57:21). Even the last verse of the entire prophecy echoes the thought of this verse: "And they will go out and look upon the dead bodies of those who rebelled against me; their worm will not die, nor will their fire be quenched, and they will be loathsome to all mankind" (66:24). All these verses are as natural to God's revelation as law and gospel. God reveals not only his grace and mercy to sinners but also his wrath and punishment to all who refuse his grace and mercy.

Since this concludes a major portion of the prophecy, let's review some of the important truths we have learned.

- The Lord asserts his superiority over all other gods again and again. This idea finds expression regularly in this section. Only he is the true God; all others are false. Lord Jehovah claims superiority over all other religious concepts because he blots out transgressions and sins. No other gods can do that.

- In addition, the Lord asserts his superiority over all other gods because in the past he has predicted the future. These are the "former things." But more important to the prophecy of Isaiah, the Lord asserts that he has new things to predict as well.

- More than a century before the rise of Babylon and before God's people are taken captive by Babylonian armies, God foretells that his people will be released from their Babylonian captivity. This portion of Isaiah concentrates on Babylon and on Cyrus. After these nine chapters, Isaiah no longer refers to Babylon or Cyrus.

- The Lord's prophet mentions Cyrus by name as the one who will bring an end to the Babylonian Empire. The fall of Babylon will signal the return of the Jews to their homeland to rebuild Jerusalem. Their return means that all the promises of the coming Messiah will also be fulfilled.

- God identifies three servants in this section. First, God calls his people Israel his servant, but they have been unfaithful, stubborn, and rebellious. Second, Cyrus is the Lord's servant who will subdue his enemies and end Babylon's dominance. As important as these servants are, they do not compare with the importance of the third servant. God introduces this Great Servant in whom he delights and on whom he will put his Spirit. The Great Servant of the Lord will become the dominant theme of the next section of Isaiah.

- The word *redeemer* appears frequently in this section and throughout the rest of Isaiah's prophecy. The word occurs more frequently in the last 27 chapters of Isaiah than anywhere else in the Scriptures except in the last three chapters of Leviticus. By this word, God identifies himself as the one who will buy back his people from their own sins. The price of this purchase will be the suffering and death of the Great Servant of the Lord.

- The Lord announces that he will redeem his people from bondage by sending the great Deliverer because of his grace and not because of anything his people have done or will do. According to God's own words, he takes action "for [his] own sake" (43:25; 48:11). Our redemption rests on grace, pure grace, and nothing but grace.

The Lord introduces his Great Servant to the world

49 Listen to me, you islands;
     hear this, you distant nations:

These words command the world to listen to an important revelation from God. The islands and distant nations represent the farthest corners of the earth, and they are to listen to this speaker. He has information important for all humanity. His announcement identifies the Great Servant of the Lord and his work. Luther wrote, "From this chapter to the end, there is nothing but Christ, and although the prophet at the same time occasionally corrects and rebukes, the scope of this treatise has to do with Christ, with the calling of the Gentiles, and with the rejection of the Jews" (LW, Volume 17, page 169).

The command for the islands and the distant nations—

yes, for all the world—to listen introduces some of the most beautiful and profound prophecy in all of Scripture. They are words. God commands humanity to listen. He tells us all we need to know in the words he has caused to be written. God's prophet Isaiah wrote down the words God gave him by inspiration. Like the other words of Scripture, they are not words taught by human wisdom but words taught by the Spirit (1 Corinthians 2:13). Peter expressed the truth of God's inspiration so clearly: "Prophecy never had its origin in the will of man, but men spoke from God as they were carried along by the Holy Spirit" (2 Peter 1:21).

The momentous words of the remaining chapters of Isaiah are before us. We too are commanded to listen. The words are God's, and they reveal the great truths of his love for all the world. Listen, because what you hear means the difference between life and death, between redemption and judgment.

But to whom are we to listen here? Who commands us to listen? Over the centuries, a great deal of debate has raged over the answer to that question. Let us listen carefully to what the speaker says of himself. He will identify himself clearly.

> **Before I was born the LORD called me;**
> **from my birth he has made mention of my name.**
> **² He made my mouth like a sharpened sword,**
> **in the shadow of his hand he hid me;**
> **he made me into a polished arrow**
> **and concealed me in his quiver.**
> **³ He said to me, "You are my servant,**
> **Israel, in whom I will display my splendor."**

The speaker claims to be the chosen servant of the Lord, who has been called before birth. Several possibilities come to mind. First, this could be Cyrus, whom Isaiah identified in chapter 45. God chose the Persian king before his birth, and through his prophet, God even mentioned him by name. God does say that Cyrus was his anointed, but the other identifying marks here do not fit the Persian king. Cyrus would come in a display of strength and might in order to subdue the nations and set God's people free. But the military triumphs of Cyrus are more than words that come from the mouth, as described in verse 2, even if the mouth and what comes out of this servant's mouth may be like a sharpened sword. In verse 3 the servant is called Israel. *Cyrus* could never be called Israel. The importance of Cyrus can be documented in ancient world history and in what he did for Israel, but how did he "bring [God's] salvation to the ends of the earth" (verse 6)? This servant is not Cyrus. We must look for someone else.

Could this servant be a special prophet sent from God? Jeremiah appeared after the time of Isaiah. God told Jeremiah, "Before I formed you in the womb I knew you, before you were born I set you apart; I appointed you as a prophet to the nations" (Jeremiah 1:5). But no single prophet could be called Israel, and the verses that follow make it impossible to identify this servant as Jeremiah or any other single prophet. For example, how could any prophet restore the tribes of Jacob and bring salvation to the ends of the earth? A prophet might announce such blessings, but he could not accomplish them.

Some have suggested that the name Israel identifies this servant as the nation of Israel, and many agree. Certainly the nation was described as the Lord's servant (42:19). But several problems prevent such an interpretation here. Israel was anything but a good example as a servant. The nation had turned away from the Lord and despised his servants,

171

the prophets. God called Israel a deaf and blind servant (42:18-20). Israel itself needed rescue and help. If we identify the servant here as the nation of Israel, then how does Israel restore itself and "bring back those of Israel I have kept" (49:6)? What this servant does helps Israel. The servant cannot be helpless Israel. In addition, the servant mentioned here is a single person. He has a mouth, and God called him from his mother's womb. The NIV translates the phrase as "from my birth." The original reads "from the womb of my mother." We might suggest that a nation can be born. We speak of the birth of our own nation. We might even say that a nation was in a womb, but we would not say that it was in "the womb of [its] mother" as an individual child. We must look for someone else to be this servant.

Who else but the Messiah fits the description here? God chose him before birth. From the beginning God's plan for the deliverance of the world involved the coming of one person. As God told Adam and Eve, this person would be the seed, or offspring, of a woman. Throughout the long history of the Old Testament, God promised the coming of such a deliverer. Abraham, Isaac, and Jacob all anticipated the coming of that one deliverer. God promised David that such a deliverer would come from his family and that this one great descendant would rule forever on David's throne. Isaiah foretold that this descendant would be the Branch from the stump of Jesse, David's father (11:1). Isaiah also identified him as a child, born of a virgin—an individual (7:14; 9:6). All the Old Testament prophecies pointed to the coming of that one Great Servant, who would deliver his people. In this text the Great Servant calls out to people at the far corners of the earth.

Consider the description of the Messiah here. God set him apart long before his birth. Jesus, the eternal Son of

God, was born in time of a woman. The Lord of free and faithful grace made the mouth of the Messiah like a sharpened sword. Remember the words of Jesus. They were often like a sharp sword cutting away pretense and unbelief, exposing sin, then applying the healing balm of God's grace for sinners. In addition, Isaiah wrote that the Messiah was hidden: "in the shadow of his hand he hid me." The God of grace did not reveal the Messiah until it was time for him to do his work on earth. Then the stars themselves joined the angels in announcing his arrival (Matthew 2; Luke 2). The Messiah is the Servant in whom the Lord would display his splendor. That is, the Messiah would come to accomplish the most glorious and wonderful blessings that God planned for all humanity. He would redeem the world from sin, death, and hell. That is the glory of God's grace, and it is tied to the Great Servant—the Messiah, Jesus Christ.

Yet we might wonder how the Messiah could be identified in verse 3 as "Israel." This Servant becomes the reason God had chosen his people Israel. The Messiah would come from the descendants of Abraham; that's why God chose Abraham. God continued to identify the origins of this Messiah through the prophecies of the Old Testament. When God calls the servant Israel, he brings all those prophecies to mind. Israel, God's chosen people of the Old Testament, existed for only one reason—to be the nation from which the Messiah for all humanity would come. The Messiah, this Servant of the Lord, would fulfill the mission God intended through Israel. He is the focal point of all Israel's history. The Great Servant therefore receives the name Israel as a title implying all God promised to bring to pass through this nation. He is the true Israel, who would bring glory to God and who stands in dramatic contrast to the historical Israel.

⁴ **But I said, "I have labored to no purpose;**
   I have spent my strength in vain and for nothing.
   Yet what is due me is in the LORD's hand,
   and my reward is with my God."

Such grand promises did not come to pass by a spectacular and triumphant campaign. Instead, it was a sad, lowly, bloody one. The Messiah set aside his glorious power and majesty in order to be a servant. He became nothing—humbled himself—and became obedient to death (Philippians 2:6-11). In the Garden of Gethsemane, all appeared lost. Eleven men surrounded Jesus; the twelfth led a band of soldiers to arrest him. After three years of ministry, after all the sermons and all the miracles, it seemed that only death awaited him. From all human perspectives, the Messiah's mission had failed. From the cross, he exclaimed, "My God, my God, why have you forsaken me?" (Mark 15:34). Yet, a few hours later, he would commit himself to the hands of the Lord: "Father, into your hands I commit my spirit" (Luke 23:46). This verse in Isaiah prophesies these events. It reminds us of the human nature of the Servant of the Lord and anticipates the Savior's words in Gethsemane.

⁵ **And now the LORD says—**
   he who formed me in the womb to be his servant
to bring Jacob back to him
   and gather Israel to himself,
for I am honored in the eyes of the LORD
   and my God has been my strength—
⁶ **he says:**
"It is too small a thing for you to be my servant
   to restore the tribes of Jacob
   and bring back those of Israel I have kept.
I will also make you a light for the Gentiles,
   that you may bring my salvation to the ends of the earth."

As empty and unsuccessful as the work of the Servant of the Lord appeared, he had entrusted his entire mission into the hands of the Lord. Isaiah recorded a prophetic dialogue between the Servant of the Lord and the Lord himself. The Servant said, "I have labored to no purpose." And so it seemed. But the goal of the Lord in sending this Servant would not fail. The Lord responded to his Servant by restating the reasons for sending him.

We note two reasons. First, the servant came to restore the tribes of Jacob. His work would focus on the ancient people God had chosen. Jesus was born in Bethlehem to "save his people from their sins," as the angel proclaimed to Joseph (Matthew 1:21). But we also note God's second reason for sending the Servant. God implied the reason in the first verse when he commanded the distant nations to listen. The Servant was also to be "a light for the Gentiles, that you may bring my salvation to the ends of the earth." God had bigger plans for displaying his splendor than merely restoring the believing Jews from captivity. The work of this Servant of the Lord would be for all people all over the world. At his birth the angels announced this wonderful news: "Glory to God in the highest, and *on earth* peace to men on whom his favor rests" (Luke 2:14). Through this Servant, God provided deliverance for all humanity. In the chapters ahead, we will see just how he did that and what it means.

> ⁷ **This is what the L**ORD **says—**
>   **the Redeemer and Holy One of Israel—**
> **to him who was despised and abhorred by the nation,**
>   **to the servant of rulers:**
> **"Kings will see you and rise up,**
>   **princes will see and bow down,**
> **because of the L**ORD**, who is faithful,**
>   **the Holy One of Israel, who has chosen you."**

The Lord continues speaking to his Servant. These words come from the covenant God, the LORD, Jehovah, "the Redeemer and Holy One of Israel"—two favorite names of God in the second part of Isaiah. The name Redeemer recalls the laws of redemption in Leviticus. If a man was forced to sell himself as a servant or sell his property to another, he could later buy back whatever had been sold. If he could not, a relative—a kinsman-redeemer—then could buy back whatever had been sold. The Lord is the Redeemer. His people had sold themselves to the servitude of sin and could not escape. Because they had nothing to offer as adequate payment, they could not redeem themselves. The Lord would offer the payment; the Servant of the Lord would suffer and die to buy back those held captive by sin and death. In addition, the Lord would redeem his people from the captivity of Babylon. Cyrus would release them from that bondage, but it would only be a preliminary event to a much greater deliverance through the Servant of the Lord.

The name Holy One of Israel appears in both the first and second portions of Isaiah's prophecy. God is indeed holy. He is separate and different from all humanity and from his people. He is without imperfection, sin, or limits and transcends all that is on earth. The Lord exists at a higher, perfect level and is therefore different and separate. But he is a God who is not content to remain in that separate and perfect existence outside the world of human activity and history. He is the Holy One of Israel. The perfect God of the universe has reached out and penetrated human history by pledging himself to Israel. He chose to create the ancient nation of Israel, to preserve it throughout the centuries, and to guide its course to serve his own purposes. His purpose clearly centers on the arrival of this Servant of the Lord from the nation of Israel. The Servant would carry out the plan of God in redeeming the world. In the Servant, God broke into the course of human events to rescue humanity. Through the Servant, God declared all the world holy and righteous and removed all that separates sinners from his holiness and therefore from his presence. Because of the Servant—and only because of the Servant—humanity can anticipate perfect deliverance and joy in the presence of this Holy One.

But Isaiah describes the Servant here as "despised and abhorred by the nation." We see the Servant rejected by his own nation, again as an apparent failure. Such a description recalls the events of the passion of Jesus Christ. His own countrymen screamed, "Crucify him." When Pilate asked what he should do with their king, the crowd answered, "We have no king but Caesar" (John 19:15).

The Servant is anything but an outwardly impressive figure. But the Lord asks us to look beyond appearances. As we listen, the Lord encourages his "despised and abhorred" Servant. Things are not what they seem to be. The Lord tells his Servant that kings and princes will bow down to him. Why should powerful heads of state bow down to this lowly, unimpressive servant? They will bow down because of the redemption he will bring to the world. The kings of the earth bow because of the unsurpassed blessing of the redemption God has provided for their people and for all the people of the earth. Note again that kings and princes outside the people of Israel—Gentiles—accord the honor to this Servant. Redemption is for all humanity.

> **8This is what the LORD says:**
>
> > **"In the time of my favor I will answer you,**
> > **and in the day of salvation I will help you;**
> > **I will keep you and will make you**
> > **to be a covenant for the people,**

> to restore the land
>> and to reassign its desolate inheritances,
> ⁹ to say to the captives, 'Come out,'
>> and to those in darkness, 'Be free!'
>
> "They will feed beside the roads
>> and find pasture on every barren hill.
> ¹⁰ They will neither hunger nor thirst,
>> nor will the desert heat or the sun beat upon them.
> He who has compassion on them will guide them
>> and lead them beside springs of water.
> ¹¹ I will turn all my mountains into roads,
>> and my highways will be raised up.
> ¹² See, they will come from afar—
>> some from the north, some from the west,
>> some from the region of Aswan."

The Lord continues to speak to his Servant in this section. Blood, disgrace, rejection by the world, death, and burial all seem to be implied in the situation of the Servant. Isaiah will describe the work of the Servant in great detail in the chapters ahead. For now, we are told that the Servant faced rejection and wondered if his work was for nothing. Yes, the Servant may have been despised by all the nations. He may have felt as if he had "labored to no purpose" (verse 4), and he may have prayed to his heavenly Father without apparent answer. Yet, "in the time of my favor," the Lord says, "I will answer you."

The promised Servant will accomplish the purposes he was sent to achieve. Of that, there is no doubt. The Lord will stand behind his Servant and pledges, "I will help you; I will keep you."

One of the purposes for which God sent this Servant was to be "a covenant for the people." Designating the Servant as "a covenant" deserves special notice. Since the Lord of the covenant—Jehovah, YHWH, the Lord—speaks, he is one of the principals in this covenant. On the other side are the people. These two parties are brought together by an agreement embodied in the Servant. He is the covenant, the agreement or contract between the Holy One and his people Israel. In this covenant of grace, God does everything, and his people receive all the benefits. The Lord would fulfill all the stipulations of the covenant in the Servant, who would suffer for the sins of the people (see chapter 53). We limit our vision if we consider this Servant to be Cyrus, one of the prophets, or even the nation itself. This servant must be the Messiah. (Consider the options presented earlier in this chapter.)

Because of the Servant's work, many blessings would flow to the people. Note how beautifully the Lord describes those blessings. Their homeland would be restored and the captives released. Perhaps we might think of the return of Judah from the Babylonian captivity. But that was only a preliminary event to a greater deliverance. The deliverance from Babylon was physical and had nothing to do with the forgiveness of sins (1:18; 43:25; 44:22) and removing the shroud of death (25:7,8) from the peoples of the earth. Christ's greater deliverance did. When we picture the return of the captives, we must remember the prophetic vision of God's prophets. They saw events in the foreground that had general outlines of greater and grander events beyond their own days and far into the future.

Here the Lord continues his description. The blessings the Lord would provide for his people through his Servant recall Psalm 23. The people "will feed beside the roads and find pasture on every barren hill." The Good Shepherd would provide rich blessings for the sheep of his flock. Remember that Jesus identified himself as the Good Shepherd (John 10).

One more aspect of this picture should not escape our attention; the Lord directs our attention to it with the word see. Look carefully at sheep of the flock that enjoys all these blessings. They come from the four corners of the earth—"from afar." The people of God may have been dispersed over all the earth and are often pictured as returning to Zion (11:12), but this picture seems to expand beyond that. Isaiah also indicated that the Lord would gather other nations to himself (2:2,3). We noted that earlier in this chapter too. This flock will be diverse, coming from faraway lands. The one region listed is difficult to identify. The NIV translates it as "the region of Aswan." It might refer to the region south of Egypt, but others suggest different regions, including a region far to the east—China. But we cannot be sure. All we know is that this flock will come from many geographic regions. God will gather them because of his compassion and will bring them great blessings.

> [13] **Shout for joy, O heavens;**
> **rejoice, O earth;**
> **burst into song, O mountains!**
> **For the LORD comforts his people**
> **and will have compassion on his afflicted ones.**

Isaiah interjects his reaction to what the Lord has just revealed. It will be so great that the heavens, the mountains, and the earth will seem to rejoice. Hallelujah! Shout for joy! Rejoice! Burst into song! God loves. He gives his people all they need. In their affliction he has compassion on them and comforts them. The grace and mercy of God for his people always generate praise

> [14] **But Zion said, "The LORD has forsaken me,**
> **the Lord has forgotten me."**

The rejoicing had one discordant note. Zion, a name

that designates God's people, complained. To God's people, it appeared as if the Lord had forsaken them. We can imagine an exile in Babylon having such a thought. From that perspective, Jerusalem lay in ruins, the Babylonians had left the temple in ruins, and God's people languished as exiles in a foreign land, while their homeland, so distant, was desolate. Surely more than one of the exiles must have said or at least thought, "The LORD has forsaken me, the Lord has forgotten me."

In the everyday world, believers experience trials and afflictions. So often at those times, God's people feel that they have been forsaken and forgotten. We find ourselves among them when we experience troublesome trials, anguishing afflictions, and persistent persecutions. "Where is God now when I need him?" we ask in our inmost hearts. Because we are weak, we need the regular reassurance of the gospel of God. Once we learn the gospel, we treasure its sweet message. But once learned does not mean we can do without hearing it again and again. Life's trials trouble us and cause us doubt, confusion, and anguish. God's people need to hear the sweet message of God's love for them as long as they live in the chaos, confusion, and conflict of human history.

What follows is such an assurance. It remains one of the most beautiful descriptions of God's love for his people. One can find no similar description in all of the world's literature. Even in the pages of God's Word, it would be difficult to find a better description of God's faithful love.

> ¹⁵ **"Can a mother forget the baby at her breast**
> **and have no compassion on the child she has borne?**
> **Though she may forget,**
> **I will not forget you!**
> ¹⁶ **See, I have engraved you on the palms of my hands;**
> **your walls are ever before me.**

The Lord's love for his people is greater than the love a nursing mother has for her child. The bond a mother has for her child is indeed strong. Such a mother will not ordinarily forget her nursing child, but she satisfies the child with the warm nourishment from her breasts as she holds the child close to her heart. She loves her child deeply and profoundly. A mother cannot suckle her infant one minute and show no compassion or love the next. Such is the picture of God's love, but his love endures more firmly, deeply, and enduringly than even the love a mother has for her nursing child.

We do not expect a mother to forget the baby at her breast, but such things do occur in this perverse world. A mother might possibly forget her children, but God will not forget his people. Such a thought is impossible for God. If he should forget his people and fail to love them, he would be denying himself, for God is love. Even when he judges the evil world, God has the welfare of his own people in mind. All things happen for the benefit of his people, as Paul wrote centuries later, "We know that in all things God works for the good of those who love him" (Romans 8:28). God will not fail to discipline his own people, as a loving father disciplines his dear children for their good (Hebrews 12:4-11). But never, never has he forgotten them. Never has he failed to have compassion on them. He loves them with a love deeper than any mother could love her nursing child.

Again God wants to draw our attention to something special. He says, "See." And what are we to see? Look at the palms of God's hands. There he has engraved, or tattooed, a remembrance of his people. The Levitical law prohibited tattoos because the use of them often indicated dedication to a foreign god, another person, or even the dead. Yet God uses the picture here to emphasize the permanence of his love and its constancy. What is on the palms of God's hands cannot be washed off as we might wash the dirt off our stained hands. God has engraved his people on his palms; his people are permanently there.

How often we see the palms of our hands in the course of a day! So God sees the reminder of his people constantly. "Your walls are ever before me," God says. Those things that his people experience are not hidden from God's attention and care. When God's people complain that the Lord has forsaken or forgotten them, he assures them. How could he ever forget his people if they are engraved on the palms of his hands? What a wonderful picture of God's constant attention to the affairs of his people! Just as we see the palms of our own hands so often each day, so God thinks of us. We need to mark well how the love of God for us burns in his heart. What a comfort to know that he has pledged to love us so!

> [17] **Your sons hasten back,**
> **and those who laid you waste depart from you.**
> [18] **Lift up your eyes and look around;**
> **all your sons gather and come to you.**
> **As surely as I live," declares the LORD,**
> **"you will wear them all as ornaments;**
> **you will put them on, like a bride.**
>
> [19] **"Though you were ruined and made desolate**
> **and your land laid waste,**
> **now you will be too small for your people,**
> **and those who devoured you will be far away.**
> [20] **The children born during your bereavement**
> **will yet say in your hearing,**
> **'This place is too small for us;**
> **give us more space to live in.'**
> [21] **Then you will say in your heart,**
> **'Who bore me these?**

> **I was bereaved and barren;**
> **I was exiled and rejected.**
> **Who brought these up?**
> **I was left all alone,**
> **but these—where have they come from?'"**

These verses tell us how God would take care of his people after the captivity. He sent them away captive, and their history revealed dark and desolate days. But the Lord would not forget them any more than he had forgotten them in Egypt when they were slaves to the pharaoh's building projects. The exile to Babylon would come to an end just as the bondage in Egypt came to an end. God's people would return from captivity.

But we must stretch this picture beyond the return of God's people from Babylon. Isaiah has used the idea of a "remnant" returning before. The group of people here is not a small, insignificant remnant but a large crowd that proclaims, "This place is too small for us." Babylon is not mentioned here, and the return from captivity is the first paragraph of a much larger chapter in the history of God's people. The Jews would return to Palestine, but we are invited to see believers gathered and coming to Zion far beyond the time of Cyrus, Zerubbabel, Ezra, and Nehemiah.

God pictures the church as a nation of people gathered together. In the Old Testament, this group of people often carried the name Zion or Israel. The New Testament believers were not only Jews. Paul was an apostle to the Gentiles, whom God gathered together with believing Jews as the church of God. God the Holy Spirit called both groups out of the world and gathered them into one church to be his own. The New Testament church is a "calling out"—the literal meaning of the Greek word used in the New Testament for *church*. What Isaiah describes here in these verses did not happen when Judah returned from Babylon. Then a small remnant returned, but here God shows us the gathering of the New Testament church.

What do the Old Testament faithful think of this development? They hear this great multitude saying that they need more space. The number of the ransomed has grown so great that the land has become too small for them. Such a thought is almost unbelievable. The realities of their Old Testament history conditioned the vision of God's ancient people. The Babylonians invaded their country, ravaged their cities, subdued Jerusalem, and led them all away captive. Only a few returned. If we extend the history even further, we note the conquest by the Romans and the second destruction of Jerusalem. Isaiah said that when the Messiah would come, the royal house of David would be nothing but a stump (11:1). How could such a multitude come into being? Where did they come from?

At times it appears that the church is bereaved, barren, exiled, and rejected. Certainly at the time of the Babylonian captivity, Judah seemed to be like a wife who was turned out, rejected, and barren. Yet the Lord has his people always before his eyes. He cares for them and continues to gather believers into the nation that Scripture calls Zion, that is, his church. As New Testament believers, we must not let our view of the church be held captive to the boundaries of our earthly vision. God continues to call, gather, enlighten, and sanctify his church and to keep it faithful to the Lord Jesus Christ through the gospel. When, at the end of time, we are assembled in the presence of the Lord Almighty, we too will be surprised. We will no doubt say, "Where did all these come from?" In our human experience, we customarily see the church as a group of believers who are often ridiculed, persecuted, and rejected as unimportant. God's reality is different from what we see in this world.

> [22] **This is what the Sovereign LORD says:**
>
> **"See, I will beckon to the Gentiles,**
> **I will lift up my banner to the peoples;**
> **they will bring your sons in their arms**
> **and carry your daughters on their shoulders.**
> [23] **Kings will be your foster fathers,**
> **and their queens your nursing mothers.**
> **They will bow down before you with their faces to the ground;**
> **they will lick the dust at your feet.**
> **Then you will know that I am the LORD;**
> **those who hope in me will not be disappointed."**

Again with the word see, the Lord points us to an important thought. This time we see what the Lord has done to gather such a crowd to himself. He has set up his banner to draw the people to himself. The banner is the gospel, and it is responsible for the conversion of the Gentiles. God gathers together those who believe. The heathen Gentiles will accompany believing children of God's Old Testament people. Even kings and queens will contribute to the joy and love that dominates this assembled group. They will love one another and support one another. The gentile kings will be foster fathers; and their queens, nursing mothers. The most powerful and the greatest will humble themselves and place their treasure and power at the disposal of the church. Those kings and queens will give the church honor and glory and in humble faith will submit to the church and its head.

Why should kings and queens do such humble service for the church? The Lord has given the church the gospel of forgiveness, life, and hope. Such treasures are tied to the

Great Servant of the Lord and his coming from Bethlehem of Judea. The Servant gave to all believers more than all the money on earth could buy. So whether believers are the powerful and dominant figures in the history of the world or the poor, lowly, and apparently inconsequential, they have what the Lord has promised. Those who hope in the Lord will not be disappointed.

> [24] **Can plunder be taken from warriors,**
> **or captives rescued from the fierce?**
> [25]**But this is what the LORD says:**
>
> **"Yes, captives will be taken from warriors,**
> **and plunder retrieved from the fierce;**
> **I will contend with those who contend with you,**
> **and your children I will save.**
> [26] **I will make your oppressors eat their own flesh;**
> **they will be drunk on their own blood, as with wine.**
> **Then all mankind will know**
> **that I, the LORD, am your Savior,**
> **your Redeemer, the Mighty One of Jacob."**

The previous verses projected a glorious vision of the church, but we can see this vision only in the Scriptures and, by faith, in what the Lord promises. In the everyday world, we see no such vision. Instead, we see a world dominated by power, money, and influence. One might wonder if anyone could gather such an assembly from the world in which we live or from the world in which God's Old Testament believers lived. They also lived in a world that seemed to be held together by the raw power of armies and the wealth of the powerful and influential. How could God's people escape the domination of Nebuchadnezzar and the Babylonians? How could any foreign kings and queens submit to the church of believers?

The answer rests in the promise of the Lord. He will

make it all happen. He will bring his people out of Babylon. He continues to gather his own from the four corners of the earth. Among those God calls are some who are by the world's standards powerful, wealthy, and influential. No matter how godless or powerful the unbelieving world may seem to be, God will gather believers to himself. The gospel will be effective, even if in the world it seems like foolishness and a stumbling block.

But not everyone who hears the gospel will believe it. Not everyone will be gathered. Some will resist; others will persecute the believers, God's special people. A terrifying picture of their fate concludes this chapter. Those who oppose the gospel and who afflict the church will "eat their own flesh; they will be drunk on their own blood, as with wine." As ghastly as the picture strikes us, the Lord announces nothing different than what his New Testament apostle related, "Whoever believes in him is not condemned, but whoever does not believe stands condemned already because he has not believed in the name of God's one and only Son" (John 3:18).

Who stands behind all these words? "The LORD, . . . your Savior, your Redeemer, the Mighty One of Jacob." The piling up of these names adds emphasis. The truth of these promises does not depend on any human effort. It depends on the Lord and his activity on behalf of his people. He promised to keep them always before his eyes. They are engraved on the palms of his hands. He pledged to love them more profoundly than any mother could love her nursing child. All rests in the God of free and faithful grace, the LORD, who will save and redeem his people. He is the Mighty One of Jacob and has the power to do as he promises.

The Lord's Servant will ransom his disobedient people

God's people have brought their misery upon themselves

50 This is what the LORD says:

"Where is your mother's certificate of divorce
　　with which I sent her away?
Or to which of my creditors
　　did I sell you?
Because of your sins you were sold;
　　because of your transgressions your mother was sent
　　　　away.
² When I came, why was there no one?
　　When I called, why was there no one to answer?
Was my arm too short to ransom you?
　　Do I lack the strength to rescue you?
By a mere rebuke I dry up the sea,
　　I turn rivers into a desert;
their fish rot for lack of water
　　and die of thirst.
³ I clothe the sky with darkness
　　and make sackcloth its covering."

The Lord had promised his people that his love was deeper than the love of a mother for her nursing child (49:15). Yet God sent Isaiah to minister to a people who were headed to captivity in Babylon. Even the return from the Babylonian captivity, as wonderful and glorious as that was to be, would see only a remnant return to rebuild Jerusalem and the Land of Promise. When God commissioned Isaiah, God sent his prophet to "make the heart of this people calloused; make their ears dull and close their eyes" (6:10). Why were such things predicted if God's love for his people was so deep? Why did God send Isaiah with such a mission? These words tell us the cause of all the trouble God would send to his people.

On the one hand, God had not forgotten them. On the

other, the sin and guilt of God's people caused all their troubles. In the first verses of this chapter, God posed some penetrating questions. First, he asked his people to produce the certificate of divorce. When a husband issued such a certificate to his wife, it declared that she was no longer bound to her husband (see Deuteronomy 24:1-4). The Lord issued no such certificate to his people. As far as God was concerned, he remained faithful and had sought no such divorce. The cause of the trouble was not God but the people. The Lord emphasized the idea with a second question: "To which of my creditors did I sell you?" According to ancient practice, if a man was helplessly caught in a debt and could not pay it, his children could be sold to the creditor in order to pay off the debt. The Lord had no such creditors. It was impossible for him to be in debt to anyone. The reason for their exile in Babylon was not because God owed something to Babylon. God says clearly, "Because of your sins you were sold; because of your transgressions your mother was sent away."

The guilt of God's people was clear. They had sinned, but God had not simply written them off because of their sin and rebellion. He sent prophets to them and called them to repentance. But they did not listen to any of his pleas, nor did they respond to the words of God's messengers, the prophets. They turned a deaf ear to God's tender and loving calls to repentance, as well as to the harsh and frightening announcements of judgment to come. They were like King Ahaz, who did not understand the gracious message of Isaiah (chapter 7).

Their troubled national history, the destruction of Jerusalem, and their deportation into exile all came because of the sins of the people, not because the Lord had changed his attitude toward them. Some might suggest that these difficulties came because the Lord was weak and unable to save his people, but the Lord says that was not the case either. He certainly did have the strength to rescue his people, and he alluded to the spectacular rescue of his people from Egypt. Back then he had dried up the sea so that his people could escape from Pharaoh's army (Exodus 14). If there should be any question about the Lord's power, he reminded his people that he controls even the sky. The Lord's power is unlimited.

All this emphasized the real reason for the misery of God's ancient people. The people themselves were responsible for their own troubles. God was not to blame. He remained faithful. What's more, God would not allow the miseries to continue. He would provide help through his Servant.

The Servant of the Lord suffers in complete and perfect obedience

4 **The Sovereign LORD has given me an instructed tongue,**
   to know the word that sustains the weary.
 He wakens me morning by morning,
   wakens my ear to listen like one being taught.
5 **The Sovereign LORD has opened my ears,**
   and I have not been rebellious;
   I have not drawn back.
6 **I offered my back to those who beat me,**
   my cheeks to those who pulled out my beard;
 I did not hide my face
   from mocking and spitting.

Just who is speaking here? Suddenly the speaker changes. In English, speakers are carefully identified, but not in Hebrew. The first verse of this chapter identified the speaker as "the LORD." But now someone else speaks, because he announces his relationship to "the Sovereign

LORD." The Hebrew mind assumed that everyone reading the passage would understand that the speaker had changed. We consider the speaker to be the Servant of the Lord, whom we have met before.

In chapter 42 the LORD, Jehovah, introduced this special Servant, "Here is my servant." This Servant was different from Cyrus, the man God chose to release his people from the Babylonian captivity, because this special Servant was anointed with God's Spirit (42:1). Once introduced, this special Servant becomes a dominant theme of Isaiah's prophecy. When he appeared next, he spoke (49:1-6). He identified himself as the Lord's special Servant. In that passage the Servant announced that the Lord had given him a mouth like a sharpened sword (verse 2).

Each of these Servant passages adds its own information about the Servant. They complement one another. When we take them all together, we gain a clearer picture of who the Servant is and what he has come to do. We have learned that he has been specially chosen by the Lord and anointed with his Spirit. His ministry will include proclaiming the Word of God, and he will not falter in his purpose, even though his work may have appeared to be in vain.

In this passage, the Servant of the Lord now adds new information. First, he clarifies what he meant earlier with the phrase "[a] mouth like a sharpened sword" (49:2). The Servant says, "The Sovereign Lord has given me an instructed tongue." Part of his ministry would be to proclaim God's Word. How can we be sure that the words of this Servant come from God? The Servant has obediently listened. "Morning by morning," that is, again and again, the Servant gave the Lord's Word his attention. But he has not just listened to the Word and then forgotten the words of God, as Israel and Judah had so often done. He willingly submitted to the Word of God. He knew what the Lord wanted, and he obeyed.

We learn a second piece of important information from this passage: the Servant will suffer. He learned the will of God, and he willingly obeyed. For this Servant, obedience meant that he would be beaten and humiliated. The Servant describes the treatment criminals experienced in the ancient East. The Servant willingly gave his back to those who struck him; he was whipped. He also gave his cheeks to those who would tear out his beard. In the ancient world, such treatment was a disgrace and humiliation, but the Servant willingly allowed it to take place because of his obedience to the Word of the Lord. His willing obedience would be evident in the way he endured reproach and spitting. In this passage, the Servant of the Lord clearly becomes the Suffering Servant.

Is there any doubt about who this Servant is? He could not be Cyrus. He could not be Israel or Judah. He could not be even the best among God's people, because no one has ever listened to the Lord's Word to the same degree as this Servant. Isaiah wrote that God's people were deaf and blind (42:18,19). Even the most obedient group of God's people or the best individual could not claim such obedience.

> No natural human being, no Christian, so long as he is still clothed with flesh and blood, can endure such things willingly and gladly without any inner rebellion. . . . Only the Holy One of God, He who was without sin, was capable of that. If the people of Israel were meant here, even Israel according to the spirit, Isaiah would be painting an untrue picture. (August Pieper, *Isaiah II,* page 391)

193

The Servant who speaks in this passage must be a special individual sent from God himself to carry out a mission that would involve proclaiming of God's truth, as well as enduring suffering and disgrace. He must be the Great Prophet promised (Deuteronomy 18:17,18) and the Great High Priest, who would offer up himself as a sacrifice for sin (Hebrews 7:26-28; 9:6-12). He is Jesus Christ, pictured here in prophecy. The truth of this identification becomes clear the more we learn about this Servant. The next verses continue the revelation.

> ⁷ **Because the Sovereign LORD helps me,**
> **I will not be disgraced.**
> **Therefore have I set my face like flint,**
> **and I know I will not be put to shame.**
> ⁸ **He who vindicates me is near.**
> **Who then will bring charges against me?**
> **Let us face each other!**
> **Who is my accuser?**
> **Let him confront me!**
> ⁹ **It is the Sovereign LORD who helps me.**
> **Who is he that will condemn me?**
> **They will all wear out like a garment;**
> **the moths will eat them up.**

The suffering of the Servant is necessary. It is a part of God's plan, which the Servant has learned from the "Sovereign LORD" himself. The Servant has also learned that the Lord would not desert him. This idea runs through these Servant passages like a golden thread. We were told, "He will not falter or be discouraged" (42:4). Then when the Servant himself appeared to labor for no purpose, he said, "Yet what is due me is in the LORD's hand" (49:4). Now he says again clearly, "I will not be disgraced." He would indeed suffer in order to accomplish his mission. Therefore the Servant resolutely faces his suffering, "I set my face like flint."

What believing saint of God can read these words without recalling how resolutely Jesus took his last journey to Jerusalem to suffer and die? He told his disciples what would happen there, but the prospect of pain and death did not deter him (Matthew 16:21; 20:17-19; Mark 8:31; 10:32-34; Luke 9:51). From the anguish in the Garden of Gethsemane, Jesus arose to face those who had come to arrest him. He willingly obeyed the Father and gave himself up to those who would inflict pain.

We note a kind of defiance in the words of the Servant here. He would endure pain and suffering, but he would remain absolutely confident that he is doing the will of the Lord and that the Lord will vindicate, or justify, him. That knowledge would enable the Servant to defy his accusers. He says, "Who then will bring charges against me? Let us face each other!" The Servant is innocent of any sin. The accusations lodged against him were intended to condemn him, but all the accusations were nothing more than a moth-eaten garment, fit only to be discarded with the trash.

So we read these passages with Jesus in mind again. Consider his words to Annas: "Why question me? Ask those who heard me. Surely they know what I said" (John 18:21). When facing the mob in the garden, Jesus said: "Am I leading a rebellion, that you have come out with swords and clubs to capture me? Every day I sat in the temple courts teaching, and you did not arrest me. But this has all taken place that the writings of the prophets might be fulfilled" (Matthew 26:55,56). Note his defiant attitude, but also note his willing obedience to the words of the Lord. His own countrymen brought many false witnesses against Jesus, but the Sanhedrin could find no evidence against him (Matthew 26:60; Mark 14:55-59). Not one of the accusations stood the test of truth.

> [10] **Who among you fears the L**ORD
> **and obeys the word of his servant?**
> **Let him who walks in the dark,**
> **who has no light,**
> **trust in the name of the L**ORD
> **and rely on his God.**
> [11] **But now, all you who light fires**
> **and provide yourselves with flaming torches,**
> **go, walk in the light of your fires**
> **and of the torches you have set ablaze.**
> **This is what you shall receive from my hand:**
> **You will lie down in torment.**

What does this Servant passage mean to the people of Israel and the world? Isaiah addresses two groups of people in these last two verses. The first group "fears the LORD." Fear of the Lord is respect for the God of free and faithful grace. The Lord has graciously promised deliverance from sin, death, and hell. As God's prophet Isaiah— yes, all of Scripture—tells us, the Lord will fulfill his promise through his Servant. Because we are all sinners, we must have this deliverance from the hand of the Lord of grace. Before God, all humans stand in absolute terror of the punishment they deserve because of their sins. But the Lord of free and faithful grace declared all sinners not guilty because of this great Servant. Believers possess deep respect and awe for the Lord; therefore, they listen to his Word. They become especially interested in the Word of this Servant, whom the Lord has sent. Those who show appropriate fear of the Lord prove it by giving ear to the Word of his great Suffering Servant. This Servant has redemption, light, and victory for all humanity. That's why he asks the world to listen to him (49:1). All who fear the Lord and trust in the Word of the Lord's Servant will find deliverance, forgiveness, and life. Consider John 3:16.

God identifies a second group. Not everyone has such a fear of the Lord. Some oppose the Word of the Lord's Servant. God pictures them here as lighting fires and preparing flaming arrows rather than obeying the Word of God's Servant. Because they oppose the Lord, have no fear of him, and do not listen to his Servant, they will not have the blessings promised by the Servant. Instead, God directs them to go into the fire of their own making. They will not be delivered but will experience the judgment of God. He will abandon them to their own folly and will bring suffering from their opposition to him and his Servant. God's bright beams of light, if rejected, turn into destroying fire.

God does not want any human being to be lost. He has provided deliverance for all humans who have ever lived or will ever live. He announced this deliverance clearly in advance through the words of his prophets. Isaiah serves as an example. Then when the deliverance was completed, he again announced it clearly. The world does not remain in the dark about the work of Jesus Christ. God's gift to the world is his Son, freely offered. And God has invited the nations of the earth to receive the gift he has so lovingly prepared. He still invites, "Believe in the Lord Jesus, and you will be saved—you and your household" (Acts 16:31). What is God to do when his invitation is rejected? The last verse of this chapter tells us: "Go, walk in the light of your fires and of the torches you have set ablaze. This is what you shall receive from my hand: You will lie down in torment." This is not God's fault. The first verses of the chapter announced that God had not given a certificate of divorce; the people had rejected him. They "will lie down in torment" because they rejected the Lord.

The Lord's deliverance approaches

51 "Listen to me, you who pursue righteousness
and who seek the LORD:
Look to the rock from which you were cut
and to the quarry from which you were hewn;
² look to Abraham, your father,
and to Sarah, who gave you birth.
When I called him he was but one,
and I blessed him and made him many.
³ The LORD will surely comfort Zion
and will look with compassion on all her ruins;
he will make her deserts like Eden,
her wastelands like the garden of the LORD.
Joy and gladness will be found in her,
thanksgiving and the sound of singing.

⁴ "Listen to me, my people;
hear me, my nation:
The law will go out from me;
my justice will become a light to the nations.
⁵ My righteousness draws near speedily,
my salvation is on the way,
and my arm will bring justice to the nations.
The islands will look to me
and wait in hope for my arm.
⁶ Lift up your eyes to the heavens,
look at the earth beneath;
the heavens will vanish like smoke,
the earth will wear out like a garment
and its inhabitants die like flies.
But my salvation will last forever,
my righteousness will never fail.

In a carefully created progression, Isaiah has been moving toward the center of the second half of his prophecy. He began with the Assyrians at the gate of Jerusalem (chapters 36 and 37) and the ominous prophecy of the coming of the Babylonians, who would carry the Jews off into captivity (chapter 39). The second half of Isaiah began with the words "Comfort, comfort my people, says your God" (40:1). From those opening verses, Isaiah has spoken words of comfort, assuring those who would eventually be held captive in Babylon that God would send them a deliverer, even naming the deliverer: Cyrus (45:1,13). But the Persian king could not deliver God's people from their sins and from death. A greater deliverer was to come in order to accomplish that rescue.

This deliverer would be the Great Servant of the Lord. God announced his coming through Isaiah in chapter 42. This Servant was the one in whom the Lord would delight and on whom he would put his Spirit. Most important, the Lord promised that this Servant would succeed in accomplishing his purpose (42:4). A few chapters later, Isaiah recorded the words of the Servant himself (49:1-4). The Great Servant's task would be difficult, and it would appear that he had spent his strength in vain. Nevertheless, the Lord would grant success to his Servant—great success that would extend even to the ends of the earth and encompass all the Gentiles (49:6).

In chapter 50, the Great Servant again speaks and reveals his absolute obedience to the Lord, even to the point of great suffering and disgrace (verse 6). The Servant is certain that the Lord will not allow him to fail and confesses his trust that he will not be put to shame. He will succeed, a common theme in the Servant passages. Isaiah introduced us to the suffering of the Great Servant, but we have not yet seen how he will accomplish his goal of rescuing God's people and all nations from their sins and from death. Certainly and carefully, Isaiah has crafted an artistic progression of thought that has been moving us in that direction. That's the center of the second half of Isaiah's prophecy, chapter 53. As humble believing readers of God's message through Isaiah, we have been marching toward that central point—the last of the Servant passages.

We are on the very doorstep of that wonderful chapter. As we take our final steps toward it, the Lord has a word of encouragement and reassurance for his faithful, those "who pursue righteousness and who seek the LORD." So often the faithful do not see triumph. Their lives are more frequently filled with trouble and defeat, even when they seek the Lord with zeal and determination. The believing Jews, who would have read these words while captive in Babylon, had no sense of victory or glory. Their homeland stood in ruins; they were not free to return. The glory of David had faded to only a memory. They may have questioned whether God had deserted them. Perhaps they asked how the promise to Abraham (Genesis 12:1-3) could ever come to pass. If Judah became extinct in Babylon, how could all nations of the earth be blessed through Abraham and his descendants? Perhaps they wondered how the great descendant of David could arise if they were captives of Babylonian power. All may have seemed hopeless.

While we may not experience exactly the same set of circumstances, believers through the centuries have faced similar dark and dreary days. Those who pursue righteousness and seek the Lord often do not move from triumph to triumph. At best, we seem to have our moments of happiness, but then we collapse again in guilt, fear, and doubt. We are sinful creatures, and our sinful human nature frustrates us. We cannot take it off and hang it up in a closet as we do our clothes. It's part of us and continues to plague us daily. Like the Jews in Babylon, we need reassurance. In these verses God assures his faithful that the deliverance he promised is not far away. In the prophecy of Isaiah, its description awaits the reader only two chapters away—37 verses from the Lord's invitation, "Listen to me."

The Lord directs his people to return to the story of Abraham and Sarah. Both of them left their homeland and traveled to a far distant land because God invited them to go and promised great things. He promised that Abraham would become a great nation and that all peoples on earth would be blessed through him. But the reality appeared so different. Abraham had no children. Sarah was barren. Both were old and past the age of having children. Yet God issued his promises to them. God did not fail to make it all happen as he said. Even though Sarah laughed at the promise of a child (Genesis 18:12), God fulfilled his promise. The descendants of Abraham and Sarah, who were captives in Babylon, were to remember the way God fulfilled his promises to their ancestors. God keeps his promises, contrary to all common sense and logic.

By faith we are also descendants of Abraham (Galatians 3:29). We are cut from the same rock, the same quarry. When our world seems barren and without hope, remember how God fulfilled his promises. He will not fail to fulfill all of them, even if it may appear impossible. Luther commented, "The prophet brings in the example of Abraham and Sarah to show that just as the Lord comforted and helped them, so He can also promote and expand the church, no matter how sterile and forsaken and lonely it may be, even in the depths of despair" (LW, Volume 17, page 197).

The Jews in Babylon may have thought that any hope of a return to Jerusalem remained a hopeless and impossible dream. Their once glorious city lay in ruins. All the beauty that once belonged to Zion and Judah had disappeared. During the period of captivity, the Promised Land remained nothing but a wasteland. Yet God promised to have compassion and to bring joy, gladness, thanksgiving, and the sound of singing again to his people. The faithful were not to despair. They were to listen to the promises of God, because God wanted to reinforce their faith with his promises. The deliverance he promised drew nearer. God promised, "My righteousness draws near speedily, my salvation is on the way."

What God had in store was not just for the Jews. "The islands will look to me and wait in hope for my arm." Verse 6 indicates the blessings God intends for all people: salvation and righteousness. God declares sinners right and holy. Through faith in that declaration, they are therefore saved from the consequences of sin. Both salvation and righteousness are God's. They do not come by human effort or intelligence. They are, instead, a gift that can come only from God. God's wonderful and gracious declaration and its consequences endure. Even the earth and the heavens will disappear and vanish but not God's righteousness and salvation.

> [7] **"Hear me, you who know what is right,**
> **you people who have my law in your hearts:**
> **Do not fear the reproach of men**
> **or be terrified by their insults.**
> [8] **For the moth will eat them up like a garment;**
> **the worm will devour them like wool.**
> **But my righteousness will last forever,**
> **my salvation through all generations."**
>
> [9] **Awake, awake! Clothe yourself with strength,**
> **O arm of the LORD;**
> **awake, as in days gone by,**
> **as in generations of old.**
> **Was it not you who cut Rahab to pieces,**
> **who pierced that monster through?**

¹⁰ **Was it not you who dried up the sea,**
the waters of the great deep,
who made a road in the depths of the sea
so that the redeemed might cross over?
¹¹ **The ransomed of the LORD will return.**
They will enter Zion with singing;
everlasting joy will crown their heads.
Gladness and joy will overtake them,
and sorrow and sighing will flee away.

As we have read the prophecy of Isaiah, God and the prophet have repeatedly encouraged us to listen and hear the Word of God. In the midst of distress, God's people are always directed to his Word, the only source of truth. The Bible asserts candidly and without apology that it is a revelation from the God of the universe. The Bible is not a collection of writings that had their origin in human imagination and intellect. The Bible claims to be a divine book disclosing what God wants people the world over to know and believe. In chapter 40, God told his prophet, "Cry out" (verse 6). Isaiah had no knowledge of what to say and asked, "What shall I cry?" *Then God delivered the message.* God gave his message first to his prophet and then through the prophet to his people. Here again we find God encouraging his faithful to hear him. In the words of God, we find life, truth, and hope. The words of man may move and inspire us, but the words of God give what no human word can. Just as God's voice created the world in which we live, his words confer blessings to humanity.

God intends his blessings for all of humanity—for the islands or Mediterranean coastlands far from Palestine, as well as his people Judah. But God does not force anyone to receive what they reject. Those who believe receive blessings. God's central principle—that is, his law, his instruction or doctrine—is justification by grace. All the Scriptures reveal this principle. They are not saved by their good works or deeds of the law.

Here in verse 7, as before in Isaiah, the term "law" means more than just the Ten Commandments. It includes all that God teaches in his Word—the law that points out sin and the gospel that gives the forgiveness of sins. The central teaching of Holy Scripture is that sinners are justified by grace through faith, not by their works or deeds. All of Scripture teaches this wonderful truth. Those who believe have that central principle in their hearts. They are justified in God's sight; their sins are forgiven; they know they are loved by God; they understand that God has chosen them for eternity in heaven. These blessings belong to them by faith, not because they have earned them. To such who believe, God speaks here and directs them to listen to him.

But not everyone believes. Those who do not believe oppose the believers, the people of God. Just as they persecuted the Great Servant when he came, unbelievers persecute those who believe God's promises and harbor his instruction in their hearts. They even killed the Servant and ridiculed him. In these words, God assures his beleaguered and persecuted people that those who ridicule them and insult them are nothing. The persecutors will disappear like wool eaten by moths. What endures beyond the things of this life and even beyond life on earth itself is God's burning zeal to rescue his people—to declare them righteous and welcome them into his presence.

But, at the time of Isaiah, God's plan had not yet been accomplished. God would bring it to pass in the future through his Great Servant. In just a few short verses, God will reveal how the Servant would fulfill all the promises of deliverance from sin and death. It would be wonderful. As an impatient believer, Isaiah calls upon God to hurry and do as he has promised, "Awake, awake . . . O arm of the LORD." To the exiles, the Lord must have seemed to be asleep and insensitive to their hopes and prayers. God's "arm" pictures his power. Isaiah calls God to action and compares the deliverance to come with the deliverance of Israel from Egypt, here referred to as Rahab. In spite of the pursuing army of Pharaoh, God dried up the sea so that his people could walk to safety. Then he closed up the sea and destroyed the enemies of his people. God's power provided deliverance. The greater deliverance to come through the Servant is not in doubt. Since God could open a path through the sea for the sake of his people (Exodus 14:21,22), he could accomplish their redemption from the bondage of sin and death. "The ransomed of the LORD will return. They will enter Zion with singing; everlasting joy will crown their heads." This verse appeared earlier in the prophecy of Isaiah (35:10). God's love runs so deep that he repeats the comfort his people so desperately craved!

> 12 "I, even I, am he who comforts you.
>   Who are you that you fear mortal men,
>   the sons of men, who are but grass,
> 13 that you forget the LORD your Maker,
>   who stretched out the heavens
>   and laid the foundations of the earth,
>   that you live in constant terror every day
>   because of the wrath of the oppressor,
>   who is bent on destruction?
>   For where is the wrath of the oppressor?
> 14   The cowering prisoners will soon be set free;
>   they will not die in their dungeon,
>   nor will they lack bread.
> 15 For I am the LORD your God,
>   who churns up the sea so that its waves roar—
>   the LORD Almighty is his name.

> ¹⁶ **I have put my words in your mouth**
> **and covered you with the shadow of my hand—**
> **I who set the heavens in place,**
> **who laid the foundations of the earth,**
> **and who say to Zion, 'You are my people.'"**

These verses contain the Lord's answer to the prophet's prayer. Isaiah had pleaded, "Awake, as in days gone by" (verse 9). God here assures all who hold his instruction in their hearts that he will indeed carry out the promises he has made. God's people have no need to fear mere men. Their deliverance rests in the hands of the Lord, who is their Maker. He created the earth and stretched out the vast expanse of the heavens. How could any of his promises fail to come to pass? Therefore, do not fear what God has created—humanity, which is as temporary as the grass. The promises issued here rest upon the faithful covenant-God, Jehovah, who has the power to churn the sea. He is the Almighty.

God addressed his comfort to those who believe and have his Word in their hearts and confess it boldly. He chose them to be his people, declared them to be his own, and placed his Word in their mouths. They proclaim the truth of God to the world. The message of redemption and righteousness announces a new heaven and a new earth to come—the hope captured in Revelation chapter 21. All who believe rest securely in the shadow of the Lord's powerful hand. He stands ready to protect his people and to destroy their enemies. God's believers are like precious jewels, over whom he holds his hand to shield and protect them. Nothing can destroy them, and no one can steal them away from him.

In the midst of persecution, God's people often forget this powerful comfort. Believers are intimidated when others ridicule them or even threaten death. Yet the pages of history are filled with stories of those who have not forgotten the Lord and who have given up their lives rather than deny the Lord, their Maker and Redeemer. Jesus also encouraged his disciples:

> Do not be afraid of those who kill the body but cannot kill the soul. Rather, be afraid of the One who can destroy both soul and body in hell. Are not two sparrows sold for a penny? Yet not one of them will fall to the ground apart from the will of your Father. And even the very hairs of your head are all numbered. So don't be afraid; you are worth more than many sparrows. (Matthew 10:28-31)

The section concludes with the comforting reassurance that God claimed the believers as his own people. God said, "You are my people."

Awake! Shout for joy! The Lord is ready to deliver his people

[17] Awake, awake!
  Rise up, O Jerusalem,
 you who have drunk from the hand of the LORD
  the cup of his wrath,
 you who have drained to its dregs
  the goblet that makes men stagger.
[18] Of all the sons she bore
  there was none to guide her;
 of all the sons she reared
  there was none to take her by the hand.
[19] These double calamities have come upon you—
  who can comfort you?—
 ruin and destruction, famine and sword—
  who can console you?
[20] Your sons have fainted;
  they lie at the head of every street,
  like antelope caught in a net.

> They are filled with the wrath of the LORD
>> and the rebuke of your God.
> [21] Therefore hear this, you afflicted one,
>> made drunk, but not with wine.
> [22] This is what your Sovereign LORD says,
>> your God, who defends his people:
> "See, I have taken out of your hand
>> the cup that made you stagger;
> from that cup, the goblet of my wrath,
>> you will never drink again.
> [23] I will put it into the hands of your tormentors,
>> who said to you,
>> 'Fall prostrate that we may walk over you.'
> And you made your back like the ground,
>> like a street to be walked over."

Isaiah had pictured the deliverance of the Lord Jehovah as fast approaching, but Isaiah had also predicted the destruction of Jerusalem and the captivity in Babylon. In the days of Isaiah, neither of those events had yet occurred. They both would come because God's people had turned away from the Lord and brought his wrath and judgment upon themselves. Once God's people had endured the just judgment of God, the deliverance would come.

Isaiah encouraged the people to awake from their stupor. They had drunk their fill of the cup of God's wrath—drained it to the dregs. Ruin, destruction, famine, and sword had come upon them because of their unfaithfulness. God's people were helpless "like antelope caught in a net." They were powerless to free themselves from the judgment. The sons of the people—the pride of any nation—fainted, unable to provide deliverance.

But God asks Jerusalem to awaken from this nightmare of judgment. God will deliver her. The judgment God sent upon his own people had reached its end. God has taken the cup of judgment that has made his people stagger from them. They would not drink of God's wrath again. Instead, God has put the cup of judgment in the hands of those who had oppressed his people. Deliverance approached. The judgment of God upon his people was over. God was about to turn his wrath upon the enemies of his people.

52 Awake, awake, O Zion,
    clothe yourself with strength.
Put on your garments of splendor,
    O Jerusalem, the holy city.
The uncircumcised and defiled
    will not enter you again.
² Shake off your dust;
    rise up, sit enthroned, O Jerusalem.
Free yourself from the chains on your neck,
    O captive Daughter of Zion.

In 51:9 the fainthearted saints had asked Jehovah, the covenant-God, to awake. Here, in contrast, the Lord asks them to rouse themselves from their hopelessness. Because of their sins and rebellion, the Lord would send Nebuchad-nezzar and the Babylonians to destroy Jerusalem and carry the people away captive. But God also promised that the captivity would come to an end. The previous chapter placed us at the threshold of that deliverance. God encour-aged his people to rouse themselves from the stupor of the captivity. God would take the cup of judgment from the hands of his people and give it to their captors. Isaiah encouraged the people to awaken from the judgment of God. The power to awaken comes from the gracious invita-tion of the Lord. He alone could supply such power.

To what were they to awaken? What would be next? In the opening words of this chapter, Isaiah repeats the encour-agement "Awake, awake, O Zion." The earlier command of the previous chapter to awaken encouraged the people to rouse themselves from their judgment. This time Isaiah, as

God's messenger, rouses the people to see beyond the judgment to what the Lord has prepared for them. They are to awaken to a new day. The old days of captivity are past.

The previous chapter had placed God's people in the dust so their captors could walk over them. Their enemies had said, "Fall prostrate that we may walk over you" (verse 23). God's people had no choice but to lie down in the dust and become "like a street to be walked over." But Isaiah encouraged them to wake up. Why? A complete reversal was at hand. They were to shake off the dust of captivity and arise to sit on a throne. Such a reversal required "garments of splendor." God's people were to awaken to a glorious and new future. Included in that future was perfect life with God. Isaiah writes, "The uncircumcised and defiled will not enter you again." The place where God's people gathered together would be a perfect world where sin and the enemies of God's people could not penetrate.

After 70 years of captivity, the people did rejoice as they returned to Jerusalem to rebuild it and to reestablish their homeland (see Psalm 126). But there's more to this than the return of these ancient people to their homes. The return from captivity served only as the beginning. Something much greater stood in the distant new day. As we look at this chapter and the next, we discover that God's people would be released from a far more serious captivity. While they may have been able to rebuild their homeland, they were still trapped in a spiritual bondage. They were dead in sin and unable to escape. The new day includes this redemption from sin and the glorious communion with Jehovah. The apostle John described this glorious new day: "Blessed are those who wash their robes, that they may have the right to the tree of life and may go through the gates into the city. Outside are the dogs, those who practice magic arts, the sexually immoral, the murderers, the idolaters and everyone who loves and practices falsehood" (Revelation 22:14,15).

That glorious new day awaits us too. We are also encouraged to awaken from the captivity of sin and death and rejoice that a new day has dawned. The Lord has prepared a new and glorious day for all his people. The Servant of the Lord secured that bright and glorious future. For those in Isaiah's day, the work of the Servant of the Lord still lay in the future. As New Testament believers, we know that the Servant of the Lord, Jesus Christ, has finished his work. The final fulfillment of this prophecy lies ahead for us. Heaven, the new Jerusalem, awaits, and we are its future citizens because Jesus has redeemed us and we are his by faith. August Pieper, one commentator on the prophet Isaiah, points us to see this broad glorious future. He wrote:

> It is the future, uninterrupted, spiritual government of the grace of the Lord in His church that is here expressed. . . . The prophet presents in a single picture the entire future of the church into all eternity—the restitution of Jerusalem after the exile being the feeble beginning, followed by the Lord's government of grace in the New Testament Church and its fulfillment in eternity. (*Isaiah II,* page 420)

³**For this is what the LORD says:**

"You were sold for nothing,
and without money you will be redeemed."

⁴**For this is what the Sovereign LORD says:**

"At first my people went down to Egypt to live;
lately, Assyria has oppressed them.

⁵"And now what do I have here?" declares the LORD.

"For my people have been taken away for nothing,
    and those who rule them mock,"
                                    declares the LORD.

"And all day long
    my name is constantly blasphemed.
⁶ Therefore my people will know my name;
    therefore in that day they will know
that it is I who foretold it.
    Yes, it is I."

In these few verses, we are reminded four times that these truths come from the Lord. It is as if four exclamation points verify the message. What could be so important that we need such emphasis? These verses tell us that God's action in bringing about the release from captivity comes by grace and by grace alone. God certainly is not obligated to bring deliverance to his people because they deserved it. Instead, they had repeatedly fallen away from the Lord and turned to other gods. The announcement of the captivity in the first place left no doubt about its cause. In chapter 50 the Lord had asserted that the sins of the people had been responsible for their judgment.

God was not obligated to redeem his people because someone bought them as one would buy a slave. No one had given God any compensation for turning over his people to the Babylonians. God says, "You were sold for nothing, and without money you will be redeemed." God did not owe anyone anything for his people. He could buy back his people because he wanted to, not because he was under obligation to pay anything. Because he owed no one anything, he could have left the people in their bondage. But he chose not to do that. Instead, by pure grace, he freely chose to redeem his people.

The idea of grace needs the emphasis of God's four assertions. The human heart wants to obligate God to act because of some special human deed done, some noble human thought or intention, or some gentle words of human kindness spoken to others. God is under no obligation to redeem humanity. All religious thought that seeks to obligate God to act on behalf of humans because of something humans individually or collectively have done is false. Human effort does not compel God to act. He acts out of his deep love for sinners who are trapped "like antelope caught in a net" (51:20).

God's grace, his undeserved love, confronts human thought at every turn. Humans want to earn God's good blessings. When they cannot, they want at least to help contribute. But they cannot do that either. When they cannot, they think that God must have acted to save them because of some good thing they might do in the future. But that is not grace. When humans look for some reason within themselves, they still obligate God to act by something a human might do. Religions that require sacrifice to court God's favor miss grace altogether. Religious thought that assumes that God will act favorably because of human kindness, tolerance, or dignity distorts grace and makes God dance to a human tune. As valuable as kindness, tolerance, and dignity are for our lives together on earth, they do not move the Lord of the universe to action. Even ideas that say that God acts by his own will, by grace, and then waits for human effort, thought, or words to complete his redemption distort grace. These ideas make God a partner with humans in saving sinners. According to this thought, God cannot complete his action until human beings add their contribution. It is by grace, and grace alone, that God acts. Nothing human obligates, constrains, or compels God to save anyone. He is not under obligation to do anything for anyone on the face of the earth. He never has been so obligated.

A look at the world in which the Jews lived reveals how helpless they were to contribute toward their own deliverance. They went to Egypt and became slaves. They could not free themselves. Centuries later, the Assyrians invaded their homeland and oppressed them. The army of Sennacherib laid siege to Jerusalem (chapters 36,37). God's people did not have the military or political strength to lift the siege or even to defend themselves. More than a century later, the army of the Babylonians would invade and destroy Jerusalem and take the Jews captive as prisoners of war. Once the Jews were captive, they could not earn their own release, nor could they fight to obtain it. Only an act of God could alter their situation in each case. He delivered them from Egypt. He destroyed the army of Sennacherib. He would send Cyrus to release the exiles from Babylon too. In each case, God could have chosen to do nothing. But he acted instead. All of these were gracious acts of God on behalf of his sinful and rebellious people.

Why? Because of his grace, his undeserved faithfulness to his people. His action has the purpose of revealing his great love and faithfulness. God says, "All day long my name is constantly blasphemed." When God saw that his name was blasphemed, he acted to vindicate his name. Those who oppressed his people began to think that their gods were better than Israel's God, Jehovah. The Lord's faithfulness to his people and his promises to them were at stake. When God acted, he acted to demonstrate his greatness and love not because he was obliged to do so. The Lord of free and faithful grace both foretold the redemption and carried it out so that all might know and believe that he and he alone is responsible for the redemption of his people and of all humanity.

⁷ **How beautiful on the mountains**
  are the feet of those who bring good news,
 who proclaim peace,
  who bring good tidings,
  who proclaim salvation,
 who say to Zion,
  "Your God reigns!"
⁸ **Listen! Your watchmen lift up their voices;**
  together they shout for joy.
 When the LORD **returns to Zion,**
  they will see it with their own eyes.
⁹ **Burst into songs of joy together,**
  you ruins of Jerusalem,
 for the LORD **has comforted his people,**
  he has redeemed Jerusalem.
¹⁰ **The** LORD **will lay bare his holy arm**
  in the sight of all the nations,
 and all the ends of the earth will see
  the salvation of our God.

Isaiah had just prophesied God's gracious deliverance of his people. In these verses, he describes the deliverance as though it has already occurred. Messengers sped forward with the good news. Their feet were beautiful because their feet carried great good news. Three terms summarize the content of their message: *peace, good tidings,* and *salvation.*

Peace does not refer to the end of hostilities with the warring nations that surrounded God's people. This peace has a meaning much deeper and more profound. It is the peace that God has established between his people and himself. God no longer burns with anger toward his people. He has removed their sin so that a condition of deep well-being exists between God and his people. This peace rests on the knowledge that the Great Servant would come to achieve it by his work on earth. The angels would announce it at his birth, "Glory to God in the highest, and on earth *peace* to men on whom his favor rests" (Luke 2:14). Jesus announced this peace with these words: "*Peace* I leave with you; my *peace* I give you. I do not give to you as the world gives. Do not let your hearts be troubled and do not be afraid" (John 14:27).

The message is *good tidings.* It is good in the absolute sense, like the proclamation of God at the creation of the world—all was good. All this flows from the LORD, Jehovah—the source of all that is good. The psalmist gave thanks for the Lord's blessings and proclaimed, "The LORD is good and his love endures forever; his faithfulness continues through all generations" (100:5). The situation between God and humanity could not be better. The blessings of God are for all humanity. No one is a slave of evil's tyranny any longer. The opposite is true. Good has replaced evil.

The third term is *salvation.* The deliverance from sin and death has been accomplished. God has come to the aid of his people. He has set them free—not from the oppression of their political enemies but from the tyranny of sin and from the dungeon of death. The release of the Jews from Babylon and their return to Jerusalem were only the first faint, rosy streaks of dawn. A much greater, more glorious freedom would brighten the sky. Paul referred to this when he wrote, "There is now no condemnation for those who are in Christ Jesus, because through Christ Jesus the law of the Spirit of life set me free from the law of sin and death" (Romans 8:1,2).

The apostle Paul also tells us that the words of Isaiah here do not simply refer to the release of the Jews from Babylon. He quotes verse 7 of this passage from Isaiah (Romans 10:15). When Paul uses these words, he refers to the messengers who proclaim the gospel of Jesus.

The final thought of verse 7 gives us the reason for all

this good news. The messengers proclaim, "Your God reigns!" During the captivity, God allowed others to rule over his people. At the end of the exile, he brought an end to the rule of the Babylonians over his people. God always remained in control. The messengers have brought that good news. But all this is not just about the exile. We know that God established a new kingdom where peace and the good news of forgiveness dominate. The reign of Jehovah included the sending of his Servant into the world. He was David's son, a king. But he entered Jerusalem as a meek and lowly person riding on a borrowed donkey. Pilate questioned him as to whether he was a king, and Jesus responded: "You are right in saying I am a king. In fact, for this reason I was born, and for this I came into the world, to testify to the truth. Everyone on the side of truth listens to me" (John 18:37). Of course, this king will return again—the next time in glory—to subdue all his enemies and judge the world. The Lord reigns. We may wonder about it from time to time, but his kingdom stands firm so that even "the gates of Hades will not overcome it" (Matthew 16:18).

The messengers proclaim their good news, and then Isaiah tells us of the Lord's coming. He asks us to look at the Lord's coming from the perspective of the watchmen who are waiting for his arrival. They are to listen and watch for the Lord. They expect that he will return to Zion. The fulfillment includes Judah's return from captivity in Babylon, the first coming of the Great Servant of the Lord, Jesus Christ, in humility, and the second coming of the glorified Lord in power and majesty. All of these arrivals are blended into one vision, and all of them bring great joy. Even the ruins of Jerusalem are encouraged to "burst into songs of joy together." We find the cause of such joy in the coming of the Lord and what he has done. He comforted his people and redeemed them.

The Lord is pictured as one who has, for a time, kept his powerful arm under the folds of his cloak. The time will come, Isaiah prophesies, when the Lord will show his power. He will "lay bare his holy arm" and will accomplish the great deliverances promised. Judah will return. Sinners will be released from the captivity of sin. The Lord will bring his faithful believers to a new and glorious Jerusalem far above all the trouble and misery of earth. The last words of verse 10 remind us that all the ends of the earth will see this salvation, or deliverance. These events are not just some obscure historical snapshots in the record of one nation, the Jews. The deliverance God promises is for all the world, and it will be made known to all the world.

> **¹¹ Depart, depart, go out from there!**
> **Touch no unclean thing!**
> **Come out from it and be pure,**
> **you who carry the vessels of the LORD.**
> **¹² But you will not leave in haste**
> **or go in flight;**
> **for the LORD will go before you,**
> **the God of Israel will be your rear guard.**

Isaiah first sees the release of the Jews from Babylon in these two verses. He encourages the faithful to leave Babylon and not be contaminated by anything unclean or impure. The Scriptures portray Babylon as the place where God's enemies dwell and a place where everything contrary to God resides. All that still remains contaminated with sin is repulsive to God, and his people are not to touch any of it. They come out of Babylon, carrying only what they need to reestablish their worship of the Lord—the vessels of the Lord. The Babylonians once stole those vessels. But when

God delivers his people, they will carry the vessels so that the faithful may use them in their worship of the Lord. They are to leave behind all else.

God had delivered his people from bondage once before. They had left Egypt quickly, pursued by the army of Pharaoh. Their departure from Babylon will be different. This departure will not be such a hasty, fearful flight. It will be a departure with quiet dignity. The reason is simple: the Lord will go before them and protect their backs. Nothing can possibly hurt these faithful of the Lord.

Isaiah saw the departure of God's people from Babylon first. But he also extended his vision forward to see God's people leaving the bondage of sin. When we come to faith in the Lord Jesus, we leave behind sin, death, and hell. The church in the New Testament is the assembly of those who have been called out of this world of sin. Believers are in the world, but they are not of the world. Still another departure awaits us all when the Lord himself will call us out of this life of tears and sorrow so that we can enter a new and glorious home above, where God "will wipe every tear from their eyes. There will be no more death or mourning or crying or pain, for the old order of things has passed away" (Revelation 21:4). We live in expectation of the Lord's return. When he comes in glory, all his faithful will depart from this world and be gathered to the glories of eternal life with the Lord of lords and King of kings. We are under his protection and in his care while we wait and as we depart. Such is the comfort that comes from the Holy One of Israel, who has redeemed us and will deliver us from all sin, from death, and from the power of the devil. Rejoice, believers! Rejoice!

The Great Servant will suffer to redeem humanity from sin and death

¹³ **See, my servant will act wisely;**
 he will be raised and lifted up and highly exalted.
¹⁴ **Just as there were many who were appalled at him—**
  his appearance was so disfigured beyond that of any man
  and his form marred beyond human likeness—
¹⁵ **so will he sprinkle many nations,**
  and kings will shut their mouths because of him.
 For what they were not told, they will see,
  and what they have not heard, they will understand.

Here is the center of the second portion of Isaiah's prophecy. The chapter divisions in our Bibles come from the 13th century; in this case the division is misplaced. The great chapter of the Suffering Servant should begin with 52:13. This is the fourth of the Servant sections, and it comes in the middle of the second half of Isaiah's prophecy. Thirteen chapters precede it, and thirteen chapters follow. Isaiah constructed the second half with this wonderful passage at the center. This should not surprise us, because the truths it presents are at the very center of all God's revelation. The central message of the Bible is Christ, and the center of this portion of Isaiah is also Christ, the Great Servant of the Lord. What the Servant of the Lord has done causes joy. The first verses of this final Servant passage encourage such rejoicing.

The Lord speaks here and says, "See, my servant." In chapter 42 the Lord had also said, "Here is my servant" (verse 1). We are directed to look carefully at one and the same Servant. He is different from such human servants as Moses and David. He does what no other servant can ever do. We have no difficulty considering ourselves to be servants of the Lord of Hosts. God's grace has called us and empowered us to serve him. But this special Servant challenges our assumptions. He is the Holy One of Israel, who appeared to Isaiah at the beginning of his prophecy (see chapter 6; see also John 12:41). This one is the Lord's Servant. He was begotten of the Father from eternity (Psalm 2:7), chosen, and sent on a mission. To appreciate the Lord's suffering and death, we must understand that he did the will of his Father, something he knew already in the temple when he was 12 years old. The mystery of the Savior's incarnation, the wonder of God and man in one person, and the resolute march toward Jerusalem and death all reside in the term "my Servant."

From the beginning of this Servant section, Isaiah tells us that this Servant achieved his goal. He will be victorious. Isaiah uses three verbs to express the exaltation of the Lord Jesus: "He will be raised and lifted up and highly exalted." Some have suggested that the verbs capture Christ's resurrection, ascension, and sitting at the right hand of the Father. The verbs clearly remind us early in this section that the suffering of this Servant will not be a defeat but a triumph—and a great triumph. Isaiah wrote, "My servant will act wisely." The verb means that the action has been successfully carried out; it has achieved its desired goal or end. So, as Isaiah tells us, this Servant did not fail to achieve the goal of his mission. He did not fail his heavenly Father. The Servant's crucifixion and death achieved what no amount of gold or silver could—the forgiveness of sins and life eternal for all the world. He has therefore been highly exalted.

The Servant's task was not easy, and we do well to remember that he completed his mission despite great difficulties. God tells us to look at the Servant, and the vision is ugly and gruesome. Many are astonished at what they see. Isaiah inserts a parenthetical description in the midst of the sentence: "His appearance was so disfigured beyond that of any man and his form marred beyond human likeness." The passion history confirms this description of the Servant. The high priest's guards and Roman soldiers beat him. No doubt his face was swollen and disfigured. Pilate invited the crowd to look, "Here is the man!" (John 19:5). This man was not a leader characterized by good looks that would attract attention and loyalty. Many were appalled at him.

Verse 15 presents us with a difficulty. The footnote to the NIV text reveals the difficulty. The NIV text says, "so will he sprinkle many nations," but another possible translation is "so will many nations marvel at him." If we translate the verb in question as "sprinkle," then the Servant purifies the nations just as the priest sprinkled oil, water, or blood in the cleansing rites outlined in the Levitical laws (Leviticus 4:6; 8:11; 14:7). Then the purpose of the Suffering Servant becomes evident already here in this verb, namely, to purify the world of sin. But if we translate the verb as "marvel," it would emphasize the amazement of the nations at the appearance of the Servant. Either translation can be defended.

Whichever translation one might adopt, the reason why kings shut their mouths is clear. "For what they were not told, they will see, and what they have not heard, they will understand." The kings behold something absolutely unheard of in human history and unimaginable by human minds. The gospel, the work of Jesus Christ, defies human reason and experience. The human heart or intellect cannot conceive of such a message. It is God's plan from beginning to end. Grace for sinners through the Suffering Servant is God's thought, God's plan, and can be grasped by the human heart and mind only with the help of the Holy Spirit.

53 Who has believed our message
and to whom has the arm of the LORD been revealed?

² **He grew up before him like a tender shoot,**
   and like a root out of dry ground.
 He had no beauty or majesty to attract us to him,
   nothing in his appearance that we should desire him.
³ **He was despised and rejected by men,**
   a man of sorrows, and familiar with suffering.
 Like one from whom men hide their faces
   he was despised, and we esteemed him not.

While the kings stood stunned in silence, Isaiah turns our attention to God's own people. The question is simple enough: "Who has believed our message?" The number of believers among Israel remained small. Paul comments on the few in Israel who believed and quotes this verse in Romans 10:16: "Not all the Israelites accepted the good news. For Isaiah says, 'Lord, who has believed our message?'" The apostle John also referred to these words to support his observation:

> Even after Jesus had done all these miraculous signs in their presence, they still would not believe in him. This was to fulfill the word of Isaiah the prophet:
>
> "Lord, who has believed our message
>   and to whom has the arm of the Lord
>   been revealed?" (John 12:37,38)

Unbelief confounds believers. Those who believe and proclaim the truth do not understand why some refuse to believe. Sadly, it happened in Isaiah's day; a part of the prophet's mission was to confirm Israel in its unbelief. Rejection of the gospel dogged the work of the apostles, and rejection of our witness will occur, even after we have proclaimed the gospel as clearly and eloquently as we can. Not all believe even Isaiah's beautiful and eloquent words.

God chose to reveal his power in a way different than

Jesus carries his cross to Calvary

what humans expect. The Lord reveals his arm not with lightning, earthquakes, fire, or wind, as Elijah learned (1 Kings 19). The Lord did not carry out his plan of salvation with armies, power, high-level diplomacy, parades, fireworks, or bands. The Lord's Servant came as Isaiah described him here. He was born in a stable and grew up in a small, unimportant village in Galilee, "like a tender shoot, and like a root out of dry ground." The root here reminds us of Isaiah's earlier prophecy concerning the coming of the Messiah: "A shoot will come up from the stump of Jesse; from his roots a Branch will bear fruit" (11:1). "Is this the great arm of the Lord?" one might ask. Isaiah and all of Scripture responded on more than one occasion with a resounding, "Yes!"

Here the prophet went on to explain more carefully. The Servant of the Lord had no physical beauty that would mark him as a leader. Israel chose Saul as its first king. The Scriptures describe him as "an impressive young man without equal among the Israelites—a head taller than any of the others" (1 Samuel 9:2). What a contrast to this Servant. He was disfigured and marred (52:14), and he was despised and rejected. "He lacked men," the Hebrew reads; that is, he was alone and without support. The prominent people did not seek him out for advice or even for company. The Messiah would live outside the circle of the rich, famous, and powerful. It has been said that, on the basis of this passage, some of the ancient rabbis thought the Messiah would have leprosy.

Luther considered this passage to be a reference to all preaching of the gospel, and the quotation of verse 1 in the New Testament confirms his view. God's power rests in the apparently weak words of the gospel. The preaching of the Word is not what people expect. First, the action of sharing the power of God through words seems wrong to the sinful human heart. Why would an almighty God work through words? Yet his Word does have power. It created the world and continues to be the power of God in the hearts of believers. Second, the content of the gospel stands opposed to all the human wisdom of the ages. Paul said the gospel appears to be "foolishness" (1 Corinthians 1:18). Yet Paul also wrote, "To those whom God has called, both Jews and Greeks, [the message of Christ crucified is] the power of God and the wisdom of God" (verse 24). God's powerful arm is Christ, and the gospel is the message of Christ. The Lord bares his powerful arm to bring some to faith, but he does it through words and sacraments. The gospel in Word and sacrament proclaims Christ crucified. But believers, including Isaiah, note with dismay and frustration that the Servant of the Lord is despised and rejected. As his messengers, we should not be surprised that the gospel we speak is also rejected and that we ourselves are despised and rejected. "A student is not above his teacher" (Matthew 10:24). The pattern is as old as our sinful human nature. If Christ himself is despised, what makes us believe that we, his servants, will fare any better?

Isaiah characterized the life of Jesus on earth very well. He was a man of sorrows and familiar with suffering. He was filled with compassion at the pain, sickness, and sorrow he saw during his ministry. He shed tears at the death of Lazarus. But more than that, he himself, in his own person, experienced all that sin brought into the world. The next verses explain this.

> **⁴ Surely he took up our infirmities**
> **and carried our sorrows,**
> **yet we considered him stricken by God,**
> **smitten by him, and afflicted.**

⁵ **But he was pierced for our transgressions,**
   he was crushed for our iniquities;
 the punishment that brought us peace was upon him,
   and by his wounds we are healed.
⁶ **We all, like sheep, have gone astray,**
   each of us has turned to his own way;
 and the LORD has laid on him
   the iniquity of us all.

Isaiah asserted the vicarious suffering of the Servant of the Lord in these verses. They are among the most treasured words of the Scriptures. One commentator on this passage wrote:

> Here is revealed the very essence of God's plan of redemption, more plainly than anywhere else in the Old Testament. . . . The entire New Testament Gospel of the righteousness of faith, as St. Paul in particular expounded it, rests upon these three verses. . . . These words are all of the New Testament Gospel in a nutshell. (August Pieper, *Isaiah II*, pages 438,439)

Meditate on these words of Isaiah. Let them fill your soul so that you may share the wonders of God's grace and fill the souls of others. Without this message of Christ's death for us and his resurrection, we have nothing to offer people except the hollow hopes of human aspiration. But this is God's Word, his message of comfort and triumph, intended not for himself but for all sinners of all times.

Part of the value of these verses lies in the contrast between the Lord's Servant and the people—between him and us. The fourth verse begins with the adverb *surely*, which points to a strong contrast. In the previous verse (verse 3), Isaiah had written that the Servant was a man of sorrows who knew pain. Now the prophet takes his readers down an unexpected path. The Servant's pain and suffering were not his own but ours. He carried *our* sorrows. The word *surely* comes first in this verse and becomes an emphatic signpost marking the important lesson of these verses. What belonged to us—Isaiah included himself—became the Servant's, and he carried it all. The first verb, *took up,* extends the idea of carrying to include carrying guilt or the debt of sin. The Servant carries not his own but "our infirmities."

The Servant's action is not what we would have expected. Isaiah continues the contrast when he begins the next phrase of the verse with the pronoun *we*. Isaiah tells us first to look at the Servant and then to look at ourselves. When Isaiah asks us to consider our opinion and our thinking about the Servant, he reminds us that we were still dominated by the theology of law, which is based on the quid pro quo principle. In other words, individuals pay for or suffer for their own evil deeds and earn their own rewards. This thinking extended to our relationship with God. The Servant suffered. We therefore concluded that he must have done something to deserve such treatment from God. We thought of him as one "stricken by God" for his own sins.

But the Holy Spirit, through Isaiah, presents the unexpected, undeserved, and unimagined. The theology of grace rests on these verses, as well as so many others. The Servant suffered for wandering sinful people. Sinful people did not suffer. He did. Verse 5 begins with that pronoun, *he*. He did not suffer for his own, but he suffered for our rebellion, the meaning of the word translated as "transgressions." He suffered for our guilt, the meaning of the word translated as "iniquities."

Both words extend the idea of sorrows and infirmities (verses 3,4). The prophet uses other words to remind us that Christ's suffering was profound. The Servant was pierced—pierced through to death. The passive form of this verb indicates that this suffering was inflicted upon him by others. This is the theology of grace. An innocent man—the Servant of the Lord—suffered for the sins of others. He substituted himself for sinners. The gospel message of these verses is consistent with the gospel of the entire Scriptures, which is so difficult for our human sinful minds and hearts to understand. Luther commented:

> It is difficult for the flesh to repudiate all its resources, to turn away from self, and to be carried over to Christ. It is for us who have merited nothing not to have regard for our merits but simply to cling to the Word between heaven and earth, even though we do not feel it. Unless we have been instructed by God, we will not understand this. Therefore I delight in this text as if it were a text of the New Testament. This new teaching which demolishes the righteousness of the Law clearly appeared absurd to the Jews. For that reason the apostles needed Scripture, *Surely He has borne our griefs*. His suffering was nothing else than our sin. These words, OUR, US, FOR US, must be written in letters of gold. He who does not believe this is not a Christian. (LW, Volume 17, page 221)

Even if the vicarious atonement of Christ defies our understanding, it remains the blessed truth of the Scriptures. Because of the work of this Servant of the Lord, we receive wonderful blessings. We could not earn peace with God or healing for our sins through the theology of law. All the gold and silver in the universe could not buy such blessings. All good human efforts and noble intentions cannot erase sin and earn peace with God. No human could remove one sinful thought, word, or action by suffering the punishment deserved. Even criminals do not remove the guilt from their record by spending years in prison or even by suffering capital punishment; they only suffer the penalty they deserve. But "one who is holy, blameless, pure, set apart from sinners, exalted above the heavens . . . sacrificed for their sins once for all when he offered himself" (Hebrews 7:26,27). Isaiah identified the blessings of the Servant's work in these precious words: *"The punishment that brought us peace was upon him, and by his wounds we are healed."* These words stand as a wonderful witness to the truth of the gospel. The pronouns are clear and unmistakable. Peace and healing come to those who have not suffered and died for their own sins. They come from him who has suffered for the sins of others. Every believer includes himself or herself in the "us" and the "we," just as Isaiah did. By the power of the Holy Spirit, every believer treasures the "him" and "his." So it has been and so it will be, as each sinner comes to claim the blessings provided by the Servant of the Lord, when each one confesses, "Jesus, crucified for me" (*Christian Worship: A Lutheran Hymnal* [CW], 319).

With the word *peace* we are reminded of the message of the messengers in the previous chapter. Their feet were beautiful because they brought good news. Isaiah wrote that they "proclaim peace, . . . bring good tidings, . . . proclaim salvation" (52:7). The gospel proclaims Jesus, who died to pay the penalty our sins deserve and rose again because he had accomplished his mission. Death could not hold him, nor can it hold any who trust in him.

Isaiah once more called upon his readers to consider

who they were in connection with this Servant of the Lord. Verse 6 begins with the phrase "We all." By nature we are like straying sheep, unconcerned about their shepherd. By nature we are unaware of the great events that took place and oblivious to the blessings won for us by the Servant. We wander, each one absorbed in his own way. What a tragic picture of human life! People are often so absorbed with themselves, their problems, their joys, and their struggles that they have no time to think about anyone or anything else. Our contemporary world seems to want to stay busy doing things so that it doesn't have to stop to think about God, death, and sin. Satan has bewitched so many to remain in a state of denial about the real issues of our relationships with God. Our sinful nature becomes his willing ally. We—and I am included by virtue of my own sinful flesh—just don't have time for all this religion stuff, and, if we do, the concept of grace robs us of our self-righteousness, so we reject it. The preaching of the cross is still foolishness and a stumbling block. We remain creatures of the law, seeking to earn the notice and favor of God by our good thoughts, intentions, and actions.

Yet God did not leave us to wander aimlessly through this life. He acted to help us. He could have given up on us. He should have. But he did not. We did not deserve God's persistence to save us. But he persisted in spite of our human penchant for wandering and self-absorption. For the first time since verse 1, we meet again the special name for God, LORD, the covenant-God of free and faithful grace. While all humans were wandering about concerned with their own affairs, he intervened and took care of everything. He acted. The LORD caused these blows to fall upon his Servant. These words are a final exclamation point to the section. They add one significant thought: the sins God placed upon his Servant were the sins of all of us. First, that included all sin, and second, it meant the sins of all people. The apostle John wrote, "The blood of Jesus, his Son, purifies us from *all* sin" (1 John 1:7). We must not think that the sins God placed on his Servant were only the sins of all the faithful. The "us all" of verse 6 included all of Judah and all who will read these words, whether they believe them or not. Remember that many Jews in Isaiah's day did not believe. The prophet was sent to them to confirm them in their unbelief. The work of the Servant included those who did not and would not believe. This thought is not limited to this passage. Paul reminds us that through Jesus, "God was reconciling the world to himself" (2 Corinthians 5:19). The "us all" includes every human, and even the Gentiles are included in these blessings. They, as well as the Jews, will be drawn to the Lord. So Isaiah's prophecy says again and again.

> ⁷ **He was oppressed and afflicted,**
>   **yet he did not open his mouth;**
> **he was led like a lamb to the slaughter,**
>   **and as a sheep before her shearers is silent,**
>   **so he did not open his mouth.**
> ⁸ **By oppression and judgment he was taken away.**
>   **And who can speak of his descendants?**
> **For he was cut off from the land of the living;**
>   **for the transgression of my people he was stricken.**
> ⁹ **He was assigned a grave with the wicked,**
>   **and with the rich in his death,**
> **though he had done no violence,**
>   **nor was any deceit in his mouth.**

Isaiah directs us again to the Servant. The Lord's Servant accepted his role without complaint. He willingly offered himself up to death. One can only think of the passion of Christ and his silence before his accusers. He did respond to the questions of the high priest and Pilate. He did challenge the first slap of injustice by the high priest's servant, but that does not violate the truth of these words. The Lord Jesus suffered silently. As they led him from the judgment hall of Pilate, he did not resist or object. As he told Pilate, his servants did not fight the Roman soldiers in hand-to-hand combat to rescue Jesus from prison or execution. Jesus moved quietly from Jerusalem to Calvary and then stretched out his hands and feet so that they might be nailed to the cross. He refused the numbing gall. As they crucified him, he prayed that the Father would forgive them.

When Isaiah compared the Servant to a lamb led to the slaughter, he chose a picture that every Jewish citizen could understand. First, in ancient Israel, people counted wealth in livestock. Abraham, Isaac, and Jacob were all prosperous herdsmen. Second, the sacrificial system God designed for his people at Mount Sinai underscored the death of livestock. The Jews celebrated the Passover with the slaughter of a spotless one-year-old lamb (Exodus 12:1-13). Consider how many Jewish families understood the meaning of a lamb silent before the slaughter. At Passover, those bringing their lambs for slaughter filled the temple. Third, many Jews outside Jerusalem in the rural areas raised livestock. They sheared their flocks for the wool and slaughtered them for their meat. These humble men and women also knew first-hand the meaning of what Isaiah wrote. So the picture was clear to Isaiah's first audience, and it is clear to us too. When John the Baptist pointed to Christ and proclaimed, "Look, the Lamb of God" (John 1:29), he tied the Savior to this passage as well as to the Old Testament sacrificial system established at Mount Sinai.

Verse 8 deals with the death of the Suffering Servant. The

judicial authorities led him away, and no one could stop his execution. At the end of the verse, Isaiah once more cites the reason for all this. The Servant did all this "for the transgression of my people." The word for transgressions used earlier in verse 5 means "rebellion." It reappears here. Our sins have caused this suffering. Each one of our sins can be considered a nail that pierced the Savior's flesh or a lash that tore his back. Every sin is an act of rebellion against God, not a simple mistake against the expectations of human etiquette or accepted human behavior. Our sins deserve severe punishment from a righteous and holy God. All that we deserved, the Servant endured. The gospel follows the law. The gospel finds expression in this entire section and here finds expression in God's claim on his people. They are still, as he said earlier, "my people." The Lord claimed them by grace, sought them by grace, and cleansed them by the blood of his Son. They are his by grace and grace alone.

Verse 9 turns to the burial of the Servant. The authorities judged this servant to be wicked and guilty of death. Capital punishment would be carried out, and it was. Ordinarily such a "criminal" would be buried with other criminals. Yet, even though the authorities would assign the Servant a grave with other criminals, God had other plans. The Servant was innocent. After his death, he did not receive a common and dishonorable burial reserved for criminals and enemies of the state. God overruled the customary practice. The Servant's grave was among the rich. This description of the Servant begins with a note of triumph. Isaiah wrote, "He will be raised and lifted up and highly exalted" (52:13). When Joseph of Arimathea and Nicodemus took the body of Jesus from the cross, they accorded him an honorable burial (Matthew 27:57-60; John 19:38-41). Matthew described Joseph as a wealthy man (verse 57).

¹⁰ Yet it was the LORD's will to crush him and cause him
    to suffer,
  and though the LORD makes his life a guilt offering,
 he will see his offspring and prolong his days,
  and the will of the LORD will prosper in his hand.
¹¹ After the suffering of his soul,
  he will see the light of life and be satisfied;
 by his knowledge my righteous servant will justify many,
  and he will bear their iniquities.
¹² Therefore I will give him a portion among the great,
  and he will divide the spoils with the strong,
 because he poured out his life unto death,
  and was numbered with the transgressors.
For he bore the sin of many,
  and made intercession for the transgressors.

The first thought we encounter in verse 10 includes Jehovah's name, "the LORD." The God of grace, who appeared to Moses and revealed his name of love and compassion (Exodus 34:6,7), willed all that his Servant endured. The Servant may have been placed in the hands of Israel's governmental and religious leaders, but the Lord devised the entire plan. He ultimately brought it all to pass. The first part of the verse leaves no room for doubt: the Lord willed, or desired, to crush the Servant. What we have read in the precious verses of this entire chapter was the plan of the Lord from eternity. He did unfold the plan as he went along, but he willed it always. He is the God of firm, steadfast, unflinching love for his creatures. His love moved him to carry out this plan in the arena of time and history. When the time had fully come, God sent his Son, and the redemption of the world was accomplished (Galatians 4:4,5), just as he had planned and just as he had foretold in the words of his prophets.

The next few words help us look at God's plan as a plan of substituting the Suffering Servant for sinners. A "guilt offering" properly offers something of value as a recompense, or compensation, for something the worshiper had withheld from God. The offering does not expiate or remove the wrong, but rather, it compensates for it. So the plan of the Lord called for his Servant to offer his life as satisfaction or compensation for the guilt of all humanity. Here we again encounter the vicarious atonement, this time from God's perspective instead of from our perspective as in verses 4 to 6. The Lord makes his Servant's life a "guilt offering." The Servant not only atones for sin, but he undoes the wrong by making restitution to God.

The verse goes on to restate the triumph announced in 52:13. The Servant has been pierced through, crushed, and assigned a grave. He is dead, "cut off from the land of the living" (verse 8). But here he sees his offspring. Who are his offspring? Those who believe—they become his children. How can a dead man see his offspring? We find the answer in the Scriptures. He will rise from the dead. His days will be prolonged. Again we read that the mission of the Servant has been successful: "The will of the LORD will prosper in his hand." Our redemption is a reality. God planned it and then carried out the plan through his Servant.

Isaiah asks his readers to view this from God's perspective. God is satisfied. He planned the redemption of sinners. He made the soul of his one and only Son the perfect guilt offering for all the sins of the world. It was enough. All this, of course, has wonderful consequences for us sinners. God says, "My righteous servant will justify many, and he will bear their iniquities." What wonderful comfort for us! The Servant is righteous. He has no sin. He is innocent and a perfect match to the will of God and the mind of God. He has not deviated from the standard of God in any point.

God then declared many to be as righteous as the Servant. To declare someone just or righteous, that is, to acquit, is a forensic act, a courtroom decree. God made this declaration, whether or not many respond to it. Remember that Isaiah has us view this act from God's perspective. God did it; his decree does not depend on any human action. Instead, it is an act of God's independent and free love. Humans are helpless, as Paul reminds us when he quotes from Ecclesiastes: "There is no one who does good, not even one" (Romans 3:12). One righteous One has changed that. Paul clarifies the forensic act of God:

> No one will be declared righteous in his sight by observing the law; rather, through the law we become conscious of sin.

> But now a righteousness from God, apart from law, has been made known, to which the Law and the Prophets testify. This righteousness from God comes through faith in Jesus Christ to all who believe. There is no difference, for all have sinned and fall short of the glory of God, and are justified freely by his grace through the redemption that came by Christ Jesus. God presented him as a sacrifice of atonement, through faith in his blood. He did this to demonstrate his justice, because in his forbearance he had left the sins committed beforehand unpunished—he did it to demonstrate his justice at the present time, so as to be just and the one who justifies those who have faith in Jesus. (Romans 3:20-26)

The final verse, also from the perspective of the Lord, announces the triumphant exaltation of the Servant of the Lord. He has achieved a marvelous victory. He has overcome sin, death, and hell. With that victory come the spoils of the conflict, the results of his efforts. His work has been so successful that the Lord will grant him an inheritance. The Servant will divide those spoils with the strong, Isaiah writes. The words translated as "great" and "strong" can also mean "numerous" or "many." The Servant's work has bought back, or redeemed, many from the bondage of sin and death. Those whom the Servant has redeemed with his suffering and death will be his eternal portion and inheritance. The Servant claims us by his work; we, as believers, are his. Isaiah repeats the reason once again: The Servant poured out his life in death and was counted with sinners. Jesus, as the Great High Priest, sacrificed himself for the sins of his people and still intercedes for them before the throne of grace.

What treasures the soul finds in these words! Luther wrote:

> Oh, we would be blessed people if we could believe this most noble text, which must be magnified. I would wish it to be honored in the church, so that we might accustom ourselves to an alert study of this text, to bring us to see Christ as none other than the One who bears and shoulders the burden of our sins. This figure is a solace to the afflicted. (LW, Volume 17, page 232)

I am among the transgressors for whom the Servant has suffered and given his life. So is everyone who reads these words or hears them. God has done everything to reconcile us to himself. He has redeemed us by grace. No other reconciliation exists. Those who believe receive all that God has done. Those who do not believe reject it and decide they have a better way to remove sin and win God's favor. That is arrogance. Those who reject God's answer must pay the penalty for accepting an answer that cannot save.

Chapter 53 occupies a central position in the second part of Isaiah's prophecy. Under the inspiration of the Holy Spirit, Isaiah has led us to this most important chapter. He has carefully arranged his material so that we arrive here with an understanding that the Lord's Great Servant would suffer and die for the sins of his people. The Great Servant would be victorious in achieving his goal. This Servant cannot be Cyrus, who could not suffer and die for the sins of God's people. Cyrus appeared in the opening chapters of this section but has since disappeared. He was one deliverer, one servant, but his role was limited to releasing God's people from Babylon. He was last mentioned in 45:13. While the Jews had yet to experience the exile, captivity, and return, Isaiah has also left Babylon behind. The last time Isaiah mentioned Babylon was in 48:20: "Leave Babylon, flee from the Babylonians!" Isaiah has been pointing us ahead to a much greater deliverance, that of the Great Servant, who delivers from sin and death.

This Great Servant is none other than Jesus Christ. But as clear as that interpretation is to us, it has been challenged repeatedly and will continue to be challenged and criticized. Some say that this servant is Israel or God's people, perhaps the best of those people, the faithful. But that interpretation ignores Isaiah's description of the servant as a single person, for example, "a man of sorrows" (53:3). In addition, the nation of Israel, even the best and most faithful citizens, could not suffer as a substitute for itself or even for the worst and most unfaithful of God's people. That would make deliverance dependent upon human effort or suffering—an idea that runs counter to so many clear passages of both the Old and New Testaments. Deliverance from sin and death is a gift of God's grace; it comes from God and God alone, in spite of the rebellion and sin of humanity.

When we identify the Servant as Jesus Christ, we tie the entire Scriptures together. God promised deliverance already in the Garden of Eden. That passage was part of the Hebrew Scriptures of Isaiah's day. In Genesis, God promised that someone would come to crush Satan's head. Who would that be? Isaiah provides a clear answer: the Servant of the Lord. The promises God gave to Abraham assumed the coming of one great descendant. God told David that one would sit on his throne whose reign would last forever. As all the Old Testament Scriptures pointed to the coming of this great Messiah, so Isaiah points to his coming and his work from the very beginning of his prophecy. He identifies him as the child of a virgin, as Immanuel, as God's Son, who would be Wonderful Counselor, Mighty God, Everlasting Father, Prince of Peace (9:6).

In chapter 53 Isaiah spells out most clearly and eloquently the great work of the Servant of the Lord. The Servant would suffer for sinners so that they might be forgiven, healed, and brought into God's eternal kingdom of joy. The New Testament claims these passages as clear references to Jesus. Who will disagree with the writers of the New Testament and with God's inspiration?

Yet some do not see Jesus here. Instead, they see the political redemption of God's Old Testament people. Such an interpretation sees the fulfillment of this chapter in the return of God's people from the exile that had been caused by their own sins. For those who see only the return of the Jews from captivity, these passages do not stretch to the cross of Calvary. But such an interpretation fails to grasp the reason for the Servant's suffering. He came to suffer for "our transgressions" and "our iniquities."

Isaiah included himself in the work of the Servant with the pronoun *our.* The Servant is not a political deliverer. He is a spiritual deliverer, a Redeemer from sin. That also fits with the promises of God to his Old Testament people. For example, the deliverer promised in the Garden of Eden was a spiritual deliverer, someone God promised to send to destroy evil and the father of all evil, the devil. Adam and Eve were not a nation that needed restoration and rebuilding. They were sinners who had disobeyed God and needed the comfort of God's forgiveness and love. God gave it to them by promising to send the Savior.

God's prophet provides more in the verses to come. Isaiah has identified the Servant of the Lord and outlined his work. The prophet does not stop at this important and significant point. The remaining chapters are just as carefully designed to help us understand the blessings that God has in store for his faithful people because of the work of his Servant. In the chapters ahead, Isaiah will turn our attention to the faithful people of God—the church, which is the assembly of all who acknowledge Christ as the Messiah.

The Lord promises to glorify his people

54 "Sing, O barren woman,
you who never bore a child;
burst into song, shout for joy,
you who were never in labor;
because more are the children of the desolate woman
than of her who has a husband,"

says the LORD.

[2] "Enlarge the place of your tent,
stretch your tent curtains wide,
do not hold back;
lengthen your cords,
strengthen your stakes.

> [3] **For you will spread out to the right and to the left;**
>   **your descendants will dispossess nations**
>   **and settle in their desolate cities.**

> [4] **"Do not be afraid; you will not suffer shame.**
>   **Do not fear disgrace; you will not be humiliated.**
> **You will forget the shame of your youth**
>   **and remember no more the reproach of your widowhood.**
> [5] **For your Maker is your husband—**
>   **the LORD Almighty is his name—**
> **the Holy One of Israel is your Redeemer;**
>   **he is called the God of all the earth.**

The Servant would succeed. Isaiah had written, "See, my servant will act wisely; he will be raised and lifted up and highly exalted" (52:13). Those words appeared at the very beginning of the great passage about the suffering of the Lord's Servant. Near the end of that section, Isaiah recorded God's words: "The will of the LORD will prosper in his hand" (53:10). As difficult and painful as the Servant's work would be, it would end in success. Isaiah now directs us to see the results of the Servant's work.

The people are described as a "barren woman." We may think of the exiles who returned to Jerusalem after 70 years of captivity. Certainly they were a ragged assembly of refugees. "Barren" might well describe the remnant that returned from Babylon. Yet God had great things in store for those people. Because of the work of the Servant, many would be added to their number. God's Old Testament people are encouraged to stretch out their tents to accommodate the increased number. The new period of their history would be an epoch of expansion.

These verses build on ideas Isaiah had mentioned earlier. First, God described his people as his unfaithful wife and identified himself as the husband. In chapter 49, God's people wondered if the Lord had forsaken them, and in the next chapter, God had asked his people to show him their certificate of divorce. But they had no certificate because God had not abandoned them. Their exile had come because of their own sins. God said, "Because of your transgressions your mother was sent away" (50:1). But what a change has taken place! The wife and her husband have been reconciled. She had been barren and desolate, but now she stands redeemed and brought back from her exile. God has atoned for the unfaithfulness of his rebellious and perverse wife and brought her back to himself. The Servant has accomplished his work. It will be helpful to remember this metaphor in the next section too. We will want to note how carefully Isaiah arranged these chapters. They are a unit, and the thought flows from one section to the next.

Second, the chapter expands on the theme of children and offspring that Isaiah had introduced at the end of the previous chapter. The Servant would see his offspring (53:10). Here they come to be part of God's people. There are so many that the tents of the church, that is, God's people, must be enlarged. The result of the Servant's work is expansion. All who believe in the Messiah come into his tent. They become part of God's people. So Isaiah takes us to Pentecost and the growth of the New Testament church. God includes us among them and has enlarged the tent to accommodate us under the protection and care of our heavenly husband. Remember how Paul makes use of this metaphor: Christ is the husband, and the church, that is, believers, are his bride (Ephesians 5:22-33).

Besides expansion, the believers have one more blessing because of the work of the Servant. God assures his people, "Do not be afraid; you will not suffer shame" (verse 4). God's people have been redeemed. They have been bought back from the consequences of their sins. They are not to fear but to rest in the undeserved and changeless love of

God. The Lord asserts the reason they should not be afraid: he is their Maker and their Redeemer. Because these faithful come under the protection of the almighty Lord of all the earth, nothing can harm them. It is as Paul wrote:

> If God is for us, who can be against us? He who did not spare his own Son, but gave him up for us all—how will he not also, along with him, graciously give us all things? Who will bring any charge against those whom God has chosen? It is God who justifies. Who is he that condemns? Christ Jesus, who died—more than that, who was raised to life—is at the right hand of God and is also interceding for us. (Romans 8:31-34)

> [6] The LORD will call you back
>   as if you were a wife deserted and distressed in spirit—
> a wife who married young,
>   only to be rejected," says your God.
> [7] "For a brief moment I abandoned you,
>   but with deep compassion I will bring you back.
> [8] In a surge of anger
>   I hid my face from you for a moment,
> but with everlasting kindness
>   I will have compassion on you,"
>   says the LORD your Redeemer.
> [9] "To me this is like the days of Noah,
>   when I swore that the waters of Noah would never again
>   cover the earth.
> So now I have sworn not to be angry with you,
>   never to rebuke you again.
> [10] Though the mountains be shaken
>   and the hills be removed,
> yet my unfailing love for you will not be shaken
>   nor my covenant of peace be removed,"
>   says the LORD, who has compassion on you.

The Lord retraced the history of his Old Testament

people, using the metaphor of the unfaithful wife and the faithful husband. How interesting that God summed up all the Old Testament history with just this short vivid passage. The Lord had married his people centuries earlier. We could consider the promises to Abraham, Isaac, and Jacob the engagement. When the people had grown in strength and number, God married himself to them. He brought them out of Egypt and made them his own. He gave them and their children a land flowing with milk and honey. Israel was the love of God's life, as any young, beautiful wife would be the love of a husband's life. But over the centuries, Israel had proven to be an unfaithful wife. They had committed spiritual adultery by worshiping other gods. God warned his adulterous wife of the consequences of her rebellion and unfaithfulness. Finally, as a faithful husband, God had abandoned his unfaithful wife. "For a brief moment I abandoned you." Isaiah's prophecy foretold the exile and captivity. God's action was just. He had faithfully loved his wife and cared for her, but she had turned away from him, spurned his love, and rejected his repeated warnings. He sent her away into exile.

All that appeared as the past in the prophet's eye, even though some of it was still to come when Isaiah wrote these words. As just as God's action against his people was, an even stronger emotion motivated him. God acted with "everlasting kindness" and "compassion." His love is deeper, wider, higher, and longer then anyone had a right to hope. What greater love can there be than God sending his one and only Son to redeem the world. He did that not when his people were good and faithful but when they were rebellious and unfaithful. We note another contrast in these verses. The affliction endured by God's people is brief. The love of God is endless, "everlasting."

God reminded his people that his love is not only deep, wide, high, and long. It is also permanent. To emphasize the point, God recalls the oath he took after the flood. When Noah and his family came out of the ark, God swore never to destroy the earth again as he had done (Genesis 8,9). That ancient promise echoes in the one God makes here: "So now I have sworn not to be angry with you, never to rebuke you again." The oath of God makes it so. Nothing can alter such an oath. Because of the work of the Servant of the Lord, Jesus, God has sworn to watch over his people. All things will work out for the good of those who love God. God's people trust in the permanent, faithful love of God.

The Lord underscores his faithful love with a comparison. The most permanent and enduring things we know on earth are mountains. They remain from generation to generation. Mount Everest may have a different name today than it did in the days of Isaiah, but it has remained the same mountain down to our own age. Even if such a mountain, or any mountain, could be shaken and removed, God's love cannot be shaken. It is a deep, permanent love—a love "for you," God says. His people are the objects of his love and compassion. From his love flow our comfort, our peace, and our confidence, no matter what the future may hold.

When God made a covenant with Noah after the flood, he placed the rainbow in the clouds as a sign of the covenant of peace he promised to Noah and all his descendants. Isaiah foretold a covenant of a far greater peace—the peace between God and his believers. The sign of that covenant is the work of the Servant described in chapter 53. In New Testament terms, the sign of that covenant is the suffering and death of Jesus Christ. Because of the Lord Jesus, we have peace with God. The peace Jesus has established between God and the sinner remains sure and certain. God will not change his mind. Those who trust in God and what he has done to redeem humanity are covered in the contract, or covenant, of peace. Nothing in all eternity will change that covenant, because nothing can change the deep compassion God has for his people. All believers of all time are included. You and I are too. This passage is among the most comforting and beautiful that God has recorded through his inspired servants.

> [11] **"O afflicted city, lashed by storms and not comforted,**
> **I will build you with stones of turquoise,**
> **your foundations with sapphires.**
> [12] **I will make your battlements of rubies,**
> **your gates of sparkling jewels,**
> **and all your walls of precious stones.**
> [13] **All your sons will be taught by the LORD,**
> **and great will be your children's peace.**
> [14] **In righteousness you will be established:**
> **Tyranny will be far from you;**
> **you will have nothing to fear.**
> **Terror will be far removed;**
> **it will not come near you.**
> [15] **If anyone does attack you, it will not be my doing;**
> **whoever attacks you will surrender to you.**
>
> [16] **"See, it is I who created the blacksmith**
> **who fans the coals into flame**
> **and forges a weapon fit for its work.**
> **And it is I who have created the destroyer to work havoc;**
> [17] **no weapon forged against you will prevail,**
> **and you will refute every tongue that accuses you.**
> **This is the heritage of the servants of the LORD,**
> **and this is their vindication from me,"**
> **declares the LORD.**

The Lord issued promises of his enduring compassion for his people to encourage them. So often God's people find themselves confronted with troubles and trials. Verse 11

247

reminds us that they are often afflicted, "lashed by storms and not comforted." But believers walk by faith and not by sight. As the writer to the Hebrews reminds us, they are like their father Abraham, who lived "like a stranger in a foreign country. . . . For he was looking forward to the city with foundations, whose architect and builder is God" (11:9,10). The glorious city of God awaits all believers. God promised such a city, and here he describes it to encourage us on our journey through life's storms.

The description of the city may remind us of the one John saw in a vision on the Isle of Patmos (Revelation 21:9-27). The turquoise, sapphires, rubies, sparkling jewels, and precious stones all communicate the incredible beauty and priceless value of the city that God has prepared for those who love him. The Hebrew for some of these terms is difficult, but the impression left by the words is unmistakable. The Lord will change the future of his beleaguered, afflicted, and storm-tossed people. He will build them into a glorious and beautiful city.

That city lies in the future. God promised that the sons and children of those who read Isaiah's prophecy will enjoy this city. It always lies ahead in the future for God's people. When God's promises are fulfilled and no longer lie in the future, the fulfillment will be more glorious than these words we have treasured can describe. While we wait, God builds up all who believe the message of the LORD, Jehovah.

Because of the Servant of the Lord, believers have great peace—the peace that surpasses all understanding (Philippians 4:7; Colossians 3:15). The faithful enjoy this peace because they are taught by the Lord himself. The next phrase reminds us that the foundation of the city is God's righteousness, his intense determination to save his people. He has declared all who are in this city to be right. They are justified. God's Servant has justified many (53:11), and they are all included in the city of peace founded upon righteousness.

This glorious city rests secure because it comes under the protection of the almighty Lord. His unfailing love and compassion for his people will not permit tyranny, terror, or attack. God's people will be protected in every possible way.

The last two verses of the chapter remind us that God controls all things. Even the enemies of God's people come under the control of the almighty Lord. A blacksmith may seem to operate completely independent of God. He may even seem to be free to forge weapons meant to harm God's people. But that is not so. God controls the blacksmith's activity too. The Lord will prevent the formation of any plan or any weapon that would destroy or harm his people. Yet in this world of affliction and storm, God's people do experience trouble and difficulty. Their enemies do persecute them and kill them from time to time. We might ask why God does not prevent disaster from falling upon the world and upon his people. The answer to the question remains beyond our understanding. God has revealed much about himself, but there are things he has not revealed to us or to anyone. We are humans with limited understanding and perception; God has no such limits. At times we must confess with Isaiah, "Truly you are a God who hides himself, O God and Savior of Israel" (45:15).

Yet no matter what the circumstances, we can be sure that God's people are always under the care of their Maker and Redeemer. He will make even the worst things we endure here turn out for the benefit of his people. The last words of the chapter stand as an emphatic exclamation point. All this rests on the LORD, Jehovah. He declares it to be so. Since his word created the world out of nothing (Genesis 1), then these promises are sure and certain too.

The Lord invites all to come

55 "Come, all you who are thirsty,
come to the waters;
and you who have no money,
come, buy and eat!
Come, buy wine and milk
without money and without cost.
[2] Why spend money on what is not bread,
and your labor on what does not satisfy?
Listen, listen to me, and eat what is good,
and your soul will delight in the richest of fare.
[3] Give ear and come to me;
hear me, that your soul may live.
I will make an everlasting covenant with you,
my faithful love promised to David.
[4] See, I have made him a witness to the peoples,
a leader and commander of the peoples.
[5] Surely you will summon nations you know not,
and nations that do not know you will hasten to you,
because of the LORD your God,
the Holy One of Israel,
for he has endowed you with splendor."

Considering what the Servant of the Lord would accomplish as Isaiah has described it in chapter 53 and the glory that God promised to his chosen people, this chapter extends God's gracious invitation to come. The first verse shouts the invitation by the series of invitations, "Come, . . . come, . . . come, buy and eat! Come, buy . . ." These invitations are addressed to "all you who are thirsty." God issues his invitation to every human, not just to his Old Testament people but to all humans, who desperately need his blessings. Just as Jesus invited "all you who are weary and burdened" (Matthew 11:28), so the Lord God invites "all you who are thirsty." Sin and death make us weary of life here and thirsty for God's blessings.

To help us grasp the invitation, try to imagine an ancient market scene where merchants have their tables and awnings set up. They shout to those who pass by, hawking their products. God is like one of those vendors, but his products are nothing like vegetables, meat, water, milk, or wine. He has spiritual blessings to dispense to everyone, and he has a fervent desire to share them with all. Not only are God's products different, but they are also free. This wonderful invitation clearly speaks of God's grace. No human can offer God anything for his blessings. Three times in this verse God emphasizes that the products he offers are free.

The second part of God's invitation asks why people spend so much effort and money to acquire things that do not satisfy their souls. Many people devote their entire attention to the things of this life. Men and women strive for the good things in life and spend a great deal of money and effort on acquiring things, preserving what they have acquired, and working to acquire more. But nothing this world can offer really satisfies; it is all simply "not bread," that is, it is not the bread of life. Without the blessings of God's grace, all humans end life like the rich fool. He had plenty of good things on earth but had nothing when he faced God (Luke 12:13-21).

We dare not forget that human beings harbor the natural inclination to purchase the gifts of God by their own effort. But God's gifts cannot be earned; they are gifts "without cost." God calls us away from every effort to earn what only he can give. The apostle Paul said it so beautifully: "It is by grace you have been saved, through faith—and this not from yourselves, it is the gift of God—not by works, so that no one can boast" (Ephesians 2:8,9). What human contribution could be placed on the scales of God that would weigh enough to buy forgiveness and eternal life? Again we see the market scene with the vendor placing human effort and possessions on a balance. But all the gold and silver in the world and all the greatest human effort and thought cannot budge the scale or even make it wiggle. Only the work of the Servant of the Lord, who "was crushed for our iniquities" (53:5), could earn the gifts of God. These gifts God now offers to all by grace. Humans become vain and silly if they think they can offer God enough for such priceless gifts.

God encourages us to acquire his gracious blessings, and he suggests an unexpected method for securing them: "Listen, listen to me." The idea of listening in the marketplace might suggest that we would have to pay attention in order to hear what we must do. But here God tells us to listen to what he has done. The contrast is again between grace and works. As we listen, we eat what is good, and we satisfy our souls on the richest fare. The words of God themselves are the feast. The rest of the chapter carries out the importance of God's Word, but here we must note these words encouraging us to listen, give ear, and hear. God calls us by the gospel— his Word. It seems so insignificant, but that's God's way. Listen and your soul will live. God's Word performs a profound miracle of grace. While we might expect to have to do something grand and magnificent for God, God says simply, "Listen." As we sit quietly in worship, we hear God's message. We so often think we have a thousand more important things to do, but God tells us here that we have nothing more important to do in all eternity than to listen. When our sinful flesh complains about the plain and sometimes dull proclamation of God's Word, we must remember that God works in our hearts through his Word. He has not promised to work in any other way to satisfy the deep spiritual needs we have.

God further emphasizes his grace when he says that he makes an everlasting covenant. We don't do it. God does! That's grace. God makes his everlasting covenant with us. For Old Testament readers of Isaiah's prophecy, these terms pointed to the coming of the Messiah. This is all grace, and lest we miss it, God tells us that this covenant flows from his faithful love promised to David. God promised that the Messiah would come from David's line (2 Samuel 7:11-16). God was not under any obligation to make such a promise, but he did so out of pure undeserved love. Once he had promised, he would be faithful and do what he said. His promises are not like those of any human; God's promises are everlastingly true.

The Son of David, Christ, completes the picture of King David as a leader and witness. Christ is David's greater Son, and he is the witness to the nations of God's undeserved love. The idea of witness here carries the idea of proclamation and points to the Messiah's office as Prophet. The words *leader* and *commander* of this verse remind us that the Messiah also serves as King. The gospel announces the undeserved love of God in Christ for sinners. The Word of God again finds a way into this text, and Christ remains the center of that Word. All Scripture points to him.

The Messiah came from heaven, and as Jesus indicated to Nicodemus, he would be lifted up so that "everyone who believes in him may have eternal life" (John 3:15). He would rule over more than just the Jewish remnant returning from Babylon. The nations would come to him—the strangers who did not know all the Old Testament prophecies. Those strangers would be brought into the fold of God's people. The words of the gospel would draw them in and cause them to hasten to the Messiah and all the promises of God.

253

What does it mean when the Lord tells the Messiah, "Surely you will summon nations you know not"? Because the Messiah is God's special Servant and God in human form—that is, Immanuel, God with us—how can he not know these nations? When we are told that the Messiah did not know the nations, God tells us that the Messiah did not know these strangers as his own people. They were outside the circle of Israel and Judah, strangers and foreigners. But even these strangers will be converted by the gospel and included in the assembly of believers—God's people.

> [6] Seek the LORD while he may be found;
>   call on him while he is near.
> [7] Let the wicked forsake his way
>   and the evil man his thoughts.
>   Let him turn to the LORD, and he will have mercy on him,
>   and to our God, for he will freely pardon.

These two verses belong with the rest of the chapter, but we pause here to draw attention to two thoughts. The first involves the invitation to seek the Lord. The gospel invitation motivates men and women to seek the Lord. They do not have the natural ability to turn to God on their own. Luther wrote, "I cannot by my own thinking or choosing believe in Jesus Christ, my Lord, or come to him" (Small Catechism, Explanation of the Third Article). God can be found by humans only as long as the gospel is proclaimed. In the gospel he comes near. God, however, does withdraw his gospel at times. Jesus withdrew himself from those who openly opposed him. His withdrawal meant a severe judgment upon them because his absence removed their opportunity to repent. On his missionary journeys, Paul would first visit the Jewish synagogue to share the gospel, but when opposition arose, he would leave and go to the Gentiles. God urges sinners to seek him before their rejection prompts his departure.

The second thought has to do with grace once more. The prophet urges sinners to turn away from their wicked ways and turn to the Lord. The end of verse 7 gives special comfort to every sinner. The Lord pledges to have mercy on the sinner and to pardon him freely. The words hold out the bright jewel of forgiveness for the grimy, stained hands of every sinner to grasp. What a comfort to every sinner! God looks tenderly upon sinners and, because of Christ, forgives them. These thoughts underscore the everlasting covenant and faithful love of verse 3.

> **8 "For my thoughts are not your thoughts,**
> **neither are your ways my ways,"**
>
> **declares the LORD.**
> **9 "As the heavens are higher than the earth,**
> **so are my ways higher than your ways**
> **and my thoughts than your thoughts.**

The connecting link between this and the previous verse are the words *thoughts* and *ways*. God speaks again and declares the superiority of his thoughts to those of any and every human. The ways and thoughts of humans are wicked and evil by nature. Moses wrote, "The LORD saw how great man's wickedness on the earth had become, and that every inclination of the thoughts of his heart was only evil all the time" (Genesis 6:5). Over the centuries nothing has changed. Jesus said, "Out of the heart come evil thoughts, murder, adultery, sexual immorality, theft, false testimony, slander" (Matthew 15:19).

Besides the problem of sin, human thoughts and ways are limited by time, space, and other factors. That principle even the ungodly can understand. Unbelievers often encounter what defies their understanding, but this text gets us deeper into the profound difference between God and humanity. Our natural perverse nature struggles against God. All thoughts that flow from us are nothing like God's thoughts. The deepest thinkers of the ages cannot achieve the high and lofty ways of God or understand God. Left alone and without God's Word, no human can imagine that God would send a Savior to die for unworthy sinners. God's grace remains a mystery to human intelligence and research. Yet God does make it known to us in his Word, as we will learn in the next verses.

Even the way God works in the human heart lies beyond the human imagination. God works the miracle of conversion through the gospel—simple words that announce forgiveness and life through Christ. The Word is powerful. For God's dealing with men and women, the Word is everything. Yet words appear so weak and ineffective—only sounds that travel through the air to an ear or a series of lines on a page perceived by our eyes. But God's ways are higher than ours. God's way works through the words of the gospel not only to convert sinners but to strengthen them and preserve their faith against the many temptations and distractions in this life. Simple words that announce God's love for sinners have more power than all human ways and thoughts because God's Word changes the heart and offers life and forgiveness to all believers.

> [10] **"As the rain and the snow**
> **come down from heaven,**
> **and do not return to it**
> **without watering the earth**
> **and making it bud and flourish,**
> **so that it yields seed for the sower and bread for the eater,**
> [11] **so is my word that goes out from my mouth:**
> **It will not return to me empty,**
> **but will accomplish what I desire**
> **and achieve the purpose for which I sent it.**

God makes contact with sinners through his Word. The Word comes from God, who authors it and sends it across time and space to the sinner. God assures us in these verses that his Word is effective. It is *his* Word because it goes out of his mouth and returns to him. As his Word, it is powerful. The writer to the Hebrews reminds us, "The word of God is living and active. Sharper than any double-edged sword, it penetrates even to dividing soul and spirit, joints and marrow; it judges the thoughts and attitudes of the heart" (4:12).

We also say that his Word is true because it comes from God. God gave his Word by inspiration, and his Word cannot lie because God cannot lie. As we read the words written by Isaiah, we can be confident that they are the very words of God. Throughout the prophecy, Isaiah noted that what he wrote had been revealed to him and that he had received his revelation from God (for example, 1:1; 2:1; 5:9; 6:1; 8:11). Jeremiah and the other prophets made the same claim. The apostle Paul wrote, "This is what we speak, not in words taught us by human wisdom but in words taught by the Spirit" (1 Corinthians 2:13). And Peter summarized the centuries of God's proclamation by reminding us, "Prophecy never had its origin in the will of man, but men spoke from God as they were carried along by the Holy Spirit" (2 Peter 1:21).

Isaiah introduces us to a precious truth concerning the Word of God. Through his prophet, God tells us how his Word works. Clearly and simply, God presents a striking comparison. His Word comes from him like the rain and snow from heaven. When rain and snow come down, they water the ground and make it bud and flourish. When God's Word comes to sinners, it too works. Paul told Timothy what the Word could do: "All Scripture is God-breathed and is use-

ful for teaching, rebuking, correcting and training in righteousness, so that the man of God may be thoroughly
equipped for every good work" (2 Timothy 3:16,17). God can
also use his Word to bring judgment. Isaiah had the difficult
task of proclaiming God's Word and watching as it made the
hearts of his listeners calloused and their ears dull (6:9,10). In
this section, however, the great accomplishment of the Word
is to convert and draw the nations to God.

God has promised to work through the external Word.
God has simply chosen the Word as the means through
which he has promised to work. Of course, he could work
through other means, but the entire Scripture maintains that
God works through the Word. These verses only emphasize
the encouragement of verses 2 and 3. There God invited
sinners to listen—listen, give ear, and hear. The phrase "give
ear" means to stretch out the ears, to strain them to catch
the words. None of this should surprise us when we realize
what God's Word can do. Whenever anyone thinks that he
or she can do without hearing the Word, such a person dis-
cards the way God works within us. We might behold the
beauties of God's created world and wonder at God's glory
and majesty, but those insights will not bring us to Christ.
Only his Word can do that.

> [12] **"You will go out in joy**
> **and be led forth in peace;**
> **the mountains and hills**
> **will burst into song before you,**
> **and all the trees of the field**
> **will clap their hands.**
> [13] **Instead of the thornbush will grow the pine tree,**
> **and instead of briers the myrtle will grow.**
> **This will be for the LORD's renown,**
> **for an everlasting sign,**
> **which will not be destroyed."**

Now look at what the Word promises. The gospel holds out joy for sinners and brings peace. God wishes to fill the heart of the sinner with joy and peace, and both come from the Word—peace with God through Christ and joy in the redemption Christ has accomplished. As this Word of promise comes from God and enters the human heart, it accomplishes God's purpose and imparts joy and peace. When Isaiah writes that God's people will go out in joy, his promise is nothing else than gospel. At first he may have in mind the exodus of God's people from Egypt, and certainly he also points to the return of the remnant from the Babylonian captivity. But those exoduses, as joyful and exciting as they were for the people of God, are nothing compared with the final exodus. All God's saints will leave the bondage of sin and death. They will be led to the Jerusalem above. In a single picture, the prophet unites both the return from Babylon and the final deliverance.

Anyone hearing the gospel longs for the eternal mansions of heaven. The overwhelming joy of God's people as they experience God's deliverance will spread to the trees and transform the wilderness from thorns and briars to pine trees and myrtles. These words do not refer to literal and physical events. Instead, they paint poetic pictures of the final deliverance of God's people from this bleak world of sorrow, pain, sin, and death.

The final section of verse 13 may have in mind the way ancient kings erected monuments to commemorate their victories and accomplishments. But later kings established different empires and often destroyed or defaced the monuments of their predecessors. Even if those monuments were not destroyed by later kings and emperors, time and weather would turn them into ruins. The deliverance of God's saints is the great accomplishment of the Lord of grace. No king will ever erase that accomplishment; no number of years or force of nature will turn it into ruins. All that God did to deliver sinners from sin and death stands forever as God's greatest honor.

The deliverance of the Lord is for all people

56 This is what the LORD says:
"Maintain justice
   and do what is right,
 for my salvation is close at hand
   and my righteousness will soon be revealed.
² Blessed is the man who does this,
   the man who holds it fast,
 who keeps the Sabbath without desecrating it,
   and keeps his hand from doing any evil."

Consider what wonderful blessings the Lord has prepared. The Servant will come and will be "pierced for our transgressions" and "crushed for our iniquities" (53:5). The blessings of his work will cause the believers to sing praise (54:1). We have read that the Lord makes these blessings available to "all you who are thirsty" (55:1). Like a merchant in a busy ancient market, the Lord encourages people to come and receive his free gift of grace: "Come, buy . . . without money and without cost" (55:1). What more can people do than to sing the praises of the Lord, the Savior-God?

Singing the praises of the Lord expresses joy and gratitude for such marvelous blessings. But the redeemed express their faith in other ways too. As this chapter begins, the Lord indicates what works will demonstrate such gratitude and joy for the blessings that the Servant offered so freely. He says, "Maintain justice and do what is right." God's people always live out of gratitude for God's gracious gifts. Behavior never earns God's gifts. We respond to God's gracious gifts by praising him and by all our activity that conforms to his righteous desires.

John the Baptist stood on the banks of the Jordan River and encouraged his audience, "Repent, for the kingdom of heaven is near" (Matthew 3:2). When his listeners had heard the announcement that salvation was near and had turned in faith to God's promises, they wanted to know what they should do. John gave them directions for their lives. At one point he encouraged, "Produce fruit in keeping with repentance" (Luke 3:8). John the Baptist cut his message from the same cloth as the prophecy of Isaiah. "Maintain justice and do what is right, for my salvation is close at hand and my righteousness will soon be revealed."

By faith we receive the blessings God freely offers. Those blessings cannot be earned by an act of human effort. Nor can any thought or emotion of human origin win over God so that he grants his blessings. We have nothing to offer God that will move him to give us anything. God gives his blessings for his own sake, as Isaiah had written earlier, "I, even I, am he who blots out your transgressions, for my own sake, and remembers your sins no more" (43:25). On account of Christ's perfect life and innocent death, God's declaration of justification is completed and real.

But faith in the Lord's promises does not earn God's declaration either. It receives his blessings and then motivates believers to conform their lives to the will of God. Because of their faith in the gracious promises of God, believers desire to think, speak, and do what God has revealed in his law. God has revealed two primary directions for the appropriate behavior of his people. First, God wants his people to maintain a proper relationship with him as their God and Redeemer. That is the message of the first table of the law (the first three commandments). Second, God wants his people to maintain proper relationships with all other humans. That is the second table of the law (the remaining seven commandments). In these words recorded by Isaiah, both tables of the law are included. God's people are those who keep the Sabbath, a requirement of the first table, and they are to keep their hands from all evil, a requirement of the second table of the law. When Jesus was asked to give a summary of the law, he replied: "'Love the Lord your God with all your heart and with all your soul and with all your mind.' This is the first and greatest commandment. And the second is like it: 'Love your neighbor as yourself'" (Matthew 22:37-39).

For the Old Testament believers, keeping the Sabbath gave expression to their relationship with the God of the covenant, Jehovah. The Sabbath was a time for God's people to rest from their weekly labors and to give God their attention. On the Sabbath they worshiped God and listened to his Word. The faithful continued to do that down to the days of Jesus. So often Jesus went to the synagogue on the Sabbath (see Luke 4:16). In New Testament days, the Lord has given his people greater freedom. We do not observe the Sabbath in the way Isaiah and the people of his day did. But God still wants us to set aside time for him and his Word. In the freedom of the gospel, Christians throughout the centuries have chosen Sunday instead of Saturday. On that day, we gather together to worship and listen to the Lord's Word. Keeping the Sabbath "without desecrating it" means to honor and observe the relationship with God—to worship. For the Old Testament believers, it meant they set aside the seventh day for rest. For New Testament believers, it means setting aside a time for God—a time to praise him and hear his Word. Like Old Testament believers, New Testament believers are to nurture their relationship with God; anything else comes from unbelief.

Believers are also to keep their hands from doing evil. Such evil does enter our human lives. Out of our own human hearts flow greed, pride, deceit, lust, and envy—to mention only a few. We are forgiven for our failures by God's grace in Christ. And our faith in Jesus motivates us to desire to turn away from all such evil. Believers today, as in Isaiah's day, desire to follow the Lord's commands. Honor your parents. Do not murder. Do not commit adultery. Do not steal. Do not bear false witness. Do not desire what belongs to someone else. Believers keep their hands from evil by obeying the commandments of God.

While no human can earn God's blessings because of his or her behavior, God has agreed to add blessings to those who do as he wishes. For example, one who keeps the Sabbath and sets aside time for God and his Word will receive additional blessings. God will work through the gospel each time a believer hears or reads it. When a believer sets time aside for God's Word, God continues to add blessings. Such a believer gains strength of faith and depth of spiritual understanding that do not come to those who do not listen to God's Word regularly. God created the Sabbath for humans, not for himself. He established it for our benefit, and he attaches blessings to every human obedience. Other examples are also evident. When a believer avoids drunkenness, God preserves him or her from the evils of alcohol abuse. A believer who avoids bitterness and anger may find that God grants tranquillity. God reminds his faithful, "Blessed is the man who does this." Psalm 1 also expresses this thought.

NOTE

Some scholars suggest that this chapter begins a third major section of the book of Isaiah. They claim that this section has a new vocabulary, a new theological position, and new subject matter. For these reasons, they claim that these last chapters, 56 to 66, were written by an author different from the one who wrote the rest of the second portion of Isaiah, chapters 40 to 55, and different also from the one who wrote the first portion of Isaiah, chapters 1 to 39. Their theory, then, suggests three different writers for the book of Isaiah instead of one. But this chapter extends the idea of chapters 40 to 56 rather than adding something completely different. Isaiah treats a new subject certainly, but with the new subject comes a new vocabulary and a new theological position. In chapter 53, Isaiah had brought us to see the accomplishment of the Servant. Now Isaiah turns his attention to the results of that great accomplishment. The two thoughts are bound together like different colored threads of the same garment, not like patches of different fabrics sewn together. All of Isaiah's prophecy demonstrates a unified design and organization rather than haphazard piecework. The author of this commentary simply finds no reason to accept the speculation of such scholars.

³ **Let no foreigner who has bound himself to the Lord say, "The Lord will surely exclude me from his people."**

> And let not any eunuch complain,
> "I am only a dry tree."

⁴For this is what the LORD says:

> "To the eunuchs who keep my Sabbaths,
>   who choose what pleases me
>   and hold fast to my covenant—
> ⁵ to them I will give within my temple and its walls
>   a memorial and a name
>   better than sons and daughters;
> I will give them an everlasting name
>   that will not be cut off.
> ⁶ And foreigners who bind themselves to the LORD
>   to serve him,
> to love the name of the LORD,
>   and to worship him,
> all who keep the Sabbath without desecrating it
>   and who hold fast to my covenant—
> ⁷ these I will bring to my holy mountain
>   and give them joy in my house of prayer.
> Their burnt offerings and sacrifices
>   will be accepted on my altar;
> for my house will be called
>   a house of prayer for all nations."
> ⁸ The Sovereign LORD declares—
>   he who gathers the exiles of Israel:
> "I will gather still others to them
>   besides those already gathered."

In the previous chapter, Isaiah had encouraged his readers, "Seek the LORD while he may be found; call on him while he is near" (55:6). The Lord said in the opening verses of this chapter, "My salvation is close at hand." The Lord extends his arms wide to embrace all who will turn to him. Since Isaiah was a Jew and he wrote for Jews, the Lord's invitation obviously applied to the Jews. But the Lord's invitation is not meant only for Jews. God intends all nations to come and receive his blessings. The work of the Servant brought benefits not just for Isaiah and his nation but also for all humanity. These verses bring us this happy truth in dramatic fashion.

One function of God's Old Testament law was to keep his people separate from the nations that surrounded them. God did not want his people to be contaminated by the pagan religious practices of the nations surrounding Israel. They were to avoid contact with Gentiles. For that reason, God's people were not to eat pork and other unclean foods. They were different. They were circumcised as a sign of their connection with Abraham and the promises God had made to him. The Israelites disdainfully referred to the world outside as "uncircumcised." One might ask whether or not God wanted these "uncircumcised" to receive the deliverance provided by the Servant.

God's law also kept others outside the assembly of his people. For example, the law was clear:

> No one who has been emasculated by crushing or cutting may enter the assembly of the LORD. No one born of a forbidden marriage nor any of his descendants may enter the assembly of the LORD, even down to the tenth generation. No Ammonite or Moabite or any of his descendants may enter the assembly of the LORD, even down to the tenth generation. (Deuteronomy 23:1-3)

Certainly the law of God commanded that some were to be excluded from God's people. Yet Isaiah is describing "a new thing" that the Lord was doing (43:19). Would the emasculated and the foreigners be able to receive the blessings of God?

In the past, some non-Jews did come to trust in the God of the covenant. Some Egyptians came out of Egypt with God's people. Rahab, a Canaanite prostitute in Jericho, believed. But what about the future? What about others? Would they receive the same blessings God gave to his own special people of Israel? The Lord answers such questions with these verses by focusing on two groups of people. First, the Lord says that no foreigner would be excluded. They were to be included when they joined themselves to the Lord, that is, when they became part of God's people by faith in the promises of God. The second group contains the eunuchs, or as the law described them, those "emasculated by crushing or cutting." They are included too. God extends his gracious arms of welcome to both groups, the eunuchs and the foreigners.

Both groups have joined themselves to the Lord. They receive the blessings God has provided through the suffering of his Servant. But not every eunuch and not every citizen of all nations will be included. Only those who have joined themselves to God's promises by faith will receive admission into the assembly of God's people. They are the people of God, true Israel. Paul clarified the idea, saying: "Is God the God of Jews only? Is he not the God of Gentiles too? Yes, of Gentiles too" (Romans 3:29) and "Understand, then, that those who believe are children of Abraham" (Galatians 3:7).

How does the faith of eunuchs and foreigners show itself? In the same way that the faith of God's Old Testament people showed itself. They keep the Lord's Sabbaths, they choose what pleases God, and they hold fast to the Lord's covenant of grace (see verse 4 and verse 6 and compare with verse 2). All believers, regardless of their circumstances or ethnic origins, are the same in God's eyes. His house, God declares, is "a house of prayer for all nations." God had in mind the spread of the gospel to all the world. When Jesus said, "Make disciples of all nations" (Matthew 28:19), he expressed the same thought that these verses express. When Paul stretched the kingdom of God to the Gentiles in Asia Minor, Greece, and Rome, God gathered other nations into his family and made them his people. As the gospel has spread throughout the world and claimed Germans, Chinese, Indians, Africans, Russians, and Japanese, the Lord has gathered still others to be his people, the assembly of believers of all nations of all times—his church.

What are the blessings God will give to those who believe? He will give them everlasting names. He will bring them to his holy mountain. They will leave behind all evil and sin and dwell with God. He will give them joy in his house of prayer. He will accept their offerings. These blessings are for all those who have joined themselves to the Lord by faith in Jesus, the Servant of the Lord.

Judgment will come upon all who do not believe

> ⁹ **Come, all you beasts of the field,**
> **come and devour, all you beasts of the forest!**
> ¹⁰ **Israel's watchmen are blind,**
> **they all lack knowledge;**
> **they are all mute dogs,**
> **they cannot bark;**
> **they lie around and dream,**
> **they love to sleep.**
> ¹¹ **They are dogs with mighty appetites;**
> **they never have enough.**
> **They are shepherds who lack understanding;**
> **they all turn to their own way,**
> **each seeks his own gain.**
> ¹² **"Come," each one cries, "let me get wine!**
> **Let us drink our fill of beer!**
> **And tomorrow will be like today,**
> **or even far better."**

Suddenly, the tone of this chapter changes. Isaiah introduced a new thought that extends into the next chapter. We have turned to a new subject, one much darker than the joyful promises to all who believe. The section begins with a gruesome invitation to the beasts of the field. They are to be instruments of God's judgment upon his unfaithful people. God invites them to come. As beasts of prey, they are to devour the unfaithful.

This invitation comes after God has graciously provided deliverance for his people through his Servant (chapter 53). God has invited his people—and all foreigners, including the eunuchs—to come and receive the blessings of his grace (chapter 55 and the first half of 56). People do not need money to purchase God's blessings. They simply could not perform enough good deeds to earn his blessings. God invites all humanity to receive what he graciously provides—forgiveness, deliverance, and life. What about those who do not believe? What is God to do with those who refuse to accept his gracious blessings and spurn his patient, tender, yet insistent invitation? Those who refuse God's gifts and blessings deny themselves the one and only solution to sin and the one and only deliverance from death. Besides the Servant, Jesus Christ, no deliverance exists. God has no choice but to bring judgment upon those who spurn his free gifts. His justice requires judgment, so he calls the beasts to come. The beasts represent the harsh judgment of God.

No one will oppose the judgment God brings. No one will sound a warning. Even Israel's watchmen, her prophets, are not able to warn the people of the coming danger. They are blind, without knowledge, and mute. A dog will bark when a stranger approaches the door or moves too close. A watchdog that does not bark when danger approaches fails to do its job. The false prophets are described as such dogs. They are more interested in lying around, dreaming, sleeping, and eating. The Scriptures so often picture God's mes sengers as shepherds who have the responsibility to care for his people. These shepherds of Israel, however, were so concerned with their own affairs that they did not warn the people of danger. As Isaiah wrote, "Each seeks his own gain." While they were so busy with their own affairs, they failed to warn of the impending danger. Their personal gain would be of no value for them, since the watchmen themselves cannot escape the coming judgment either.

Isaiah even pictured one of these false shepherds calling to his fellows. He invited them to a drunken party. Sadly, it was not one isolated instance. The drunken revelry continued day after day, and their intoxication got worse and worse each day—all the while the beasts approached to devour them and the people. The false shepherds have rejected God's invitation. They have not kept the Sabbath or joined themselves to the Lord by faith. Judgment must come to them. Because of their unfaithfulness, God's people stand without warning in the path of God's judgment.

57 **The righteous perish,**
    and no one ponders it in his heart;
  devout men are taken away,
    and no one understands
  that the righteous are taken away
    to be spared from evil.
  ² Those who walk uprightly
    enter into peace;
    they find rest as they lie in death.

In this world God's people live among the unfaithful. The previous verses painted a gruesome picture of the beasts coming to devour those who had turned away from the Lord. As gruesome as the reality of the coming judgment is, those who be responsible for the safety of God's people are anything but responsible. Not only do they fail to give an alarm, but they are involved in drunken parties. What a sad state of affairs. One might wonder if anyone has remained faithful to the Lord and what will happen to them as the judgment approaches. These two verses shift our attention to the righteous who live among the unrighteous. The Lord still has his faithful, just as in the days of the prophet Elijah. Elijah had anguished over the ungodliness of his day. He thought he was the only faithful servant of God left, but God reminded him that he still had seven thousand in Israel who had not worshiped Baal (1 Kings 19).

The righteous are those whom God has declared righteous on account of the Servant. They believe and struggle to live righteous lives in gratitude for their blessings. "The righteous perish," that is, they die. That may not sound like any kind of an advantage, but the righteous are in the hands of the Lord. He cares for them, and one of his strategies takes them out of this world of trouble to himself. As the judgment approaches, God removes his faithful out of harm's way and leaves the ungodly and unrighteous.

From the perspective of the ungodly, the righteous believers disappear and life goes on. The ungodly do not consider what the departure of the righteous means. The unrighteous are more concerned about drunken orgies than doing the will of God who has redeemed them. Sadly, their lives remain untouched by the witness and example of the righteous. In verse 4 we discover that the ungodly are more interested in ridiculing the righteous than in heeding their message or following their example of godliness.

But we find another perspective. What fate awaits the righteous who die? These verses give us some wonderful comfort. Two things happen. First, the righteous believers are removed from the judgment. The beasts God has called will not devour them because God has spared them from such judgment. But a second blessing applies to those the Lord takes in death. They enter peace. For them, death is not the end; they will enter a new world where peace dominates. The Hebrew word for "peace" connotes total well-being and happiness, a blessing that cannot be found outside of God. For the wicked there is no such peace (48:22; 57:21), but those believers whom God has taken to himself in death have such peace. "They find rest as they lie in death." So God promises to all those who die in faith, "Then I heard a voice from heaven say, 'Write: Blessed are the dead who die in the Lord from now on.' 'Yes,' says the Spirit, 'they will rest from their labor'" (Revelation 14:13).

The believers are under the protection of the Lord of heaven and earth. He has not forgotten them as he describes the coming judgment. The faithful are always in the hand of God, and he will do whatever is best for them and for his church, even in the face of harsh judgment upon the ungodly.

> ³ "But you—come here, you sons of a sorceress,
>   you offspring of adulterers and prostitutes!
> ⁴ Whom are you mocking?
>   At whom do you sneer
>   and stick out your tongue?
> Are you not a brood of rebels,
>   the offspring of liars?
> ⁵ You burn with lust among the oaks
>   and under every spreading tree;
> you sacrifice your children in the ravines
>   and under the overhanging crags.
> ⁶ The idols among the smooth stones of the ravines are your
>   portion;
>   they, they are your lot.
> Yes, to them you have poured out drink offerings
>   and offered grain offerings.

In the light of these things, should I relent?
[7] **You have made your bed on a high and lofty hill;**
   there you went up to offer your sacrifices.
[8] **Behind your doors and your doorposts**
   you have put your pagan symbols.
Forsaking me, you uncovered your bed,
   you climbed into it and opened it wide;
you made a pact with those whose beds you love,
   and you looked on their nakedness.

The prophet shifts our attention once more back to the ungodly upon whom the judgment comes. They are called "sons of a sorceress" and "offspring of adulterers and prostitutes." These unbelievers have turned completely away from the Lord. They have turned to witchcraft and magic. They are not content with the message of God, which he delivered through his prophets, and they have abandoned God's Word. Instead of listening to God, they have adopted ideas, revelations, and religious practices of their heathen Canaanite neighbors. Baal worship combined religious worship with adultery and prostitution. Clearly, God addresses all those who have turned away from him and commands them to come closer to hear his message.

The description of the ungodly and wicked is graphic. These ungodly people have sneered at God's faithful people. They have stuck out their tongues in derision. Their immorality grows like weeds under "every spreading tree." They even sacrificed their own children. The spiritual and moral climate had become so polluted that they "made a pact with those whose beds [they] love." One can hardly imagine a people more opposed to God. Instead of seeking the Lord at his temple, they have worshiped somewhere else. Instead of following the proscribed directions for worship, they have invented their own patterns. They have ridiculed God's people and given themselves over to their own sexual appetites. In addition, they have sacrificed their own children, killing them without remorse. Human sacrifice was one facet of the Canaanites' worship, by which they hoped to gain Baal's blessing of fertility.

Several difficulties arise in these verses, but no difficulty remains in understanding the message. We do not know what the "smooth stones of the ravines" means. It could refer to some kind of stone worship or some paraphernalia of heathen worship. Whatever it means, the people have brought their offerings to these dead stones to gain the favor of the gods. The attitude of the unrighteous comes through clearly even if we don't know exactly what these "smooth stones" were.

We don't exactly know what it means when the Lord says, "Behind your doors and your doorposts you have put your pagan symbols." It could very well mean that the people hung a kind of phallic symbol, a pagan fertility charm, behind the door. It could also mean that the people removed the little box containing a passage from the Scriptures, which traditionally every Jewish household placed on the front doorpost. Instead of attaching Scripture to the front door, these people hung it inside, *behind* the doorposts, so no one could see it. Yet in spite of these difficulties and others, we have no difficulty understanding the description of a society that had abandoned the Lord. They were "a brood of rebels" and "the offspring of liars," burning in lust. They did not care for the Lord and the blessings he provided through his Servant. God tells us all this so we can understand why he sent judgment upon them.

> ⁹ **You went to Molech with olive oil**
> **and increased your perfumes.**
> **You sent your ambassadors far away;**

you descended to the grave itself!
¹⁰ You were wearied by all your ways,
but you would not say, 'It is hopeless.'
You found renewal of your strength,
and so you did not faint.

¹¹ "Whom have you so dreaded and feared
that you have been false to me,
and have neither remembered me
nor pondered this in your hearts?
Is it not because I have long been silent
that you do not fear me?
¹² I will expose your righteousness and your works,
and they will not benefit you.
¹³ When you cry out for help,
let your collection of idols save you!
The wind will carry all of them off,
a mere breath will blow them away.
But the man who makes me his refuge
will inherit the land
and possess my holy mountain."

The description continues, and so do the textual difficulties. Molech was the god of the Ammonites, Israel's neighbor across the Jordan, a god who was worshiped with human sacrifice. But the word the NIV translates as "Molech" can also be translated as "the king." This author prefers to translate it as "king" here because the context directs us away from the religions practices of the unfaithful people to their political practices. Instead of depending on the Lord for help and protection, they had sent ambassadors to whatever king would offer them help. Ahaz sent envoys to Tiglath-Pileser (2 Kings 16; 2 Chronicles 28; Isaiah 7). When God had told Ahaz and his people to depend upon him for help, they had turned away and sought alliances with foreign powers. They had so utterly abandoned the Lord that they would go to great lengths to find help, even "descend[ing] to the grave itself." But they refused to turn to the Lord.

Verse 10 deserves comment. These people had rejected the Lord and all his blessings and chosen a direction contrary to the Lord. The human heart by nature remains so perverse that it prefers any path rather than to follow the Lord's. The inclination of the human heart is evil (Genesis 8:21) and resists the Lord and rebels against his way. Without the change worked by God's grace, humans remain addicted to anything that is contrary to the Lord. But the sinful human path is difficult. Consider the effort it took to create idols. Consider the cost of sacrificing one's own children. Consider the efforts of those who attempt to appease God by their religious effort. This situation has not changed since the days of Isaiah. People weary themselves by their false religious practices. Yet in spite of the effort, the sinful human heart will not admit that such things are hopeless. Instead, humans find some satisfaction in trying to appease God by their great efforts. They grow proud of their achievements and conclude that God must be pleased with such great sacrifice and so much effort. Such thinking deludes so many and characterizes all the activity of humanity that is contrary to the Lord's path.

While all this continued, God remained silent. That silence in itself became a judgment. God allowed them to grow bold in their opposition to him. He remained silent so that the measure of their rebellion could be complete. These people have moved past the rebuke of the Lord. When he rebuked them, they did not listen. Instead, they persisted in their unbelief. So God abandoned them to their own imaginations. When no one corrects or disciplines sin, it grows. Without God's corrective discipline, rebellion against God only becomes stronger and more arrogant. No one is more difficult to correct or change than the one who has escaped punishment again and again. Such a person grows bolder, harder, and more stubborn with each passing disobedience. These people have not pondered the Lord because he has abandoned them to their own sins. The Lord remained silent, and sin grew.

This section announces the coming judgment. And it will come. When it does, nothing can help those who rebel against the Lord and follow their own paths. Whatever such rebellious sinners consider to be righteous and whatever they think deserves to be noticed by God will provide no benefit. Deliverance always comes by grace, freely given by God, not as a reward for works. These people have decided that deliverance must be earned. They work to earn it and worship their own gods to secure it. But neither the works they have performed nor the idols they have collected will offer them help in the face of God's judgment. Isaiah has often told his readers how useless and futile it is to trust other gods (44:6-20, for example). Here God says that "a mere breath will blow them away." The judgment approaches. Since these people have turned away from the Lord, they are without excuse and without help.

This section concludes with a word of comfort to the faithful. After all that the Lord threatens upon the rebellious, he encourages his faithful: "But the man who makes me his refuge will . . . possess my holy mountain." This section has been filled with judgment upon the unrighteous, but it concludes with a word of comfort. The next section will be filled with comfort for the righteous, but will conclude with a word of warning to the wicked.

The Lord will heal the contrite

14And it will be said:

"Build up, build up, prepare the road!

Remove the obstacles out of the way of my people."
¹⁵ **For this is what the high and lofty One says—**
   he who lives forever, whose name is holy:
 "I live in a high and holy place,
   but also with him who is contrite and lowly in spirit,
 to revive the spirit of the lowly
   and to revive the heart of the contrite.
¹⁶ **I will not accuse forever,**
   nor will I always be angry,
 for then the spirit of man would grow faint before me—
   the breath of man that I have created.
¹⁷ **I was enraged by his sinful greed;**
   I punished him, and hid my face in anger,
   yet he kept on in his willful ways.
¹⁸ **I have seen his ways, but I will heal him;**
   I will guide him and restore comfort to him,
¹⁹   **creating praise on the lips of the mourners in Israel.**
 Peace, peace, to those far and near,"
   says the LORD. "And I will heal them."

The faithful among the readers of Isaiah's prophecy read the condemnations and warnings with fearful hearts. But God wanted to encourage his faithful who lived in the midst of such perversion and wickedness. He desired to call others to repentance so that they may turn from their evil paths and embrace the gift of forgiveness won by the Servant. The Lord intends this section for the faithful and for those who will yet be called to repentance. God always remains more interested in turning the sinner to repentance than in bringing judgment upon the unrepentant.

The speaker of this invitation is none other than the Lord. He identifies himself as the "high and lofty One." He is far above all the created world. He lives forever and his name is holy. In other places in Isaiah's prophecy, the Lord has identified himself as the Holy One of Israel. He is perfect in every way, without sin and defect. But he is more than that. He is separate from all the created universe—high above all we see and perceive with our human senses and far beyond what our intellects can comprehend. He is holy and lives "in a high and holy place." We might expect such from the great God of the universe. Ordinarily we would not expect him to be concerned with what happens here on this little planet we call earth. Nor would we expect such a high and holy God to be concerned with human beings, who live a mere 70 or 80 years (Psalm 90:10).

But God, the high and lofty One, does what we would not expect. He chooses to live with the contrite and lowly. He loves his creatures more deeply than we can imagine. Isaiah announced that God would dwell with his people when the child of the virgin, Immanuel, was born (7:14; 9:6,7). He did not leave his people without hope and without help. Isaiah also promised that this child would be the Servant of the Lord who would suffer and die for the sins of the world (chapter 53). God did not leave humanity alone to its own destruction. He intervened.

All that God did to dwell with his people in Christ becomes a pledge of another dwelling with them. He comes to the lowly and contrite with grace and blessing. Remember Zacchaeus. Jesus called him to come down from the sycamore tree and then dwelt with him. Jesus brought forgiveness and joy. Even if he does not sit in our homes as he once did, he comes to all the contrite and lowly with the same forgiveness and joy. He encourages us all to welcome him into our hearts and lives. "Here I am! I stand at the door and knock. If anyone hears my voice and opens the door, I will come in and eat with him, and he with me" (Revelation 3:20).

His purpose in coming to live with the contrite and lowly is to revive them. Like Zacchaeus, the contrite and lowly carry a heavy burden of guilt. The law condemns all humanity, for not one human being does what is right. "All have sinned and fall short of the glory of God" (Romans 3:23). If God should deal with us as we deserve, we could anticipate only judgment and condemnation. But God deals with us in a way we do not deserve. Because of Jesus Christ, the Servant of the Lord, God has justified us, that is, he has declared us right and holy in his sight. We are forgiven. We are revived and encouraged when we know God has forgiven us because of Jesus.

This does not mean that the Lord simply excuses the sins of the contrite and does not excuse the sins of the unrepentant. He is "enraged" (verse 17) by the sins of all people. They must all be punished. Every last sin must be punished. God punished the sins of all people when his Servant, Jesus, substituted himself for all humanity and suffered the punishment deserved by the whole world. That vicarious punishment and death heals the guilt of human sin. Those who believe it receive the healing. They are the contrite and lowly who know their sins and by the power of God's grace turn toward him in faith. The proud, rebellious, and ungodly sense no need for forgiveness. They have turned away from the Lord. God does not dwell with them. Instead, he chooses to dwell with the lowly believers.

To the lowly believers, God will restore comfort. How? He will cause the lips of his faithful to speak the gospel. They will speak of peace, the peace that surpasses human understanding. Such a peace exists between this high and holy God, who is rightly angry at sin and all those who sin. Because of Christ, God's peace rests in his forgiveness. God is no longer angry with the faithful who trust in the promises of God concerning forgiveness. He is dismayed that so many refuse to believe. Yet he continues to proclaim peace to all those far and near. He promises to heal them. Those who continue to refuse his invitation and fail to turn to the Lord in faith can expect no forgiveness but only the judgment they deserve. They have refused the healing peace that God freely offers.

> ²⁰ **But the wicked are like the tossing sea,**
> **which cannot rest,**
> **whose waves cast up mire and mud.**
> ²¹ **"There is no peace," says my God, "for the wicked."**

Saint Augustine paraphrased this passage when he wrote, "Our hearts find no peace until they rest in you." (*Confessions* I:1, New York: Penguin Books, page 21). The wicked are as restless as the sea. Stand at the seashore any time of the day or night, and you can hear the rhythmic rush of the waves. The sea never rests. Even on a calm day it moves. For the wicked who do not know the forgiveness of Christ, there is no rest. What's worse, the turmoil and unrest of their lives stirs up "mire and mud." Nothing of peace. Nothing of beauty. Nothing of consolation. Isaiah's text presents a vivid and classic picture, even if the wicked do not understand it to be so. There simply is no peace for the wicked.

Verse 21 marks the end of a major section of the prophecy of Isaiah. A similar passage appeared at the end of the previous major section (48:22), and it signals the end of another section here. Before we move on to the last section of Isaiah, let's review the highlights of this section.

- The section begins (chapter 49) with the second of the four Servant passages. Isaiah introduced this special Servant in chapter 42 and distinguished him from other servants, including Cyrus. The Servant passage at the beginning of chapter 49 tells us that the Lord chose this Great Servant and, through him, he would display his splendor.

- Chapter 50 contains the third of the Servant passages. This time God reveals that the Servant will be obedient to his mission. He will suffer, giving his back to be beaten. Yet the Servant will triumph.

- The fourth of the Servant passages, in chapter 53, stands as the most important passage of this section. The passage actually begins at 52:13. The Servant of the Lord will be stricken, smitten, and afflicted for the sins of the people. He will die in order to pay for the sins of the people, and the Lord will be satisfied with his sacrifice. This passage marks the central truth of the second half of Isaiah and of the entire Scriptures.

- Because of the work of the Servant, God promises future glory to his people.

- God cannot keep this great accomplishment a secret. He invites "all you who are thirsty" to come and receive his blessings (55:1). What God offers cannot be bought because they are free gifts of his grace.

- The blessings accomplished by the Servant, Jesus Christ, are not just for the Jews. They are for all people. God invites foreigners and eunuchs—those who would normally be excluded—to come and enjoy the fruits of the Servant's work.

- Those who do not believe and who remain rebellious can expect no peace and no forgiveness. Since they have rejected the work of the Servant, judgment will come upon them.

The Lord promises his new Zion eternal glory

Rejoice in the sincere worship of the Lord

58 "Shout it aloud, do not hold back.
       Raise your voice like a trumpet.
Declare to my people their rebellion
    and to the house of Jacob their sins.
² For day after day they seek me out;
    they seem eager to know my ways,
as if they were a nation that does what is right
    and has not forsaken the commands of its God.
They ask me for just decisions
    and seem eager for God to come near them.
³ 'Why have we fasted,' they say,
    'and you have not seen it?
Why have we humbled ourselves,
    and you have not noticed?'

This last major section (chapters 58–66) of the book of Isaiah, God's prophet, begins with a command. All three major sections of this second part begin with a command. Chapter 40 began the first section (chapters 40–48) with "Comfort, comfort my people." The second section (chapters 49–57) began, "Listen to me, you islands; hear this, you distant nations." This section begins with a command to spread the message: "Shout it aloud, do not hold back." In each section, the Lord has a message that people need to hear. The first two sections began with good news of God's promised deliverance and grace. But this last section begins with a message of rebuke, not a message of comfort or deliverance. The Lord commands his prophet to "declare to my people their rebellion." With these words, the Lord forcefully calls his people to repentance.

What have they done to warrant such words of rebuke? The prophet Isaiah had been called to warn of the coming judgment upon the people of Judah for their unbelief, idolatry, and rebellion. At the same time, God commissioned Isaiah to announce the most comforting news that Judah and the world could ever hope to hear. Immanuel would come, born of a virgin and ruling on David's throne (7:14; 9:6,7). Isaiah explained the comfort of this great news when he announced that Immanuel would also be the Servant of the Lord (42:1-9; 49:1-7; 50:4-9; 52:13–53:12). This Servant would accomplish deliverance from sin and death. He would be stricken, smitten, and afflicted and would die for the sins of the people. The iniquity of all the world would be laid upon him, and by his suffering all the world would be healed. All this is a gracious explanation of 43:25, "I, even I, am the one who blots out your transgressions, for my own sake, and remembers your sins no more."

Most of those at the time of Isaiah failed to understand the gracious redemption God promised for his people and all the world. But even worse, they perverted God's message of deliverance. In their own religious practices, including their fasting, they had changed God's gracious gift into a deliverance earned by their own good behavior.

The Lord himself speaks as the chapter begins. He commands a loud and unrestrained shout "like a trumpet" to proclaim the rebellion of his people. Notice how Isaiah described this rebellion. On the one hand, it seemed as if the people were eager to know the ways of the Lord. From all outward appearances, they were a righteous nation "eager to know [the LORD's] ways." No doubt that meant that they observed the worship regulations, including fasting, outlined in the Law of Moses, and they observed the Sabbath. But on the other hand, God described them as rebellious and sinful and their worship as unacceptable.

The people asked God for "just decisions" and seemed "eager for God to come near them." They looked for God's deliverance. All this seems to be as God would demand, but something was deeply wrong. What was it? The people say, "Why have we fasted, . . . and you have not seen it? Why have we humbled ourselves, and you have not noticed?" They were expecting God to reward their fasting and humility. These people did not understand the grace of God and the undeserved promises of redemption through the Servant. They trusted in their works to earn the notice of God and his rewards. They perverted and destroyed God's grace. Deliverance, in their thinking, became a reward for their religious fervor.

What was wrong with such a thought? First, it was absolutely arrogant. God is holy, perfect, and separate from everything human—far above all creation. What could any human offer to God to earn his favor and be worthy of his notice? What great human effort could move God? All humanity together cannot offer enough sacrifices or deeds of kindness to move the mind and heart of a holy God. One small and insignificant human cannot offer anything that deserves God's blessing. Grace, and grace alone, remains the only reason God shows compassion and concern for anything human. He decides to do so on his own; he loves not because we love him or do anything righteous. He loves for his own sake. We only receive the great blessings of his undeserved concern for us and his deep love for his creatures. It is arrogance to think that we could do something so good or so great that we would earn his love as due compensation. These people had taken on the attitude of the Pharisee in the temple as he recited the good things he had done to deserve God's notice and blessing (Luke 18:9-14).

In this most important matter, the people had missed the mark; they had sinned. Their devotion to God served only their own desire for deliverance. They served God from selfish motives—hoping to win deliverance.

The attitude of the people was wrong from another perspective too. Their attitude opposed God's clear message. The last Servant passage (52:13–53:12) very clearly proclaimed the vicarious atonement. The Servant suffered for the people. That served as the basis of God's declaration of righteousness, the justification of sinners. Isaiah had written, "After the suffering of his soul, he will see the light of life and be satisfied; by his knowledge my righteous servant will justify many, and he will bear their iniquities" (53:11). Human effort could not earn such blessings, but so many at the time of Isaiah chose to pervert the message, rebel against it, and substitute their own doctrine of blessings earned by human effort. That was and is rebellion against God and a perversion of God's expressed and clear Word. Deliverance from sin and death cannot be earned by human effort; it can only come as a free gift of God to undeserving sinners. These people did not believe the Scriptures; they did not believe what God told them about themselves or about the deliverance from sin and its consequences.

In effect, these people had erected another idol. They worshiped a god different from the LORD, Jehovah, the God of grace. They had created a god who rewarded their fasting and religious fervor with blessings. That concept of god makes God no different than all the gods created by all cultures of all times. In many ancient cultures, when the crops were bad, people believed that their god was angry with them and that they had to appease him or her. When things were good, they imagined that they had done what the god wanted them to do and that the god was rewarding them for their devotion and zeal.

But a subtle and dangerous difference remains between the gross idolatry of the heathen and the concept of God held by these Jews. The heathen nations fashioned statues of wood, stone, or metal and worshiped them. The idolatry of the Jews was more subtle. They believed that God rewarded their efforts. That was the principle of all false religions and all idolatry. Some of the Jews did bow down to worship the idols of the heathen, but others did not bow down to physical idols. Instead, they worshiped a different God than the God of the Scriptures. The God they worshiped rewarded them for their good effort and punished them for their evil. He rewarded their fasting and noticed when they humbled themselves. For them, the God of free and faithful grace had become a god of works. It was as if they had taken the pure gold of grace, made a plaster replica of it, and painted that with a bright color. They no longer saw the God of free and faithful grace. Instead, they worshiped the painted plaster replica, the god who rewards humans with deliverance because of their behavior. They had the notion that they would earn God's love by what they did.

This false concept of God persists in our own age and will persist until the end of time. As sinners, we are infected by pride and arrogance. We believe that what we do matters in the court of God's justice. We want to be noticed, and we want our good deeds to be noticed. Even after we know God's free gift of grace in Christ, we are still influenced by our old sinful nature. We have a tendency to pervert the grace of God and make it into law. So many Christian churches abandon the God of grace and adopt the concept of a god in heaven who rewards human effort. Others concentrate so much on Christian virtues and behavior that they no longer talk of Christ, the one who delivers us from sin, death, and hell. In effect, they hide the gold of grace with the bright paint of human effort. They fall into the same sin and rebellion as these people who wondered why God had not noticed their fasting and humility.

We are all subject to the temptation of exchanging the grace of God for the delusion of works. The Galatians, who were taught by the apostle Paul himself, fell into that trap. The apostle corrected them sharply: "You foolish Galatians! Who has bewitched you? Before your very eyes Jesus Christ was clearly portrayed as crucified. Are you so foolish? After beginning with the Spirit, are you now trying to attain your goal by human effort?" (3:1,3). Deliverance from sin and death by our own efforts entices our sinful human hearts. It flatters the natural human spirit. It sidesteps the harsh demands of God's holy law and avoids the confrontation with the just punishment all sinners deserve from God. Humans find it very difficult to give up the belief that they can earn divine favor through human merit and effort. They gladly hear that deliverance from sin and death can be earned by their own works. Only regular repentance turns us away from our efforts toward God's mercy. Only regular repentance turns our boast about how much we have done for God to the humble plea of the publican, "God, have mercy on me, a sinner" (Luke 18:13).

This section begins with this loud and clear denunciation of salvation by works. God did not build the church upon the doctrine of human effort. Instead, by his grace he built the church upon Christ and his saving work. Isaiah understood this truth very clearly and proclaimed it so eloquently. His own people rebelled against grace and worshiped a god who rewarded human works instead of the

Lord Jehovah, the God of free and faithful grace. Without Christ, no one can find deliverance from sin or death. Every other concept of God hides the gold of God's grace in Christ. Without Christ, religion becomes only idolatry, rebellion, and perversion.

The chapters ahead concentrate on the faithful believers and the gracious glory God has in store for them. Before Isaiah turned his attention to the blessings God reserved for his people, he took time to define God's people. God wants us to know that his people are not those who depend on their own religious practices. Instead, God's people are those who by faith humbly receive the blessings accomplished by the Lord's Servant, Jesus Christ. That's the church—people who believe in Jesus. No substantial difference exists between those who believed in the days of Isaiah and those who believe today. They believed in the Servant who would come; we believe in the Servant who has come.

> "Yet on the day of your fasting, you do as you please
>   and exploit all your workers.
> 4 Your fasting ends in quarreling and strife,
>   and in striking each other with wicked fists.
> You cannot fast as you do today
>   and expect your voice to be heard on high.
> 5 Is this the kind of fast I have chosen,
>   only a day for a man to humble himself?
> Is it only for bowing one's head like a reed
>   and for lying on sackcloth and ashes?
> Is that what you call a fast,
>   a day acceptable to the LORD?

No religious fervor or pious life can earn the blessings only God can give by grace. Every human work, even the most noble and noteworthy, is flawed. When confronted with the harsh demands of God's holy law, the human spirit can only make one of two false choices. Either the soul deflects the harsh demands of God's law and becomes self-righteous, or the soul abandons all hope and turns to despair. God, of course, supplies the only true alternative—Christ has suffered what human sin deserved and achieved forgiveness and deliverance from the consequences of sin. The people described in this section chose the first of the two false choices. They believed that they could do what God demands and God would reward them for their goodness and their devout fasting. But such people did not understand themselves. They did not know that their righteousness was only a sham and hypocritical. God corrected them here.

God demands perfect obedience; no human can comply. The people had taken pride in their fasting, but as devout as their fasting may have appeared, it was not sincere. They still retained the desire to exploit their works. They did as they pleased, not as the Lord demanded. Their fasting ended in quarrels, strife, and brawling. These hearts and lives had not been changed by the worship of the Lord. No compassion, generosity, humility, or love marked their lives. They remained combative, arrogant, selfish, and greedy. Yet they imagined that God would reward them for their religious fasting and devotion.

By nature we are all combative, arrogant, selfish, and greedy. These are fruits of the sinful nature for which the Servant of God suffered and died. God wants to transform human hearts so that they are loving, humble, generous, and kind. That transformation comes only when the Spirit works within and one believes in the God of grace. But sadly, even after we believe, we retain our sinful nature and so often fall into quarrels, strife, and greed. Our transformation will not be complete until we enter the glory of heaven. Here on earth we struggle against the tendencies of our own sinful nature and wrestle sometimes hard and long to do as God desires. When we fail, we turn to God for forgiveness and find in his love and grace the strength to continue the fight against the sin within.

These people rejected God's grace. They abandoned what God had told them about the Servant and were trying instead to earn God's blessings by their fasting. That's impossible. So God revealed their hypocrisy. Without Christ, God accepts no human effort (Hebrews 11:6), no matter how good it appears. With Christ, human effort comes to the favorable attention of God, who forgives the failings and sins. God sees the blood of his own Son instead of the stain of the believer's sin. Then, by virtue of his love for sinners in Christ, God empowers his faithful to persist in their struggle against sin and in their efforts to live as he desires. These people had no concept of God's grace in the Servant, Christ.

> ⁶ **"Is not this the kind of fasting I have chosen:**
> **to loose the chains of injustice**
> **and untie the cords of the yoke,**
> **to set the oppressed free**
> **and break every yoke?**
> ⁷ **Is it not to share your food with the hungry**
> **and to provide the poor wanderer with shelter—**
> **when you see the naked, to clothe him,**
> **and not to turn away from your own flesh and blood?**

The Lord exposed the hypocrisy of those who refused his grace and sought to earn his blessings by their religious effort. Next the Lord turned to provide a positive example of what he wanted from his people. They were not to be hypocrites but sincere believers who showed their faith by their actions. The writer to the Hebrews wrote, "Without faith it is impossible to please God" (11:6). Those who trust in the Lord Jehovah recognize the wonderful blessings they have received from his gracious hand. They have no illusions about earning God's blessings by their behavior, even if their efforts correspond to the description in these verses. They are so grateful for the undeserved gifts of God that they desire to show their gratitude by their activity.

Consider the sheep on the right hand of the Lord of glory (Matthew 25:31-46). They wondered when they had ever done the things that the glorious King noticed in their behavior (25:37-39). Certainly they did not think that their behavior deserved the notice of God. How different they are from those in this chapter who wondered why God did not notice their fasting. Those on the right in the Savior's description of the final judgment were righteous and holy because God declared them to be so; he justified them. Their behavior only served as evidence that they believed, that they were forgiven for their failures, and that they had gratefully struggled to live as the Lord wanted. Such behavior is never enough to earn deliverance. Even Isaiah would later write, "All our righteous acts are like filthy rags" (64:6). At the same time, religious zeal and pious living are the natural result of faith in the grace of God. Believers who know that they have forgiveness, life, and salvation only through the grace of God desire to thank God by their actions. Believers joyfully dedicate themselves to God as living sacrifices (Romans 12:1).

> [8] **Then your light will break forth like the dawn,**
> **and your healing will quickly appear;**
> **then your righteousness will go before you,**
> **and the glory of the LORD will be your rear guard.**
> [9] **Then you will call, and the LORD will answer;**
> **you will cry for help, and he will say: Here am I.**
>
> **"If you do away with the yoke of oppression,**
> **with the pointing finger and malicious talk,**

The Lord of grace promises wonderful blessings to those who trust in him and who accept the forgiveness, life, and salvation he provides through the Servant. Those who believe and trust in the promises of forgiveness in Christ are washed white and clean of their sins (1:18), and they are new creations of God's grace (2 Corinthians 5:17). They live by the Spirit, who gives them power to do as God desires. These are the church of God—believers in Christ, the Servant. The chapters that follow reveal the wonderful blessings God provides for them. Here begins that wonderful catalog of blessings.

Verse 8 begins with "Then," that is, when true sincere faith and trust in God's grace capture the hearts of the sinners and motivate them to do what God described in verses 6 and 7. Then a special relationship exists between God and his believers. When faith enters our hearts and we understand the word of reconciliation, we become God's ambassadors (2 Corinthians 5:20). The light within the hearts of such believers shines. So Jesus encourages his faithful, "You are the light of world. . . . Let your light shine before men, that they may see your good deeds and praise your Father in heaven" (Matthew 5:14,16). As ambassadors of the Lord who reconciles sinners by his Servant, Christ, believers have the gospel, the word of reconciliation, the only hope for spiritual health. They proclaim it wherever they go.

As believers trust in Christ, proclaim the gospel, and live godly lives, the Lord goes with them. The righteousness of God, which has been imparted to the faithful by faith, directs their paths. While the righteousness of the people goes before, the glory of the Lord follows. God's faithful believers are surrounded by the care and concern of the Lord. The prophet pictures an army or caravan on the move. Just as God cared for his people in the wilderness after he delivered them from Egypt, so the Lord will care for his faithful because he has delivered them from sin and death. They are on the march, saints of God, living in the wilderness of this world, on their way to eternal glory. As they journey, God surrounds them with pledges of his deep and abiding love—righteousness and glory.

As God's saints move through life, they pray. The Lord encourages them to call upon him in their needs (Psalm 50:15; 91:15), and he promises to hear them. A special relationship exists between the Lord and his believers. He always remains interested in what troubles them and encourages his faithful to bring their troubles to him. He promises to be present at every difficult turn in the road with his help. In these verses, he pledges to say to his people in their needs, "Here am I." What a comfort for believers! We can cast our cares upon him, and he will listen. (See such New Testament promises as Matthew 7:7; Hebrews 4:14-16; and 1 Peter 5:7).

> [10] **and if you spend yourselves in behalf of the hungry**
> **and satisfy the needs of the oppressed,**
> **then your light will rise in the darkness,**
> **and your night will become like the noonday.**

Is the Lord here suggesting that his blessings are the reward for human effort after all? The Lord still speaks, "If you do . . . then your light will rise in the darkness." The verses seem to suggest that God grants blessings on the basis of human effort. But God is still a God of grace and will always be a God of grace and not a God of works. The Lord speaks here to his believers, those who already trust in the redemption achieved by the Servant. If these believers spend their efforts on behalf of the hungry and oppressed, they let their light shine in the world. Kindness and compassion are great lights in the darkness of a self-centered, greedy, and cold world. The passage only describes the result of godly behavior and does not make God's blessings dependent upon human effort. These verses provide an encouragement for God's people to produce fruits of the Spirit (Galatians 5:22-26).

> ¹¹ **The Lᴏʀᴅ will guide you always;**
> **he will satisfy your needs in a sun-scorched land**
> **and will strengthen your frame.**
> **You will be like a well-watered garden,**
> **like a spring whose waters never fail.**
> ¹² **Your people will rebuild the ancient ruins**
> **and will raise up the age-old foundations;**
> **you will be called Repairer of Broken Walls,**
> **Restorer of Streets with Dwellings.**

More promises to the faithful! How could anyone do enough to earn these promises from the Lord Jehovah? What could the people of Isaiah's day do to deserve the guidance of the Lord? What can anyone do to earn such a blessing? God guides those who have humbly accepted his redemption. While the rest of the world wants to create a god that rewards human effort, believers understand God's grace. Believers understand the deep love of God. They know that he loved them so deeply and profoundly that he sacrificed his own Son as an atonement for the sins of the world. The Lord will guide those believers and satisfy them with everything they need.

In these two verses, the Lord uses two pictures to describe his people and to promise them his blessings. First, God's people will be like *an oasis* kept alive and green by a never-ending spring. That picture is especially beautiful for God's Old Testament people living in Palestine, a dry and arid place. Water is essential to human life.

Wherever rainfall is limited, rivers and streams are important. God promises to supply his people with what is essential to their lives. The second picture is that of *a rebuilding*. God's people will rebuild what had been destroyed. This is a promise of the return of God's people from captivity. What the Babylonian army broke down and destroyed will be rebuilt by those who return. The picture promises that God's people would reestablish their land and live in the homes they longed for during the years of captivity.

> [13] **"If you keep your feet from breaking the Sabbath**
> **and from doing as you please on my holy day,**
> **if you call the Sabbath a delight**
> **and the LORD's holy day honorable,**
> **and if you honor it by not going your own way**
> **and not doing as you please or speaking idle words,**
> [14] **then you will find your joy in the LORD,**
> **and I will cause you to ride on the heights of the land**
> **and to feast on the inheritance of your father Jacob."**
> **The mouth of the LORD has spoken.**

We note here again that God says, "If you [do] . . . I will . . ." But God does not retract his grace. The Lord is speaking here to his faithful who have received the blessings of his grace. He speaks to them in much the same way that he spoke to his people after the Exodus. After God had graciously delivered his people from the bondage of Egypt and had cared for them on their journey to Mount Sinai, he issued his commands. When they were assembled before Mount Sinai, God reminded them of his gracious deliverance, "I am the LORD your God, who brought you out of Egypt, out of the land of slavery" (Exodus 20:2). Because they knew God's gracious deliverance, God provided guidance for their daily lives. He issued the Ten Commandments. They could not earn the deliverance from Egypt by their behavior; that had already been given to them. So here God speaks to those who already know that the Servant was "crushed for [their] iniquities" (Isaiah 53:5). They could not deserve that redemption from sin any more than the Israelites at Sinai could have earned the exodus. Because they knew the grace of God and the deliverance it offered, God gives them guidance and direction.

Why does the Lord choose to mention the Sabbath law here? God set aside the Sabbath as a day of rest, but more important, he set it aside as a day of worship. On that day God's people gathered together to listen to the Scriptures. They heard the wonderful promises that God recorded in the Old Testament Scriptures. On that day God's people nurtured their relationship with the Lord Jehovah, the God of grace. As they gathered together and heard the words of God, the Lord promised to bless them. Because God promised to work in the human heart through the gospel, great blessings come to those who hear and read the Scripture and gather to worship the Lord together. Here God promises that they will "find [their] joy in the LORD, and I will cause [them] to ride on the heights of the land." Through their worship, God would keep them faithful to his promises. He promised to touch their hearts by his grace as they listened to the gospel. Such blessings God promises to all who faithfully use his Word and worship him.

This promise can be understood by thinking of the relationship between any two people. Two people maintain a close relationship when they give each other time and attention. Relationships fragment when one party neglects the other. Marriages suffer when spouses neglect each other and so does every other relationship. God desires to continue in the warm and loving relationship he has with his faithful people. He promises never to abandon the relationship, but God also knows that some of his people will take the relationship for granted and will be tempted to neglect it. God warns them not to do "as you please." Instead, the Lord of grace encourages his people to set aside time for worship so that they might renew their relationship with him. When and if they failed to give God regular time, and when and if they failed to listen to the gracious words of God, they stood in danger of losing all his blessings. Therefore, God encourages them. "Give me regular time," he says. "Seize opportunities to hear my Word. In other words, observe the Sabbath and I will continue to bless you."

Isaiah mentions the Sabbath for another reason too. The Lord told Moses:

> Say to the Israelites, "You must observe my Sabbaths. This will be a sign between me and you for the generations to come, so you may know that I am the LORD, who makes you holy. The Israelites are to observe the Sabbath, celebrating it for the generations to come as a lasting covenant. It will be a sign between me and the Israelites forever, for in six days the LORD made the heavens and the earth, and on the seventh day he abstained from work and rested." (Exodus 31:13,16,17)

When the Israelites rested on the Sabbath, they confessed that they knew the Lord Jehovah. They rested from all their work and partook of the rest and refreshment that God himself observed at the creation of the world. The Sabbath pointed to the greater rest of the gospel (Hebrews 4:1-11). By faith in the gospel, believers rest from the arduous tasks of trying to earn God's favor. They receive peace and rest in the forgiveness of their sins through Jesus. When they observed the Sabbath, they confessed faith in the God of free and faithful grace. They were his and their actions gave testimony to their faith.

At the conclusion of the chapter, Isaiah adds his familiar emphatic period: "The mouth of the LORD has spoken." Therefore, the message stands true and reliable. This message does not come from any human mind or mouth but from the Lord himself.

The Lord will come to save his people

59 Surely the arm of the LORD is not too short to save,
nor his ear too dull to hear.

In this life the promises of God often seem to lie just beyond the reach of his people. The previous chapter ended with the great promise that God would make his people "ride on the heights of the land." In their day-to-day lives, such a promise appeared as either an exaggeration, a vain dream, or a faraway reality to be fulfilled at some distant future time. For God's people, fulfillment of his promises waits just beyond the horizon of human vision, experience, and knowledge. Yet one reaction to God's promises questions whether God would ever do as he promised and complains about his apparent delay in providing help. Another reaction abandons the promises of God and trusts in human efforts to gain security, peace, and deliverance.

King Ahaz had chosen the second approach when he depended on the armies of Assyria to deliver Jerusalem from his enemies (Isaiah 7; 2 Chronicles 28). Ahaz concluded that the Lord could not save Jerusalem and that deliverance required that he make an alliance with Assyria. Later, others in Jerusalem at the time of Isaiah depended upon an alliance with Egypt to save them from the Assyrians (Isaiah 30; 36:3-8). The Lord had demonstrated his power to deliver his people. In spite of King Ahaz, the Lord did rescue him and his people from their enemies. Certainly the policy of Ahaz did not bring about any real deliverance. The Assyrians proved to be more of an oppressor than a deliverer. They brought trouble instead of deliverance (2 Chronicles 28:16-25). Then later during the reign of Hezekiah, the son and successor of King Ahaz, the Lord destroyed the proud Assyrian army at the very gates of Jerusalem (2 Chronicles 32:1-23; Isaiah 37:36,37). The Lord's arm was not as short as so many had thought. The Lord could indeed deliver.

After Assyria faded as a regional power in the Middle East and Babylon took her place, God's people again wondered about the promises of God. Isaiah foretold the captivity of God's people in Babylon. In their captivity, they wondered about the promises God had given for redemption and deliverance. They were captives and powerless. The Lord's deliverance appeared to be nowhere in sight except in the words of the prophets. No doubt some among God's people complained that the Lord's promises seemed to be only empty words—a dream that existed on the edge of reality. But Isaiah reminded God's people that the Lord was not too weak to save. He only delayed his deliverance until the appropriate time. Just as God once heard the prayers of his people when they were slaves in Egypt, he would hear the anguish of his people in the future.

The lesson remains valuable for God's people of all times. The Lord has given us wonderful promises of triumph over death and eternal glory in his presence. These lie in the future, beyond our vision and experience. Even our forgiveness of sins before the throne of God rests on promises we have not seen and cannot test with empirical tools. We may wonder if God really means what he says. When we experience pain, misery, and loss, we confront the same choices people have always faced. Do we believe what God says or take matters into our own hands? Do we believe God means what he says, even though he appears unable or unwilling to help us? Isaiah reminded the people of his day, and us too, that the Lord will indeed save his people and will listen to their cries for help and deliverance.

Even if God had appeared to abandon his people in their Babylonian captivity, nevertheless he had not lost his power to save. He had promised that a remnant would return. In addition, he had promised very clearly in the previous chapters that his Servant would come and would redeem his people. Those promises, for the people of Isaiah's day, were off in the distant future. Israel must wait for the release from captivity and the Servant's coming. As they waited they were to trust in the Lord's power to fulfill his promises.

> **² But your iniquities have separated
>   you from your God;
> your sins have hidden his face from you,
>   so that he will not hear.**

In the previous chapter, God told his people that the promise of this future deliverance could not be earned by their fasting. Their fasting may have been outwardly appropriate, but it was still imperfect and seriously flawed. It could not earn the deliverance of God. It was and still is arrogant for anyone to think that human effort—even if done in compliance with God's law—can achieve the notice and attention of God. God acts by grace, not because humans deserve his promises or his deliverance. It is not only arrogant to think that human behavior can earn the blessing of God; it is also foolish. Human beings need to understand the depth of their own sinful nature. The behavior of God's people was not just imperfect but also perverse and evil.

Sin separates humans from God. He is holy, perfect, and separate from all imperfection. Humans are sinful, imperfect, and profane. This was true for Adam and Eve after their disobedience. It was true for Abraham. It was as true for Isaiah and the people of his day as it is for us. On one level, this verse and those that follow apply to the people of Isaiah's day. But the apostle Paul stretches these words beyond that narrow historical situation. In Romans chapter 3, Paul convicts Jews and Gentiles of sin and quotes verses 7 and 8 of this chapter from Isaiah as proof (see Romans 3:9-24). All have sinned. The sinful nature of every human separates him or her from God. A great barrier stands between God and humanity. That barrier exists because of "your iniquities" and "your sins."

In this section, God's prophet preaches the law in all its severity. The reason God did not hear the call of his people was because of their sin. As we read this chapter, we will gain a clear picture of sin. Each word broadens our thinking about sin. Isaiah used two words here. The word he used for "iniquities" views sin as crooked behavior or perversion. The word includes the deed and its consequences. As a plural, it indicates the multitude of deeds that are in violation of God's law. The NIV translates the second word as "sins." This word considers sin as an attitude or action that misses

God's mark. The plural again emphasizes the great number of actions that miss the mark of God's demands. Both words imply that God, the Creator, has established an absolute standard for the behavior of his creatures. He has revealed that standard as his law, and he requires perfect obedience. Anything less than that is sin. The verses that follow will explain the depth of human sin.

> ³ **For your hands are stained with blood,**
>> **your fingers with guilt.**
> **Your lips have spoken lies,**
>> **and your tongue mutters wicked things.**
> ⁴ **No one calls for justice;**
>> **no one pleads his case with integrity.**
> **They rely on empty arguments and speak lies;**
>> **they conceive trouble and give birth to evil.**

In these verses, Isaiah explored the way sin corrupts human behavior. Sin sets one against God and against other humans. Isaiah showed the evidence. Sin has no respect for human life. Human hands are stained with blood as wars, abortion, and violence all testify. Sin so perverts the human heart and mind that it corrupts speech. Instead of speaking truth, humans lie. Dictionaries regularly define *lies* as "falsehoods without a basis in fact"; they are ideas and concepts founded on nothing but human imagination. Isaiah added more. Instead of speaking what God wants and what contributes to the good of others, the tongue also speaks "wicked things." This term carries the meaning of injustice, a deed contrary to what is right and contrary to God's character and will.

Human sin also subverts the legal system. Justice and integrity disappear. In their places come empty arguments, lies, trouble, and evil. The word Isaiah used for "empty arguments" here is the same word that God used to describe the universe on the first day of creation. Then the earth was empty, or void. Israel's legal system had been reduced to an empty exercise that had no more sense than chaos. God chose a different word for "lies" in verse 4 than the one he used in verse 3. In verse 4, the word means "vanity" and "emptiness" and refers to anything that disappoints the hope promised. As the description continued, Isaiah said that sinners conceive trouble and give birth to evil. The trouble that sinful humans conceive produces only misery, toil, and labor. The evil to which they give birth results in nothing but the painful aftermath of sin. Such evil achieves nothing but sorrow, idolatry, wickedness, and emptiness.

> **⁵ They hatch the eggs of vipers**
> **and spin a spider's web.**
> **Whoever eats their eggs will die,**
> **and when one is broken, an adder is hatched.**
> **⁶ Their cobwebs are useless for clothing;**
> **they cannot cover themselves with what they make.**
> **Their deeds are evil deeds,**
> **and acts of violence are in their hands.**
> **⁷ Their feet rush into sin;**
> **they are swift to shed innocent blood.**
> **Their thoughts are evil thoughts;**
> **ruin and destruction mark their ways.**
> **⁸ The way of peace they do not know;**
> **there is no justice in their paths.**
> **They have turned them into crooked roads;**
> **no one who walks in them will know peace.**

When God looked at the world before the flood, he noted "how great man's wickedness on the earth had become, and that every inclination of the thoughts of his heart was only evil all the time" (Genesis 6:5). The description in these verses confirms that observation. From the sinful human heart comes vipers, cobwebs, violence, and evil. Not one good thing flows from the sinful human heart. Jesus also observed, "Out of the heart come evil thoughts, murder, adultery, sexual immorality, theft, false testimony, slander" (Matthew 15:19). When Paul marshals his arguments to convict all the world of sin, he quotes verses 7 and 8 (see Romans 3:16,17). Sin perverts every aspect of human life.

Verse 7 uses still another word for sin. This word does not mean evil in a general sense but evil that causes injury. This evil represents the opposite of good and the opposite of peace. How different all this is from what God wants for the people of the world! Ruin, destruction, and the absence of peace and justice mark sin's way.

On the other hand, peace and justice mark God's way. Both *peace* and *justice* also have special meanings. The Hebrews did not limit peace to just the absence of war and the quiet that comes at the end of conflict. This peace is a perfect and full sense of well-being that comes from deliverance. Such peace comes only through the Redeemer. Jesus said: "Peace I leave with you; my peace I give you. I do not give to you as the world gives. Do not let your hearts be troubled and do not be afraid" (John 14:27). Isaiah had said that there would be no peace for the wicked (48:22; 57:21). The thought reappears here. The wicked do not know "the way of peace."

In addition, justice does not mark the path of the wicked. *Justice* here means more than the equal and fair application of the law. It denotes the judgment that God pronounces and that conveys freedom, life, and eternal happiness. Such judgment comes because God declares the world righteous through the perfect life and sacrificial death of his Servant, Jesus Christ. One cannot find such peace or judgment anywhere but in Christ. Within the human heart, only sin reigns by nature; therefore, the human heart cannot produce peace or justice. The sin within the human heart perverts every person. Paul concluded, "There is no difference, for all have sinned and fall short of the glory of God" (Romans 3:22,23).

> ⁹ **So justice is far from us,**
> **and righteousness does not reach us.**
> **We look for light, but all is darkness;**
> **for brightness, but we walk in deep shadows.**
> ¹⁰ **Like the blind we grope along the wall,**
> **feeling our way like men without eyes.**
> **At midday we stumble as if it were twilight;**
> **among the strong, we are like the dead.**
> ¹¹ **We all growl like bears;**
> **we moan mournfully like doves.**
> **We look for justice, but find none;**
> **for deliverance, but it is far away.**
>
> ¹² **For our offenses are many in your sight,**
> **and our sins testify against us.**
> **Our offenses are ever with us,**
> **and we acknowledge our iniquities:**
> ¹³ **rebellion and treachery against the LORD,**
> **turning our backs on our God,**
> **fomenting oppression and revolt,**
> **uttering lies our hearts have conceived.**
> ¹⁴ **So justice is driven back,**
> **and righteousness stands at a distance;**
> **truth has stumbled in the streets,**
> **honesty cannot enter.**
> ¹⁵ **Truth is nowhere to be found,**
> **and whoever shuns evil becomes a prey.**

Up until these verses, all the descriptions for sin were of the sins of others: "*Their* deeds are evil deeds. . . . *Their* thoughts are evil thoughts" (verses 6,7). But we do not classify Isaiah as a hypocrite or a Pharisee. He knew that sin lurked within his own human heart too. So he included himself among those convicted of sins: "So justice is far from *us,* and righteousness does not reach *us.*" Sin separates humans from God. The words *justice* and *righteousness* both refer to the deliverance, rescue, or salvation from the consequences of sin. Because of sin, deliverance becomes impossible from the human side of the barrier that exists between God and humanity. Nothing any human can do will result in any real deliverance from sin, any victory over death, or any rescue from the eternal consequences of sin.

Sin is also spiritual blindness. In a vivid picture, Isaiah described his spiritual condition by nature as a blind man groping with his hands for a doorway through a wall. He can see nothing and must feel his way. Such futile effort will result in no deliverance. Even in the brightest light, no one can find deliverance by his or her own effort. Instead, humans stumble about in the dark, yearning for deliverance, even growling like hungry bears, but they find no deliverance. The more we grope in our sin for deliverance, the farther away from God we wander and the deeper we descend into our misery. Deeper and deeper we blindly fall into sin and rebellion against God. We cannot find deliverance. Such deliverance comes down only from God to earth. Human effort not only cannot achieve deliverance; it cannot even find it. Deliverance remains a gift of grace from above.

Verse 12 uses three words for sin that summarize what we have learned about sin. The NIV translates the first word as "offenses." Isaiah used this word twice in the verse, and our translation uses *offenses* both times. It means rebellion against God's law and covenant. Verse 13 pictures sin as a breach in our relationship with God. Human beings commit many such sins of rebellion against God. We choose to obey the sin within and reject the will of God. The second word is translated as "sins." This word we have encountered before in the chapter (verse 2). The word identifies sin as missing the mark or falling short of the standard God has set for us. The third word is translated as "iniquities." We have seen this word in this chapter, once translated as "iniquities" (verse 2) and once as "evil" (verse 4). The word means "crooked behavior" and includes the burden of guilt that comes as a consequence of sin. In each case, the word identifies sin as a deviation from God's standard, either a rebellion, a failure, or a perversion.

Summary of words for sin in Isaiah chapter 59

Translation	Reference	Definition
iniquities	verses 2,12	an act that incurs guilt, crooked behavior, perversion
sins	verses 2,12	miss the mark, failure to live up to God's absolute standard
evil	verses 4,6	empty, vanity, falsehood, fraud
sin	verse 7	moral deficiencies that injure oneself or others, inferior quality that does not meet standards
offenses	verse 12	rebellion, breach of relationship

Isaiah stood with the people of his day in their sin, for he too was a sinner. But Isaiah took a remarkable step. God's law had convicted him, and he confessed his sin. He acknowledged his iniquities. He understood his position before God. When God called Isaiah in chapter 6, Isaiah encountered the holy, majestic, and powerful Lord Jehovah. Then he confessed, "Woe to me! . . . I am ruined! For I am a man of unclean lips, and I live among a people of unclean lips, and my eyes have seen the King, the LORD Almighty" (verse 5). God is holy; Isaiah was not. Isaiah's attitude was that of all believers in Christ. Believers know their sins. They understand that they have failed to live as God has demanded. They know that their sins are many, that they sin daily, and that they deserve God's just punishment.

Because of sin they can find no peace, justice, righteousness, truth, or honesty. By human effort no one finds deliverance from the damning guilt of sin or from its persuasive power. One might "shun evil," yet the evil in this world attacks such efforts. The unbelieving world will not allow even those who may still be faithful to the Lord to speak his truth. Human sin wishes to silence those who speak of God's plan of redemption. Isaiah observed, "Truth is nowhere to be found, and whoever shuns evil becomes a prey." On the human side of the barrier, no human can find redemption or deliverance. Instead, humans seek to prevent the proclamation of the truth and persecute those who proclaim it.

> The LORD looked and was displeased
>> that there was no justice.
> [16] He saw that there was no one,
>> he was appalled that there was no one to intervene;
> so his own arm worked salvation for him,
>> and his own righteousness sustained him.
> [17] He put on righteousness as his breastplate,
>> and the helmet of salvation on his head;
> he put on the garments of vengeance
>> and wrapped himself in zeal as in a cloak.
> [18] According to what they have done,
>> so will he repay
> wrath to his enemies
>> and retribution to his foes;
>> he will repay the islands their due.

If deliverance has to come from any human effort or thought, we must despair. Human beings arrogantly think that human effort is good enough for the holy, perfect God of the universe. It is foolish to think that any human effort can rise above the deep corruption that infects every human heart and life. The first portion of this chapter should make that clear. Our sins are so many, and they show themselves in so many varied ways. We are hopelessly doomed if we look for deliverance from ourselves. All of humanity by itself could not generate one Savior. Paul wrote, "There is no one righteous, not even one" (Romans 3:10). Through his prophet, God paints a bleak and dark picture of human existence.

But we ought not despair. God reached across the barrier to deliver us. Human effort cannot reach across the barrier that separates us from God. Only God can provide a solution, a rescue, a deliverance, a salvation. His plan called for the coming of the Servant on whom the Lord would lay "the iniquity of us all" (53:6). That Servant we know as Jesus Christ "bore the sin of many, and made intercession for the transgressors" (53:12). God's plan had been clearly set forth in the earlier chapters of this section. In this section Isaiah emphasizes that only the Lord himself could provide a solution to human sin. The Lord found no one among all of humanity; even among his chosen people, there was no one. But the Lord's own zeal to save us designed a plan to rescue us from the consequences of our own sins (verse 16).

In order to accomplish this deliverance from sin, God clothed himself with four things. Two of them are comforting to every sinner, and two of them strike terror in the heart of every sinner. First, Isaiah says that God clothes himself in "righteousness as his breastplate." The piece of armor closest to God's heart is righteousness. This righteousness comes from the undeserved love of God for sinners, the grace he has promised. He declares all the world righteous because of the work of the Servant, Jesus. Instead of counting all the sins mentioned in this chapter, God reconciles "the world to himself in Christ, not counting men's sins against them" (2 Corinthians 5:19). He declares them all to be people who have met his requirements, and he pronounces them not guilty; he justifies them. The second piece of armor is the "helmet of salvation." The helmet covers the head. God planned and carried out the deliverance of humanity from sin. God did not haphazardly or hurriedly plan the deliverance of humanity. From eternity God planned that the death of his own Son would rescue the world from sin, death, and hell. These two pieces of armor shine and glitter with the wonder of his love and grace for sinful humanity.

But the Lord also clothes himself with two items that must cause every sinful human heart to shudder. First, he puts on the "garments of vengeance." God has provided the only solution to human sin. His deliverance is a free gift to all humanity. He has done everything necessary, and he offers this free gift to all. What will happen to those who refuse God's gift? God's vengeance will punish those who do not accept his free gift. Their refusal means that they believe that God's gift is unnecessary or unimportant. They will suffer the consequences of their rejection.

Finally, Isaiah tells us that God has wrapped himself in "zeal as in a cloak." He will not grow cool in carrying out his plan to save humanity nor will he grow cool in bringing judgment upon all those who reject the salvation he has so freely offered. God will make sure it all happens; he is clothed with zeal. These verses describe God as a God of law and gospel. He remains serious about sin and its punishment. At the same time, he continues to be serious about his deep love and mercy for his unworthy creatures.

311

¹⁹**From the west, men will fear the name of the L**ORD**,**
  and from the rising of the sun, they will revere his glory.
  For he will come like a pent-up flood
  that the breath of the LORD **drives along.**

²⁰ **"The Redeemer will come to Zion,**
  to those in Jacob who repent of their sins,"
                                      declares the LORD**.**

The Lord has dressed himself with four things and
revealed both law and gospel. Yet the Lord has been and
always will be essentially a gracious and loving God. In
Exodus, the Lord identified himself as "The LORD, the LORD,
the compassionate and gracious God, slow to anger,
abounding in love and faithfulness, maintaining love to
thousands, and forgiving wickedness, rebellion and sin"
(34:6,7). The prophet Ezekiel wrote: "As surely as I live,
declares the Sovereign LORD, I take no pleasure in the
death of the wicked: but rather that they turn from their
ways and live. Turn! Turn from your evil ways!" (33:11). So
Isaiah directs our attention away from vengeance and judgment toward the gracious promises that God has revealed
to those who repent.

The Lord will not permit humanity to wipe its feet on
his grace and mercy. He will bring judgment on all who
reject his grace and continue in their sins. But he promises
grace and every blessing to those who believe and turn
from their sins. Isaiah saw these converts—these believers—in this passage. They come from the west and the
east, two directions that imply all directions. In other
words, those who "fear the name of the LORD" and "revere
his glory" come from every corner of the earth. They do
not experience the vengeance or judgmental zeal of the
Lord. Instead they have the gracious promise of God concerning the Redeemer.

How have these people come to believe and stand in

awe of what the Lord has done to save them? The breath of the Lord has come upon them. That is the Spirit of the Lord. He will come powerfully, like a flood driven by a powerful wind. One can hear the implication of Pentecost in these words. The activity of the Spirit has worked to bring many to faith in the Lord. The work of the apostle Paul demonstrates the power of the Spirit. His letters to Philippi, Colosse, Rome, and other gentile congregations illustrate the work of the Spirit in bringing many from the east and west to trust in the Lord and revere the salvation he provided through Jesus. Wherever the Word of grace persists, there the Holy Spirit becomes a powerful force in breaking down the pride of unbelief and in creating the miracle of faith. His work continues to our own age; believers who were once dead in sin are now alive in faith because of the Holy Spirit's power.

All believers are included in this wonderful promise. All believers are included in Zion and "those in Jacob." They are not limited to those who have ethnic and cultural ties to the ancient people of Israel. All who repent of their sins are included. The deliverance from sin and its consequences has come because God has provided it. The Redeemer came. Isaiah has used the term *redeemer* so often that we may take it for granted. But this Redeemer provided what no human could. He bought back all who were trapped in the bondage of sin. How aptly this fits into the picture of the kinsman-redeemer described in the Levitical laws (Leviticus 25). When someone became hopelessly entangled in obligations, the kinsman-redeemer could come and free him from those obligations. He could buy the freedom of his helpless relative. Now consider what the Lord, our brother and Redeemer, has done. We have become entangled in our own sins and are helpless to release ourselves or to gain our own deliverance. God sent our Redeemer to release us from our bondage. He paid for our release by his life and his death. We are free of sin because God is our Redeemer.

²¹"As for me, this is my covenant with them," says the LORD. "My Spirit, who is on you, and my words that I have put in your mouth will not depart from your mouth, or from the mouths of your children, or from the mouths of their descendants from this time on and forever," says the LORD.

The Lord has always remained the same. The covenant he promises here is not different from the covenant of grace he had established when he chose Abraham. In Genesis 15 when God makes a "covenant" with Abraham, it is God alone who passes through the sundered parts of the animals. It is God who calls down on himself the curse of death if this "covenant" is broken. Here God makes a testamentary promise to die. And this promise he fulfills in the incarnation and death of Christ. The patriarch Abraham was the forefather of the people from whom the Redeemer came. The words that introduce this covenant are the same as those that introduced the covenant with Abraham (Genesis 17:4). God promised that his covenant with Abraham would be "an everlasting covenant between me and you and your descendants after you for the generations to come, to be your God and the God of your descendants after you" (Genesis 17:7). This covenant is nothing new. The promises of God and the work of the Spirit created generations of believers. Although many in Judah had abandoned the Lord, he still had his faithful among them. They were the true sons and daughters of Abraham because they believed in the promises God made to Abraham. He is, after all, the father of all believers (Romans 4:16,17).

Let us note what God promises as his part of the agreement or covenant. God promises that his Word would not depart from his faithful believers through all time, from one generation to another and "from this time on and forever." What a blessed promise that is. We could know nothing about redemption and Christ unless God revealed it to us. So he has. The Scriptures speak the same message from beginning to end—Christ. Because God's Word announces Christ, his Word becomes a means through which the Holy Spirit comes into human hearts and minds in order to create and nourish faith. Without the Word, the Spirit has not promised to work; and without the Spirit, no faith can arise within the human heart. When God promises to give his believers the Word perpetually throughout time, he promises that he will continue to call, gather, and enlighten his people. He promises to nurture them as they face the trials and temptations of this temporary existence we call life.

The treasure of the church today remains the Word of God. God himself stands behind this promise and says that he will give his people "my words that I have put in your mouth." The only reliable source of information about God, sin, and eternity remains God himself. He knows the truth, and he has communicated the truth to us in his Word, the Scriptures. Those who know the truth listen to the voice of Jesus (John 18:37). Though others attack and despise God's Word, yet God promises that it will not disappear from the mouths of his children. God's Word will be spoken and communicated to others by the mouths of his believers. Through the Word of the gospel, the Holy Spirit will work to create new believers, who in turn will confess and witness to the truth. By the power of the Spirit, their witness will cause others to believe, and the cycle will continue. Believers today are the fulfillment of this promise; those who will still come to faith in the future will be an additional fulfillment. Finally we will all be gathered together in the presence of the Lord and sing his praise forever. Our mouths will rejoice in the grace of the Lord forever, and this promise will be completely fulfilled.

The glory of the Lord will shine upon his people

60"Arise, shine, for your light has come,
and the glory of the LORD rises upon you.
² See, darkness covers the earth
and thick darkness is over the peoples,
but the LORD rises upon you
and his glory appears over you.
³ Nations will come to your light,
and kings to the brightness of your dawn.

The prophet issues two striking commands: "Arise, shine." Both call God's people to attention. The people appear to be lying in the dust and in the darkness. They are by nature like all other people of the earth. They are troubled and despondent. But something spectacular has happened. Their light has come; the glory of the Lord rises upon them. What does that mean? The Old Testament generally means something special when we find the phrase "the glory of the LORD." It usually refers to the Lord's wonderful brilliant grace in Christ. "The glory of the LORD" visibly displays the presence of the Savior-God of the covenant, Jehovah, and announces some significant aspect of his plan of salvation. (For more information, see *Isaiah 1–39,* in The People's Bible series, pages 372,373, and August Pieper, "The Glory of the Lord," in *The Wauwatosa Theology,* Volume 2, pages 417-497).

Consider what we have learned in the previous two chapters. God's people had tried to earn God's favor by their fasting (chapter 58). But that fasting could not

The gentile wise men worship the Christ Child

deserve the notice of God. In fact, it was shallow and hypocritical. The next chapter (chapter 59) presented a correct view of their relationship with God. The sins of the people had erected an impassable barrier between them and God. They could not penetrate the barrier by their own effort; there simply was "no one to intervene" (verse 16). But God responded; "his own arm worked salvation for him" (verse 16). God himself had to provide the deliverance his people needed. The chapter concluded with the announcement of God's gracious covenant, his solemn contract with his people. He would be their Redeemer and come to Zion.

This chapter begins with two commands. The people should "arise" and "shine" because God's promised deliverance was about to arrive. Thick darkness and gloom covered all the people of the earth, including God's own people, but deliverance was on the way. The Lord himself brought the deliverance. Isaiah wrote that "the glory of the LORD"—the deliverance through Christ—rises upon "you" and it becomes "your light." How does this deliverance belong to God's people? That should not surprise us at all. Jesus reminded the Samaritan woman that "salvation is from the Jews" (John 4:22). God had long promised that the Messiah would come from the descendants of Abraham (Genesis 22:18), from the tribe of Judah (Genesis 49:10), that he would be born in Bethlehem (Micah 5:2), and be a descendant of King David (2 Samuel 7; Isaiah 9:7). Isaiah includes all the Old Testament prophecies to God's people when he says the light rises upon "you" and is "your light."

Yet God intends the wonder of this deliverance for all people of the world. The Messiah did indeed come, and he lived in Palestine among the Jews. The Messiah was born a Jew, but the light of God's grace attracts the attention of all nations. Even kings will come to the brightness of God's grace in the Messiah. This entire chapter draws a vivid picture of the New Testament church. When Christ ascended, he told his disciples to proclaim the good news to all the world. From Jerusalem the gospel spread out into the gentile world of Greece and Rome through the apostle Paul. No doubt it spread in other directions as the believers fled persecution, carrying the gospel with them (Acts 8:4). That was only the beginning. The brilliance of God's grace beams brightly for us too. We trust in Jesus today because God has claimed us through the gospel.

Some, however, suggest that we must read these verses as a prophecy of the return of the Jews from Babylon. After 70 years of captivity, the Jews were downcast and despondent. When they were allowed to return to rebuild Jerusalem, they were surely joyful (Psalm 126). But the prophecy forces us to look beyond that one deliverance from captivity. No foreign nations were drawn to God's people because of that one historical deliverance of the Jews. The edict that King Cyrus issued in 538 B.C. did not dispel the gloom and darkness that covered the entire earth. It created joy in the hearts of the small remnant that returned to rebuild Jerusalem. In addition, it set the stage for the greater deliverance that came for all the world when the Messiah arrived in Bethlehem. Yet a greater light rises in these verses than the light of the return of the remnant. Isaiah looked far beyond 538 B.C. and stood with the shepherds who were terrified when "the glory of the Lord shone around them" (Luke 2:9).

> [4] **"Lift up your eyes and look about you:**
>   **All assemble and come to you;**
>   **your sons come from afar,**
>   **and your daughters are carried on the arm.**

⁵ **Then you will look and be radiant,**
your heart will throb and swell with joy;
the wealth on the seas will be brought to you,
to you the riches of the nations will come.
⁶ **Herds of camels will cover your land,**
young camels of Midian and Ephah.
And all from Sheba will come,
bearing gold and incense
and proclaiming the praise of the LORD.
⁷ **All Kedar's flocks will be gathered to you,**
the rams of Nebaioth will serve you;
they will be accepted as offerings on my altar,
and I will adorn my glorious temple.

⁸ **"Who are these that fly along like clouds,**
like doves to their nests?
⁹ **Surely the islands look to me;**
in the lead are the ships of Tarshish,
bringing your sons from afar,
with their silver and gold,
to the honor of the LORD your God,
the Holy One of Israel,
for he has endowed you with splendor.

The glory of the Lord has brought great deliverance. The Servant of the Lord has offered his back to those who beat him, and he has obediently set his face like flint to carry out the Lord's plan (50:6,7). The Lord has laid upon him the iniquity of all humanity (53:4-6). But the Suffering Servant would also be raised, lifted up, and highly exalted (52:13); he would accomplish his task. Through this Servant, death was swallowed up forever, and the Lord Jehovah promised to wipe away the tears from all faces (25:8). Isaiah pictures this great deliverance as having already arrived. It all came because God faithfully fulfilled the promises he made to his Old Testament people. God chose them and preserved them through the centuries for one purpose—to bring this deliverance to pass for all the world.

Neither God's Old Testament people nor any other nation deserved such great deliverance. God's people had abandoned the Lord and his great promises. Isaiah fills his prophecy with indictments of the people of his age for their sin and rebellion. The heathen nations surrounding the Jews were no better than idolaters. But the Lord of free and faithful grace provided deliverance in spite of their sin and rebellion. Isaiah does not picture a misty, vague possibility of deliverance. He sees the deliverance as an accomplished fact and encourages God's people to look at the results of the great deliverance.

First, Zion should look around and see that so many come to her because the glory of the Lord has risen upon her. We see here a gathering of believers who come to enjoy the deliverance God provided. Sons and daughters have been recalled from their sins and rebellion and become believers. They come to Zion in faith and repentance. These sons and daughters are the Jews and Israelites who had been scattered to the far corners of the earth. Isaiah saw them coming to Zion from the places to which they had been scattered. In the early days of the New Testament church, God graciously gathered the Jews through the spread of the gospel. Paul regularly went to the synagogues in the Mediterranean world to announce the gospel to them. Many believed and became a fulfillment of this prophecy.

But more come. Zion has become also a light for the nations. The Lord Jesus, the Light of the world, came as God promised. Jesus was a Jew who lived in Galilee and traveled to Jerusalem. But God never intended that the deliverance he brought from sin and death would be limited only to Jews. God always intended this deliverance for all the world. Already on Pentecost, the gospel won converts from all nations. During his ministry, Paul did not limit his work to preaching only at the Jewish synagogues. He proclaimed the gospel on the street corners and in gentile cities (Acts 13,14,16–20,28).

Isaiah pictured these converts expressing their faith by bringing gifts to Zion. When we look around, as Isaiah encourages us to do, we see gifts from all over the world coming to Zion—the wealth of the seas, the riches of the nations, herds of camels, gold, incense. Moving majestically toward Zion with rich cargoes of silver and gold, the ships of Tarshish look "like clouds, like doves." Believers bring all these lavish offerings out of gratitude for the deliverance of God's grace. Those who come proclaim the praise of the Lord and bring offerings to adorn the Lord's glorious temple (verses 6,7). Even the Arab nations would come bearing gifts in faith. While we may have difficulty identifying the exact locations of the homelands of the people Isaiah mentions, the overall impression is not in doubt. Many besides the Jews believe in the deliverance the Lord provides, and they show their faith by their offerings.

So the New Testament church has received gifts from the faithful. The offerings gathered by the apostle Paul's missionary team serve as but one example (1 Corinthians 16:1-4; 2 Corinthians 8,9). Over the centuries many have offered much from their treasures to thank the Lord for his deliverance. So many from so many nations have come to know the God of Israel. Because of what God has provided through his Servant, Jesus Christ, these nations overflow with generosity. The people who come laden with gifts do so "to the honor of the LORD your God, the Holy One of Israel, for he has endowed you with splendor"—the splendor of deliverance through Christ from sin, death, and hell.

Through the centuries, the church has read the first verses of this chapter as the Old Testament reading for the festival of

Epiphany. How fitting! The church set aside Epiphany as the day to remember that the Magi came to Jerusalem looking for the King of the Jews. Gentile kings came to worship Immanuel, the child of Bethlehem, and to honor the Lord God of Israel. When they found him, they presented him with gifts of gold, frankincense, and myrrh (Matthew 2:1-12).

Nothing can give greater joy to Christians than to see so many others praising the God of grace. "Your heart will throb and swell with joy" because of all who come to honor the Lord and proclaim his praise. Through the gospel, God continues to call sinners to faith and adds them to his church. If we look around at our own lives and churches, such joy may, at times, be in short supply. We do not see such large crowds coming to faith and confessing their faith in Jesus. The conversion of unbelievers most often occurs on a much smaller scale than pictured here by Isaiah. Yet thousands upon thousands have turned to the Lord in faith over the centuries. In the day-to-day life of God's people, those conversions occur through the witness of Christians. God makes believers one at a time and sometimes more slowly than we would like. But each soul that trusts in Jesus joins this great assembly and brings joy to the faithful, even to the angels of heaven, as Jesus said, "There is rejoicing in the presence of the angels of God over one sinner who repents" (Luke 15:10).

> [10] **"Foreigners will rebuild your walls,**
>   **and their kings will serve you.**
> **Though in anger I struck you,**
>   **in favor I will show you compassion.**
> [11] **Your gates will always stand open,**
> **they will never be shut, day or night,**
> **so that men may bring you the wealth of the nations—**
>   **their kings led in triumphal procession.**
> [12] **For the nation or kingdom that will not serve you will perish;**
>   **it will be utterly ruined.**

In Isaiah's day the Assyrian army invaded Judah and besieged Jerusalem. The military force of Assyria wanted to raze the walls of Jerusalem and destroy the city. Sennacherib, the king of Assyria at the time, wanted to make the Jews his servants. He had no interest in serving them. Isaiah also looked into the future and saw the coming of the Babylonian army. The Babylonians also would besiege Jerusalem, destroy the city, and carry the Jews off into captivity. But Isaiah's vision looked beyond the Babylonian invasion. His vision stopped briefly at the return of the Jews from Babylon. The Jews did rebuild Jerusalem, and the Persian king even assisted in making it possible. But Isaiah saw beyond even that event. The prophet saw a city, however, not built with bricks and mortar or one that has walls and streets. God does not promise that the city of Jerusalem in Judea will be built again as a glorious and holy city. Such ideas continue to divert our attention from the real vision. We do not look for a millennial kingdom on earth that has Jerusalem as its center and capital. Instead, Isaiah sees a spiritual gathering of people—the New Testament church.

When Isaiah says that "foreigners will rebuild your walls," he means that foreign converts will help build the church. Believers from all nations will contribute to the growth of God's gracious rule in the hearts of his believers. So we pray with each repetition of the Lord's Prayer, "Your kingdom come." God's prophet sees kings serving his people. How different that picture is from the one Isaiah knew! He watched the Assyrians mass outside Jerusalem, intent on military victory. Yet, by the power of the Holy Spirit, he also saw foreign kings converted to the truth and working to build the city, that is, the church of God.

In Isaiah's experience, the gates of Jerusalem were closed and barred to prevent a foreign army from entering the city. These verses picture the opposite. The gates are open. They are never shut. God's invitation to believe always presents an open door for any sinner. Those who believe may enter, and when they enter by faith, they willingly and readily serve the Lord. They bring their gifts to the Lord. Men, women, and children of all stations in life—including the powerful, that is, the "kings" as Isaiah pictures them—have come to trust in Jesus and have entered his church. The Lord always welcomes people. He never excludes anyone who believes. Therefore, the gates stand open.

God has furnished wonderful blessings for all people of the earth. Jesus came for all the world. The gates of his church stand open in welcome to all, but what of those who do not wish to enter those gates? What happens to those who remain outside in unbelief? Isaiah reminds us, "The nation or kingdom that will not serve you will perish." The prophet says the same thing Jesus said, "God so loved the world that he gave his one and only Son, that whoever believes in him shall not perish but have eternal life. Whoever believes in him is not condemned, but whoever does not believe stands condemned already because he has not believed in the name of God's one and only Son" (John 3:16,18).

> [13] **"The glory of Lebanon will come to you,**
> **the pine, the fir and the cypress together,**
> **to adorn the place of my sanctuary;**
> **and I will glorify the place of my feet.**
> [14] **The sons of your oppressors will come bowing before you;**
> **all who despise you will bow down at your feet**
> **and will call you the City of the LORD,**
> **Zion of the Holy One of Israel.**

The ancient world valued Lebanon for its trees. Solomon imported the timber of Lebanon to build a magnificent temple (2 Chronicles 2:8-10). As Isaiah pictures the New Testament church of God's saints, he describes it as a beautiful place. The description of the church continues in these verses. Besides the wood of Lebanon, we note two other truths.

First, the church will include former enemies of Judah and Jerusalem. Isaiah says that "sons of your oppressors will come bowing before you." At a future time, some descendants of the ancient enemies of God's Old Testament people will come to faith.

Second, these converts will confess their faith in the truth. They will call the church "City of the LORD, Zion of the Holy One of Israel." The foreigners use two names for the Lord that are special in the Old Testament: "the LORD," that is, the special name for the God of free and faithful grace; and "the Holy One of Israel," that is, a special name Isaiah has used throughout his prophecy. These foreigners are believers who share the same faith and treasure the same truths as Isaiah and all God's Old Testament believers. The one church of believers includes believers of all time.

> ¹⁵ **"Although you have been forsaken and hated,**
>   **with no one traveling through,**
> **I will make you the everlasting pride**
>   **and the joy of all generations.**
> ¹⁶ **You will drink the milk of nations**
>   **and be nursed at royal breasts.**
> **Then you will know that I, the LORD, am your Savior,**
>   **your Redeemer, the Mighty One of Jacob.**

The description of the church continues here, and we pause to note two more things. First, because of the glory of the Lord, God would make his people an "everlasting pride." Only one thing could possibly make God's people an everlasting pride: the Messiah's coming from their midst. Salvation has come from the Jews, and the effects of the Lord's deliverance extend to eternity. When we believe, we have eternal life.

The prophet continues to describe how the nations will nourish the church. The rich milk of the nations will give the church strength and vitality. So God uses the talents, treasures, and energy of believers from all nations to build his church. Note also the list of names God uses for himself at the end of verse 16. The One who has gathered the church and who continues to provide such rich blessings to his people is none other than "the LORD, . . . your Savior, your Redeemer, the Mighty One of Jacob." God bases his fame and glory on the fulfillment of his promises to save and redeem sinners from sin, death, and hell. His mighty power has accomplished that wonderful deliverance, and he continues to call and gather believers together into his church.

> [17] "Instead of bronze I will bring you gold,
>> and silver in place of iron.
>> Instead of wood I will bring you bronze,
>> and iron in place of stones.
>> I will make peace your governor
>> and righteousness your ruler.
> [18] No longer will violence be heard in your land,
>> nor ruin or destruction within your borders,
>> but you will call your walls Salvation
>> and your gates Praise.
> [19] The sun will no more be your light by day,
>> nor will the brightness of the moon shine on you,
>> for the LORD will be your everlasting light,
>> and your God will be your glory.
> [20] Your sun will never set again,
>> and your moon will wane no more;
>> the LORD will be your everlasting light,
>> and your days of sorrow will end.

By the power of the Holy Spirit, Isaiah saw the return of God's people from Babylon. He paused briefly at that historical event, but he also looked beyond it to the arrival of the Messiah. Isaiah pictured the New Testament church as God would gather it, protect it, and nourish it through the centuries. It is almost as if the word *everlasting* in verse 15 has refocused the attention of Isaiah on God's people in heaven after the Last Day. Verse 17 begins with a promise that God would make things better than they had been. The promises of God are framed in the language and thought of the Old Testament, but Isaiah saw what no one in his age could have known by experience.

It would be well for us to read these words of Isaiah with the words of the apostle John in mind:

> I heard a loud voice from the throne saying, "Now the dwelling of God is with men, and he will live with them. They will be his people, and God himself will be with them and be their God. He will wipe every tear from their eyes. There will be no more death or mourning or crying or pain, for the old order of things has passed away."

> The city does not need the sun or the moon to shine on it, for the glory of God gives it light, and the Lamb is its lamp. The nations will walk by its light, and the kings of the earth will bring their splendor into it. On no day will its gates ever be shut, for there will be no night there. The glory and honor of the nations will be brought into it. Nothing impure will ever enter it, nor will anyone who does what is shameful or deceitful, but only those whose names are written in the Lamb's book of life. (Revelation 21:3,4,23-27)

21 **"Then will all your people be righteous**
     and they will possess the land forever.
   They are the shoot I have planted,
     the work of my hands,
     for the display of my splendor.
22 **The least of you will become a thousand,**
     the smallest a mighty nation.
   I am the LORD;
     in its time I will do this swiftly."

Finally, Isaiah lets us look inside this great and glorious city in order to see the inhabitants. The people within are all "righteous." How can this be? Isaiah had written, "Your iniquities have separated you from your God" (59:2). But those who are within God's glorious church are free from all their iniquities and sins. Because of the work of the Servant, God has declared them to be righteous and holy. Because Christ would bear the transgressions, sins, and iniquities of all, God has announced, "My righteous servant will justify many" (53:11). All those who are within the walls of God's city, all who believe and enter his church, are righteous because God has declared them to be righteous. "This righteousness from God comes through faith in Jesus Christ to all who believe" (Romans 3:22). God has made it so. The believers are the work of his hands, and he planted them so that they may proclaim the Lord's praise in time and for eternity.

What wonderful promises we have in this chapter. For the people of Isaiah's day, of course, the fulfillment of all this lay in the future. It would happen. The Lord assured his people that it would happen at the time that he determined. And it did. In the fullness of time, it happened as God promised. We can be assured that the eternal future of all believers remains secure. Just as the Servant has come and God has gathered us into his church through the gospel, so he will take us to the eternal mansions of heaven.

The Lord will send his Servant to announce good news

61 The Spirit of the Sovereign L<small>ORD</small> is on me,
because the L<small>ORD</small> has anointed me
to preach good news to the poor.
He has sent me to bind up the brokenhearted,
to proclaim freedom for the captives
and release from darkness for the prisoners,
² to proclaim the year of the L<small>ORD</small>'s favor
and the day of vengeance of our God,
to comfort all who mourn,
³   and provide for those who grieve in Zion—
to bestow on them a crown of beauty
instead of ashes,
the oil of gladness
instead of mourning,
and a garment of praise
instead of a spirit of despair.
They will be called oaks of righteousness,
a planting of the L<small>ORD</small>
for the display of his splendor.

Who speaks in these verses? Whom has the Lord anointed and sent to preach good news? Isaiah identified the speaker in several earlier passages. In 11:2, the prophet wrote that the Spirit of the Lord would rest on the Branch from the stump of Jesse. In 42:1, the Lord promised that he would put his Spirit upon his Servant, who would bring "justice to the nations." In 50:4, a part of one of the Servant passages, the Servant claims to have an "instructed tongue, to know the word that sustains the weary." Just after another of the Servant passages in 49:8,9, the Lord promised to recall the captives and free those in darkness, two things God anointed the speaker in these verses to do.

As this chapter begins, the speaker says, "The Spirit of the Sovereign L<small>ORD</small> is on me." Is there any reason to doubt who speaks these words? The speaker is none other than the Servant of Jehovah, the Branch from Jesse, that is, Jesus Christ. One important New Testament passage removes all questions. When Jesus attended the synagogue in Nazareth, he received the scroll of the prophet Isaiah and read this passage. After he had finished reading, he rolled up the scroll and sat down. Then Jesus said, "Today this scripture is fulfilled in your hearing" (Luke 4:21). It was a dramatic moment for everyone in the synagogue. They were amazed and so furious that they sought to throw Jesus off a cliff. But their reaction did not change the fulfillment. Jesus identified himself as the one who fulfilled these prophecies.

So Jesus speaks here in prophecy and announces that the Spirit of the Lord is upon him. That Spirit descended upon him visibly at his baptism (Matthew 3:13-17; Mark 1:9-11; Luke 3:21,22). In these words from Isaiah, Jesus identifies the Spirit as the Spirit of the "LORD," that is, the God of the covenant, who has promised grace and mercy. In addition, this is the Spirit of the "*Sovereign* LORD." This identifies the Spirit as coming from the all-powerful God, who carries out the promises he makes. Jesus did not come on his own. The God of free and faithful grace sent him and endowed him with his Spirit. We note the implied reference to the Trinity: the Lord, the Spirit, and the Servant, or the Anointed One.

Jesus became the Anointed, that is, the Messiah. He has come to announce good news. His entire mission centers on the "good news," or the gospel. We should not forget that God did not send his Messiah to restore the earthly kingdom of David and Solomon or even to establish a new, better kingdom on earth. The speaker tells us that he has come "to preach . . . to proclaim . . . to comfort . . . to bestow." He descended with a message of good news, healing, and freedom. He came to address that good news to the poor, the brokenhearted, and the prisoners. The larger context of these words drives us to view them as spiritual problems rather than physical ones. Isaiah had written that the iniquities of the people had separated them from God (59:2) and that darkness covers the earth (60:2). In the previous chapters, God promised wonderful relief from sin and the darkness. In this chapter he tells us who will bring that relief and deliverance. The Messiah brings this deliverance because "the Spirit of the Sovereign LORD is on [him]." Not only did the Messiah come to achieve the deliverance from sin and death (chapter 53), but he also came to proclaim it clearly to all who were so afflicted.

On one level, the prophecy anticipates the return of God's people from their Babylonian exile. The remnant heard the announcement of "freedom," and they returned to Jerusalem to rebuild their land. But that deliverance became only the prelude to a much larger deliverance from captivity—the captivity of sin and death. On another level, the Messiah came to proclaim the healing message of forgiveness from God. He bandages brokenhearted sinners with his soothing message of forgiveness. He removes the burden from guilty consciences. He releases sinners bound in the hopeless dungeon of their own depravity. He breaks the bondage of Satan's controlling influence over human lives. His message announces the wonderful deliverance from sin, death, hell, and Satan.

All humans need to hear the good news of Jesus. Human lives are often filled with misery and trouble. We endure defeat and failure more often than we triumph. Our hearts are broken. We are disappointed again and again. Our loved ones suffer pain and die. Sometimes those we love inflict pain upon us and then desert us. We are captives. Either we cannot escape the consequences of our own failures, or we are controlled by the mistakes of others. We suffer from the bitterness of a spouse, the loveless attitude of a parent, and the harsh criticisms of others. Our lives are often a series of episodes of mourning and grief. Moments of happiness and joy pass all too quickly, and we mourn another loss or another failure. Lives are often filled with greed, jealousy, pride, lust, envy, hatred, and anger. At the end of human life stands death—inescapable, dark, and undeniable. All humans are heirs to such conditions because of their own sins, rebellion, and guilt.

The Lord, however, does not want any human to be abandoned to such a fate. He has sent his own Anointed to announce the good news of a different future. The third verse sets up a series of opposites that bring joy to every human heart. On one side we have mourning, grieving, ashes, and despair. On the other side, we find comfort, a crown of beauty, the oil of gladness, and a garment of praise. The Lord knows when tears stream down our cheeks and when our lives appear colorless and drab because of our sins. He has provided the alternative—the good news of his love in Christ. Words—spoken, written, and remembered—express the good news. The gospel is the power of God (Romans 1:16). The Lord chooses to work in human hearts through the gospel. Through those words, God imparts comfort, joy, freedom, and strength.

The Messiah was sent to announce the message of God's love for weary sinners. One description of his work tells us that he proclaims the year of the Lord's favor and the day of vengeance. The message of God is always both law and gospel. The phrase "the year of the LORD's favor" comes from the law of the Year of Jubilee in ancient Israel. In the Year of Jubilee, property that had been sold reverted to its original owner, debts were forgiven, and those who had been enslaved for their debts were released (see Leviticus 25:8-55). In contrast to such good news, God threatened a "day of vengeance." We should not forget to notice that the Lord's favor extended throughout a year and his vengeance, for only a day. God wants to be known more for mercy and compassion than for vengeance. But for all those who refuse his mercy, there will be judgment and vengeance. The entire Scriptures make that clear (see Exodus 34:5-7; Mark 16:16; John 3:16-18; 2 Peter 3:8-10).

Verse 3 concludes by pointing us to the results of the preaching of this good news. Those who have heard the Messiah's message and believe it are called "oaks of righteousness." The oak, or terebinth, of the ancient world was a strong and durable deciduous tree. The Scriptures picture believers as such trees. Here they are trees of "righteousness" because they find their righteousness in the Messiah, not in their own good works. The righteousness of God gives them their strength and life.

The Lord has done everything for them. They are "a planting of the LORD for the display of his splendor." With this phrase we can recall the end of the previous chapter: "Then will all your people be righteous. . . . They are the shoot I have planted, the work of my hands, for the display of my splendor" (60:21). The proclamation of the gospel creates faith in the hearts of some. They are God's saints, righteous and strong in this world, but strong only because God has declared them righteous. God's saints have grown strong because they are nourished on the promises of the Lord. They are enduring trees in a world of chaos, violence, and evil.

⁴ They will rebuild the ancient ruins
and restore the places long devastated;

> they will renew the ruined cities
>> that have been devastated for generations.
> ⁵ Aliens will shepherd your flocks;
>> foreigners will work your fields and vineyards.
> ⁶ And you will be called priests of the LORD,
>> you will be named ministers of our God.
> You will feed on the wealth of nations,
>> and in their riches you will boast.

We continue to look at the results of preaching the good news of the gospel. Those who have been converted by the Holy Spirit through the gospel will be gathered together into the one holy Christian church. Through these converts, God will build the church. The Old Testament nation would be transformed into the New Testament church. In Isaiah's day, God kept his Old Testament people separate from aliens and foreigners, but in the age ushered in by the Messiah, aliens and foreigners will have a part in the building of God's church. Not only will outsiders be included because of their faith in the Messiah, but God's Old Testament people will also have a part. Together, gentile converts and Jewish believers will live on the wealth of the nations (see 60:5-7).

> ⁷ Instead of their shame
>> my people will receive a double portion,
> and instead of disgrace
>> they will rejoice in their inheritance;
> and so they will inherit a double portion in their land,
>> and everlasting joy will be theirs.
>
> ⁸ "For I, the LORD, love justice;
>> I hate robbery and iniquity.
> In my faithfulness I will reward them
>> and make an everlasting covenant with them.
> ⁹ Their descendants will be known among the nations
>> and their offspring among the peoples.
> All who see them will acknowledge
>> that they are a people the LORD has blessed."

The Lord promised abundant blessings to his people. In a Jewish family, the firstborn inherited a double portion. All God's people will be treated with the special honor and blessings accorded to the firstborn. God's Old Testament people endured shame and disgrace. In this life, God's people always experience the same things. But their fortunes will change. The Lord promises joy—everlasting joy. We note the everlasting covenant and the inheritance in the promised land. The prophet does not tell us that believers will receive a double portion of the physical land of Palestine. God has something much greater in mind. He promises that his elect will have an everlasting inheritance in the new Jerusalem, which Jesus referred to as "my Father's house" (John 14:2).

Law and gospel are again evident. The Lord loves justice and hates robbery. Those who believe the gracious gospel will rejoice in their inheritance. But those who do not believe will not receive such a blessing. Even those who may appear to worship God and present him with their offerings, but who have remained hypocrites and dependent on their own good works, can expect no blessing from the Lord.

But we direct our attention here to the believers. They are God's chosen people, a people belonging to God (1 Peter 2:9). The Lord has called them out of the world, and they are different from the world. Their light of faith shines (Matthew 5:16) so that "all who see them will acknowledge that they are a people the LORD has blessed."

> ¹⁰ **I delight greatly in the LORD;**
>   **my soul rejoices in my God.**
>   **For he has clothed me with garments of salvation**
>   **and arrayed me in a robe of righteousness,**
>   **as a bridegroom adorns his head like a priest,**
>   **and as a bride adorns herself with her jewels.**
> ¹¹ **For as the soil makes the sprout come up**
>   **and a garden causes seeds to grow,**

**so the Sovereign LORD will make righteousness and praise
spring up before all nations.**

The Messiah spoke in the opening verses of this chapter,
but someone else speaks here. These words cannot be the
words of the Messiah. Instead, they are the words of someone who has received the benefits of the Messiah's work.
Isaiah described this speaker as one clothed in the "garments
of salvation." The Messiah brings forgiveness and peace with
God and dispenses it to sinners, who need these blessings.
The Messiah has no need of these blessings himself. The
words remind us of the "Song of Mary" when she heard that
she would be the mother of the Messiah: "My soul praises
the Lord and my spirit rejoices in God my Savior" (Luke
1:46,47). The words recorded here by the prophet Isaiah are
the words of a believer who has received the great blessings
of God. Great joy fills the heart of such a believer.

Every believer may rejoice that God has covered his or
her sinful life with the robe of righteousness. Jesus fashioned this robe from the threads of his perfect life. Then
he wove it on the loom of the cross and colored it with his
own red blood. God freely gives the cloak of his Son's perfect life to the sinner, and it covers every sin, rebellion,
and deviation from God's standard. This robe of Christ's
righteousness is long and wide enough to cover every
twisted human thought, word, and deed. But this robe
comes only from God. No human can erase a single sin.
Left to ourselves, we walk about as Lady Macbeth did. She
killed the king, and her sins haunted her conscience and
heart. Like Shakespeare's character, we vainly attempt to
wipe our own sinful hands clean. If we are honest, we will
conclude as she did: "Here's the smell of the blood still; all
the perfumes of Arabia will not sweeten this little hand"
(*Macbeth* 5.1.52-54). Only God's grace in Christ can cover

human sin. Forgiveness cannot be achieved by human effort, no matter how godly that effort may appear to other human eyes. We are justified, that is, we are declared righteous, freely by grace. By faith we put Christ's spotless robe on our shoulders and make it our own. So we sing:

> Jesus, your blood and righteousness
> My beauty are, my glorious dress;
> Mid flaming worlds, in these arrayed,
> With joy shall I lift up my head. (CW 376:l)

Because this robe covers the deepest stain of human sin, it becomes also a garment of salvation. Humans stand before God dressed in this robe. God sees the believer clothed with the perfection of his own Son and welcomes the believer into his presence. Without the righteousness of Christ, we are turned away from God and sent to the eternal torment of hell. But the perfection of Christ mantled about us by faith brings eternal life and deliverance from judgment. We rejoice because God has given such a garment of salvation to us and claimed us as his own.

The last verse of the chapter assured God's Old Testament readers that this would all come to pass. Just as the soil brings forth green grass and beautiful flowers, so surely will the "Sovereign LORD" make "righteousness and praise spring up before all nations." The soil may look barren and lifeless, but after a time the seed sprouts and grows. For the Jews of Isaiah's day, Jerusalem would be destroyed and God's people led away captive. But, in God's good time, they would return. Beyond that return, further into the future, the Messiah would come and proclaim the good news of the gospel. All the words of this chapter, as well as all the other prophecies, would then bloom into fulfillment.

The Lord takes an oath to bless the redeemed

62 For Zion's sake I will not keep silent,
 for Jerusalem's sake I will not remain quiet,
till her righteousness shines out like the dawn,
 her salvation like a blazing torch.
² The nations will see your righteousness,
 and all kings your glory;
you will be called by a new name
 that the mouth of the LORD will bestow.
³ You will be a crown of splendor in the LORD's hand,
 a royal diadem in the hand of your God.
⁴ No longer will they call you Deserted,
 or name your land Desolate.
But you will be called Hephzibah,
 and your land Beulah;
for the LORD will take delight in you,
 and your land will be married.
⁵ As a young man marries a maiden,
 so will your sons marry you;
as a bridegroom rejoices over his bride,
 so will your God rejoice over you.

Chapter 61 opened with the words of the Messiah and closed with a song of praise by one clothed with the garments of salvation. This chapter opens with the words of the Lord himself concerning his church. He created the church by his grace though the Word, and he cannot keep silent about it. He will not keep silent "for Zion's sake" and "for Jerusalem's sake." The blessings he prepared for his people are too important and too wonderful to keep hidden.

Zion and *Jerusalem* refer to the church of God. If we apply these terms to the earthly kingdoms of Judah and Israel, we miss the point of the Lord's message. Interpretations looking for fulfillment in those physical kingdoms misfire in the harsh light of history when again and again the earthly kingdoms failed to bring the peace and prosperity the citizens hoped would come. In order to match prophesy and history, some have even suggested that Zion and Jerusalem will one day enter a millennial age when all these prophecies will be fulfilled literally on earth. But God does not announce the wonders of any political entity named or conceived as "Zion" and "Jerusalem." Nor is he concerned about any other visible organization, including the organized Christian church. *Zion* and *Jerusalem* refer to the invisible church, the assembly of believers in Jesus Christ. This Zion will always be hidden from our physical sight—invisible while we are here on earth. We recognize it now because its citizens assemble to hear the message of the grace of God in Christ and to receive Christ's sacraments. But in the world of history, the church does not appear glorious by comparison with everything else. Instead, we see it persecuted and ridiculed in the world.

But this does not stop the Lord from proclaiming the message of his grace and mercy, which creates and sustains the church. By grace alone, the Lord provided his people with forgiveness and peace. The Messiah, Jesus Christ, died and rose to accomplish this. God's efforts created the people who have become his Zion and Jerusalem, the people he has called out of the darkness to be his chosen holy nation (1 Peter 2:9). They are his people here in this world, and after this life is over, they will enter the new Jerusalem that awaits believers (Revelation 21:3,4). The Lord does not want the message of his grace in Christ, which created his church, to be a secret to the world. He wants all people to hear and believe the message of his love for sinners. So he will not keep silent until the righteousness that belongs to all believers shines so brightly that all the nations see it.

How does the Lord announce this? Of course, the Scriptures provide that clear announcement, but God works through his people too. Jesus told his disciples, "You will be my witnesses" (Acts 1:8). So God works through the proclamation of his people. First, he gives them the power to speak of his grace, as Stephen did before the crowd that stoned him. Second, God works through their proclamation of the gospel to call others to see and believe. The entire process becomes one grand cascade—a continuous cycle. By the gospel, God empowers his people to speak and works through their message to bring others to faith. Then he empowers these new believers to speak and works through their message again to bring still others to faith. The cycle has persisted through the centuries to the present; God has not kept silent. Because the good news of God's mercy in Jesus Christ has come from the voices of God's people, his gospel continues its glorious work.

The Lord is not indifferent toward his people, whom Isaiah here calls Zion and Jerusalem. God delights in his people. He has created them, protected them, and promised them wonderful blessings. Isaiah pictures God's people as "a crown of splendor" and "a royal diadem." Since the Lord holds the church, pictured as this crown, in his hand, the church is his work of art—his creation, which he desires to display to the world. God works as the artist who has done everything to make his church beautiful. He invested time in fulfilling the prophecies made throughout the pages of Scripture. He has invested the holy precious blood of his one and only Son to wash away the sins of his church. He has worked through the gospel to call people and has made them his own. Now he continues to give the church the power to proclaim the sweet message of forgiveness and eternal life. God wants to display the workmanship and effort he has invested in his church.

In the history of this world, however, the church seems more desolate and deserted than glorious. Just as Isaiah's readers were directed to look ahead, so all God's people look ahead, not to a new chapter in world history and politics but to the end of the world's book and the dawn of God's glorious new Jerusalem. In this world, God's people have no lasting city, but they are looking forward to the one waiting for them (Hebrews 13:14). The church knows that this glorious city lies beyond time and space because God promised it. Here we find another of those promises. The promises give believers a taste of what awaits them. The believers trust in the grace and mercy of God, which he shares with them through the Word. Through it, believers know of his love for them and are refreshed by it in the world, where disloyalty and desertion play so prominently. Even if it appears so, believers are not deserted now. They are in God's hands, and he promises his presence and protection. Yet they await a future time when the presence of God will be complete and immediate.

Through Isaiah, God reminds believers of the blessings to which they are heirs. While they may be called desolate and deserted here, yet God delights in them, and they have a new name. Isaiah will be more specific about that name at the end of the chapter, but here the new names are Hephzibah, meaning, "my delight is in her," and Beulah, meaning, "married." The Lord's own commentary on these names speaks of his love for his people and the joy they experience because of his grace. The metaphor is that of marriage and anticipates Paul's words in Ephesians chapter 5 about the church being the bride of Christ. God's people are married to Christ so that they may be cared for, protected, and no longer abandoned. They are subject to him, enjoy his love, and find happiness in the relationship. God also finds joy in his church, to the point that he himself will "rejoice over [it]."

Perhaps some confusion may persist in this passage because the sons marry the bride, but the larger picture depicts the great rejoicing caused by the relationship between God and his church. God will rejoice over his people. Believers will rejoice over God's grace. Believers will even rejoice over one another, as Paul did: "What is our hope, our joy, or the crown in which we will glory in the presence of our Lord Jesus when he comes? Is it not you? Indeed, you are our glory and joy" (1 Thessalonians 2:19,20). The New Testament church fulfills the promises, but the glory and joy of the eternal church in heaven surpasses anything we know today. The church now proclaims the grace of God in a world of darkness and must endure times of desolation and decay. Only in the church above will the words of God through Isaiah be fulfilled completely.

> 6 **I have posted watchmen on your walls, O Jerusalem;**
> **they will never be silent day or night.**
> **You who call on the LORD,**
> **give yourselves no rest,**
> 7 **and give him no rest till he establishes Jerusalem**
> **and makes her the praise of the earth.**

Some commentators have put the first verses of this chapter into the mouth of the prophet Isaiah. But here in verse 6, the speaker posts watchmen on the walls of Jerusalem, something that the prophet could not do. The Lord speaks here.

Notice how the Lord works to proclaim his message. He posts watchmen on the walls. These watchmen cannot remain silent: "They will never be silent day or night." The passage tells us that they stand on the walls, but the walls of Jerusalem have long since tumbled at the hands of more than one invading army. Walls here must refer to the spiritual Jerusalem, God's holy church.

Who are these watchmen? First, they are the prophets, who are often pictured as watchmen. The prophets announced God's message to God's people. The job description for such a watchman included warning God's people against error and false doctrine, announcing God's wrath against sin, and holding out the consolation of God's love and forgiveness. Those who were God's watchmen proclaimed God's message, no matter what the consequences. Again and again they had to oppose the false prophets, who spoke a message different from God's. The true prophets condemned sin, soothed the troubled, nurtured the weak, strengthened faith, and converted the lost. How? By speaking the Word of God. Because the power remained in the Word, they could not be silent.

The prophetic office came to its fulfillment in Christ, who is God's best messenger to his people. Jesus entrusted this prophetic office to the New Testament church. Through the church, God continues to place watchmen over his flock to guard it against those that would destroy it, to warn against error, to lend counsel, and to preach and teach God's truth. When his people choose someone to serve them, God calls watchmen to mount the walls of his church. In the freedom of the gospel, God's people determine the scope of work for each person called. Only those so designated by the church should speak as the church's public ministers. Most commonly, pastors and teachers are the contemporary fulfillment of Isaiah's prophecy. At every point in the history of his church, such watchmen are needed, and God has supplied them. Because Satan continues to roar his threats and falsehoods, looking for souls to devour, the Lord will continue to supply watchmen until the church reaches glory. Like Peter and John, those watchmen cannot remain silent: "We cannot help speaking about what we have seen and heard" (Acts 4:20).

The watchmen God gives his church may be viewed as leaders who have a special responsibility to proclaim the truths of God. Yet every saint of God has the ministry of the keys and shares God's truth, counsels those needing guidance, warns against falsehood, and points others to the grace of God in Christ. While the saints of God determine who will be their public watchmen, every believer serves as a watchman. The church is one body with many different parts working to accomplish the goal mentioned here—to establish Jerusalem, or the church, and make her the praise of all the earth. Everyone in the church has to work to reach those high goals.

So that believers don't forget that, the Lord provides a word of encouragement to all saints. He tells them, "Give yourselves no rest . . . till he establishes Jerusalem and makes her the praise of the earth." The task before God's people requires constant attention in this life. No one can sit idle. Not one believer can remain silent. Together believers will support the mission outreach to the nations of the earth. Simply, believers are to be active in looking for the extension of the church.

The prophet begins, "You who call on the LORD," reminding us of the passages that encourage every believer to pray to the Lord. Even as they are active in witnessing where they live in this world and in sending missionaries to other parts of the world, they should give the Lord no rest either. Their prayers should pester God with requests for blessings upon every announcement of law and gospel by every watchman everywhere. The task will be finished only when God reveals the new Jerusalem at the end of time. Then the church will be seen as the glorious bride that God has described in his Word. On that day, the saints of God will stand before all the nations of the earth, and the Lord will say, "Come, you who are blessed by my Father; take your inheritance, the kingdom prepared for you since the creation of the world" (Matthew 25:34).

The prophecy sees the final glory of the church, but in the course of time, the history of the church unfolds gradually. The Word is proclaimed, new souls are added to the church, and new leaders are called to function as watchmen. Those in the church at any given time have work to do. They are to be zealous as witnesses and fervent in prayer. What a contrast to the watchmen of Israel who were blind, without knowledge, and mute and who loved to sleep and dream (56:10)! Such watchmen will see the glory of the church, but they will not enjoy it.

> 8 **The LORD has sworn by his right hand**
>   **and by his mighty arm:**
>   **"Never again will I give your grain**
>   **as food for your enemies,**
>   **and never again will foreigners drink the new wine**
>   **for which you have toiled;**
> 9 **but those who harvest it will eat it**
>   **and praise the LORD,**
>   **and those who gather the grapes will drink it**
>   **in the courts of my sanctuary."**

All the promises of God come to us in the frail vessel of words. The Lord works through those words because his Word is powerful. At the beginning of time, God called the physical world into being by the words of his mouth. Earlier in the chapter, the new name of the people of God comes from the mouth of the Lord. When God speaks, it is so. Yet words fill the world in which the church lives. Some of those words are promises by powerful people. Others are cruel words of hatred and prejudice. Still others are spoken to catch our attention and move us to a course of action.

In this world of good intentions, broken promises, and empty words, God underscores his promises with an oath. He swears by his right hand and his mighty arm, both symbols of his power and strength. When a court officer administers an oath, the witness raises his or her right hand to emphasize the solemnity of the oath. God's oath emphasizes his promise. It will be done. Nothing can alter that fact. The promises of God are not wishful hyperbole; he has sworn to bring them to pass.

God's oath here recalled how his people experienced oppression in this world. One might think of Gideon needing to thresh grain in a winepress to hide the crop from the Midianites (Judges 6). Such oppression was common in the ancient world. God's oath implied deliverance and freedom. No foreigners would take advantage of God's people any longer. The gifts of God's grace could not be taken away.

The fulfillment of this promise will lead God's people to "praise the LORD" and to drink the wine "in the courts of [his] sanctuary." These terms refer to the offering of firstfruits and tithes proscribed in the Mosaic Law (Deuteronomy 26:1-15; 14:22-29). One of the key features of the Mosaic Law in this case was to eat and drink "in the presence of the LORD your God" (Deuteronomy 14:23,26). The blessings God promised would form the basis of worship and thanksgiving and would point to the final worship and praise in the eternal glorious presence of the Lord.

On one level, the blessings God promises here include the blessings of food and drink; on another, the blessings of peace and prosperity; and on a third level, communion with God in worship. Each time God's people enjoy the earthly fulfillment of these promises, they can look forward to the final, permanent, and complete fulfillment in the new Jerusalem. Every expression of worship and praise is imperfect and temporary for the church on earth, but each expression reminds us of the perfect praise that the saints offer in heaven (Revelation 7:9-17). From time to time, God's people on earth have enjoyed such blessings as prosperity, freedom, and peace. At other times God has withheld those blessings for his own purposes; these trials do not void the promises of God. Periods of conflict, famine, and oppression will come to a final end, according to God's promise. He has taken an oath to verify its fulfillment.

> **[10] Pass through, pass through the gates!**
> **Prepare the way for the people.**
> **Build up, build up the highway!**
> **Remove the stones.**
> **Raise a banner for the nations.**
> **[11] The LORD has made proclamation**
> **to the ends of the earth:**
> **"Say to the Daughter of Zion,**
> **'See, your Savior comes!**
> **See, his reward is with him,**
> **and his recompense accompanies him.'"**
> **[12] They will be called the Holy People,**
> **the Redeemed of the LORD;**
> **and you will be called Sought After,**
> **the City No Longer Deserted.**

The artistry of these exhortations includes the customary parallelism of Hebrew poetry but adds a repetition that emphasizes not only the concept but the sound of the words. In English we would call it assonance. While its effect is lost in English, the translators perhaps attempted to capture it with the prepositions attached to the verbs: "pass *through*" and "build *up*." The repetition and the sound give expression to an emphatic and enthusiastic response to the oath of the Lord. He swears to fulfill his promises; the church responds with deep gratitude and excitement.

As we labor in this world and hear the firm promises of God, we long for their fulfillment. The last book of the Bible concludes, "Amen. Come, Lord Jesus" (Revelation 22:20). In verse 10 here, the prophet appears to be the speaker encouraging God's people to prepare for the fulfillment of all the promises God makes. God's people, his church, will be gathered from the far reaches of the earth. These future converts will come; prepare the way for them! Remove every obstacle! Raise a banner for them to follow! The spirit of the exhortations seems to be "Consider all these wonderful promises for Jerusalem and Zion. Wow! Let's go and enjoy them all." Isaiah recorded a similar exhortation in 57:14. In addition, the words here allude to the words of 40:3,4. There the way is prepared for the Lord. Here the way is cleared for the people.

The return of the exiles from Babylon provides one fulfillment of these words. When Cyrus issued his edict, the Jews returned to rebuild Jerusalem. Historical and political realities marred that joyful return to the city of God. Many Jews made long pilgrimages to Jerusalem for one of the festivals. For many of them, the journey became the highlight of their religious lives. Consider the Jews from all the nations who were in Jerusalem on Pentecost morning. Yet all their pilgrimages—no matter how wonderful and uplifting—were pale, imperfect reflections of the gathering of the church from all nations. The prophet urged God's people to pass through the gates of their own cities, including Babylon, and gather together in the city of God. Each pilgrimage became a reminder of the great gathering of all God's people. Even the entrance of Jesus into Jerusalem on Palm Sunday gives us only a foretaste of the return of the Lord in glory when he will gather all his people to himself and receive their shouts of praise and thanksgiving.

Isaiah's inspired words take us to a point far into the future. The holy Christian church throughout the world hears the proclamation of the Lord: "See, your Savior comes!" The time of redemption has arrived. Isaiah saw it as a historical fact, even though for him it remained centuries in the future. The prophet recorded the same announcement in 40:10. The scattered people of God will hear the proclamation. The Savior who comes will bring with him the reward he has won. He offers it freely to his people. *Reward* implies that someone earned something for an act accomplished, a quid pro quo, such as wages for a job performed. But in the city of God, no citizen can earn the reward. The Savior has earned it. He dispenses it freely, and his people receive it by faith. God delivers from sin, death, and punishment. No individual member of God's people, or even all of them together, can save a single sinner. Note that the proclamation comes from the Lord. Again, words announce the wonderful deliverance from sin, death, and hell that he has accomplished.

A new name, "the Holy People, the Redeemed of the LORD," characterizes God's people. The church of God is not a secular institution concerned with taxes, tariffs, social reform, political agendas, or other worldly affairs. God's people focus on moral, spiritual, and eternal issues, all connected to the redemption earned by the Savior and to the forgiveness of sins, which washes away every stain of evil. Whenever the institutional church alters its focus so that it concentrates on something other than these blessings of the Savior, it ceases to be the holy and redeemed people of God.

The city of God, his church, so often looks impover-ished in this world. The church seems to be stagnant and curiously mismatched in the world of power politics, materi-alism, and practical needs. So often it has been opposed and persecuted. The grand cathedrals erected in previous ages now appear empty and, in many cases, amount to nothing more than museums. But God changes things. No longer will his people be called deserted and be viewed as desolate. God's people have forgiveness and eternal life— the gifts of God sought after by thousands throughout his-tory. The church of Jesus Christ is not desolate. She is not deserted. God still has his legions of the faithful. Finally, when all the people of God are gathered from the nations of the world, no one will say the church is deserted and has no members. Instead, the feet of the saints will march glori-ously into the presence of God. Luther writes, "Formerly you [the people of God] were forsaken and despised by your enemies. The ungodly perish and then the church remains. . . . This is one sermon concerning the promises given to the church" (LW, Volume 17, page 351).

The Lord has brought vengeance and redemption

63 Who is this coming from Edom,
　　from Bozrah, with his garments stained crimson?
Who is this, robed in splendor,
　　striding forward in the greatness of his strength?

"It is I, speaking in righteousness,
　　mighty to save."

From the opening verse of chapter 60 to the end of chapter 62, Isaiah has revealed the unsurpassed glory that will belong to God's redeemed people. As Isaiah looked into the future, he saw these things: "the glory of the LORD" would rise upon the faithful (chapter 60), the Servant would bring good news and great blessings (chapter 61), and Zion would receive a new, glorious name (chapter 62). What wonderful blessings await the faithful of the Lord!

With all those wonderful blessings fresh in the reader's mind, Isaiah saw a startling figure approach. The figure of a man that Isaiah saw walked confidently as a victor "striding forward in the greatness of his strength." He was "robed in splendor." His appearance implied a powerful, confident, and triumphant figure. But we notice something unusual about him. He wore stained clothing. We might expect that he would be sweaty or dirty, like a warrior, because of difficult exertion. But the detail that catches our attention is that his splendid garments were stained red.

The person Isaiah saw came from Edom, an ancient enemy on Israel's southern border. Through the long history of God's people, Edom remained one of Judah's most implacable enemies. Edom here represents all the forces aligned against God and his people. Bozrah was an important city of Edom and no doubt was a stronghold. The name Bozrah may mean "unassailable." As Isaiah saw the figure approaching, he asked, "Who is this?"

The powerful figure answered boldly and confidently, "It is I, speaking in righteousness, mighty to save." These words help us identify the figure. He speaks in righteousness and is "mighty to save." The Lord has a fervent zeal to save sinners; he is righteous. Because of his righteousness, he planned the deliverance of his people and the deliverance of all the world. God's plan was to send the Servant who would substitute himself for a world of sinners under God's judgment. Because of the Servant, God could "justify many" (53:11), that is, he could declare them not guilty. When the figure claimed to speak "in righteousness," he did so in connection with the plan of God for the deliverance of the world. The figure Isaiah saw also claimed to be the powerful author of salvation. Who but the Lord is "mighty to save"? Throughout his prophecy Isaiah has been describing God's great claims to glory and to his superiority over all other gods and all other theologies. Simply, the Lord is superior to all others because only he blots out the sins of his people. God says, "I, even I, am the LORD, and apart from me there is no savior" (43:11). Who else can this be but the great Savior of God's people?

The Suffering Servant, whom we first noted in Isaiah chapter 53, no longer appears bruised and beaten. He has triumphed. He who was crucified no longer remains lowly and meek. He has become powerful and glorious. "The stone the builders rejected has become the capstone; the LORD has done this, and it is marvelous in our eyes. This is the day the LORD has made; let us rejoice and be glad in it" (Psalm 118:22-24). We are not in doubt about the identity of this figure, but a question still remains.

> ² **Why are your garments red,**
> **like those of one treading the winepress?**
>
> ³ **"I have trodden the winepress alone;**
> **from the nations no one was with me.**
> **I trampled them in my anger**
> **and trod them down in my wrath;**
> **their blood spattered my garments,**
> **and I stained all my clothing.**
> ⁴ **For the day of vengeance was in my heart,**
> **and the year of my redemption has come.**
> ⁵ **I looked, but there was no one to help,**
> **I was appalled that no one gave support;**
> **so my own arm worked salvation for me,**
> **and my own wrath sustained me.**
> ⁶ **I trampled the nations in my anger;**
> **in my wrath I made them drunk**
> **and poured their blood on the ground."**

The blood-spattered garments of the figure reminded the prophet of someone who stamped out grapes. During harvesttime the ripe grapes were gathered and put into a winepress, where workers stomped on them with their bare feet. The annual task was messy, and the clothes the workers wore naturally became spattered and stained with the juice of the crushed grapes. The stains upon the Lord's garments reminded the prophet of that annual event. So he asked for an explanation. Why are the garments of such a dominant figure stained red like those of someone at the time of the grape harvest?

The Lord's answer deepens the contrast with the previous chapters. The Lord has indeed taken part in a harvest, but not a harvest of grapes. It is a harvest of judgment. The Lord has stamped out his enemies, and his garments are stained with their blood. He has completed the "day of vengeance." The picture Isaiah draws for us here assumes that the judgment was already accomplished and the Lord is returning from its completion. The picture of the bloody Messiah may surprise and revolt us. We discover that he is not covered with his own blood. If that were the image, we could find comfort in it because we know that Jesus shed his blood to cleanse us of our sins. But in this picture, the blood of his enemies has stained his garments, and he wears his bloodstained garments as a badge of honor.

He defeated—thoroughly defeated—his enemies. The Lord makes it clear that no one helped him with the gruesome task of judgment. Just as no human being can help the Lord in his work of saving sinners (59:16), so no one can help bring about judgment. No human was, is, or will be righteous and holy enough to stand beside the Lord and assist in either case. The Lord himself, alone and without the aid of anyone else, has accomplished both salvation and judgment.

Once God accomplished that judgment, however, the deliverance of his faithful is assured and certain. As brutal as this picture may be, we find words that speak of God's grace—"righteousness" and "mighty to save" (verse 1), "my redemption" (verse 4), and "salvation" (verse 5). God's plan has always called for punishment and deliverance. God's message has always been a message of law and gospel. He thoroughly condemns his enemies, but he also graciously redeems his faithful.

Who are those enemies? Remember where the Lord had been. Isaiah had seen the Lord come from Edom and Bozrah (verse 1). The judgment he has accomplished had been completed there. Edom was an ancient enemy of God's Old Testament people. Isaiah had used Edom as an illustration of God's enemies in the first portion of his prophecy too. In chapter 34, Isaiah had described a bloody scene of judgment: "My sword had drunk its fill in the heavens; see, it descends in judgment on Edom, the people I have totally destroyed. The sword of the LORD is bathed in blood" (verses 5,6).

Why Edom? Because they constantly opposed God's people (see *Isaiah 1–39*, in The People's Bible series, pages 366-368). In the future, when the Babylonians would defeat the Jews, sack Jerusalem, and carry the population into exile, Edom would gloat. A later psalmist referred to their reaction: "Remember, O LORD, what the Edomites did on the day Jerusalem fell. 'Tear it down,' they cried, 'tear it down to its foundations!'" (137:7). Such opposition to God and his people meant that they refused the blessings of salvation the Lord had graciously offered through Judah and the house of David. Edom therefore is a symbol of all who refuse to believe in the Messiah. The Lord does not focus his judgment only on Edom. He stamps out "the nations" (verse 6), that is, all people who reject his gracious offer of deliverance, through the Messiah, from sin, death, and hell.

In Isaiah's vision, the Lord had carried out the day of vengeance—judgment day. The Lord said that such a day was "in my heart"—a part of his plan from the beginning. Jesus did not shrink from telling his disciples and others about that day of judgment (see Matthew 24,25). The day of vengeance was but one side of the Lord's righteousness; he promised another side too. Here Isaiah pictures it as "the year of my redemption." Judgment would surely come, but when the Lord defeated and destroyed all his enemies, he would bring about the great redemption, the peace and joy he had prepared for his faithful believers. These six verses remind us of what will happen to all who do not believe. Luther comments, "This is the meaning of this little chapter, that at the close of the promises it brings terror, as if to say, 'If you do not want to have salvation and Christ, receive Him from Edom with stained garments'" (LW, Volume 17, page 354). Christians readily sing:

> Saints, behold! The sight is glorious—
> See the man of sorrows now,
> From the fight returned victorious!
> Ev'ry knee to him shall bow.
> Crown him! Crown him!
> Crowns become the victor's brow. (CW 216:1)

Many scholars, including Luther, believe that there should be a chapter division at the end of verse 6. The description of the bloody and glorious Lord does provide an important conclusion to the entire second half (chapters 40–66) of Isaiah's prophecy. In many ways, it closes this section in a way similar to that in which Isaiah concluded the first half (chapters

1–39) of his prophecy. In the first half, chapters 34 and 35 concluded the prophetic portion. Chapters 36 to 39 recorded the historical events of Assyria's invasion and its aftermath. Chapter 34 had referred to God's judgment on Edom. This second half concludes at this point with a reference to Edom too. The chapters that follow present a prayer spoken by a representative of God's people and God's answer to that prayer. A logical break occurs here at verse 6.

From the opening verse of chapter 40, God has provided rich comfort to his people through the message of his prophet Isaiah. He promised that he would send deliverance (40–48), he described how he would deliver his people through the Servant (49–56), and he outlined the wonderful blessings that would come to his people because of the work of the Servant (57:1–63:6). Before we go on to the remaining chapters, let's review what we have learned in this section.

- The Lord reminded his people that they could not earn his blessings through their fasting. Sadly, their worship was flawed by insincerity and by their own greed. Redemption cannot be earned. God's people are not to be characterized by their religious activity, or even their religious zeal, but by repentance and faith.

- The iniquities of all humanity separated them from God. Isaiah used several different words to describe sin (see chapter 59).

- "The glory of the Lord" would rise upon his faithful people and bring them joy. The Savior would also draw the Gentiles to himself. The Gentiles would bring their wealth and power into the church to be used in the service of the Lord.

- The Lord would continue to announce to all the world what he had done for all sinners. The believers would enjoy great blessings and would be called God's holy people and the redeemed of the Lord.

- The glorious, triumphant, and bloody Lord would bring about the judgment upon all his enemies because they were also enemies of his people. The destruction of his enemies would bring deliverance for his people.

A believer prays for deliverance

⁷ **I will tell of the kindnesses of the LORD,**
  the deeds for which he is to be praised,
  according to all the LORD has done for us—
 yes, the many good things he has done
  for the house of Israel,
  according to his compassion and many kindnesses.
⁸ **He said, "Surely they are my people,**
  sons who will not be false to me";
  and so he became their Savior.
⁹ **In all their distress he too was distressed,**
  and the angel of his presence saved them.
 In his love and mercy he redeemed them;
  he lifted them up and carried them
  all the days of old.

All the blessings God's prophet promised were still in the future. In Isaiah's day, the reality of life in Jerusalem was anything but a glorious, joyful, or triumphant existence. Sin still dogged their lives. Greed, envy, pride, ambition, and rage still clogged all their relationships. Drunkenness and sexual immorality brought temporary pleasure but then returned to bite with the fangs of guilt and misery as these sinful pleasures only wasted lives and potential. Death remained the victor over every human effort. In the world of history and politics, the Assyrian army may have retreated during Isaiah's day, but eventually a new threat would appear. The Babylonians would come and destroy everything. All these realities sound so contemporary.

Some suggest that this prayer came from the heart of an exile after the Babylonians had carried the Jews away captive. They claim that Isaiah could not have written it. For proof they cite verse 18, in which the speaker of the prayer describes the temple as "trampled down." The speaker also describes Jerusalem as "a desolation" (64:10) and the temple as "burned with fire (64:11). Such conditions did not exist until long after Isaiah was dead and buried. Indeed, the prayer may well be placed into the mouth of an exile during the Babylonian captivity. Yet that does not mean that Isaiah did not write it. God's prophet wrote very clearly about the Messiah seven hundred years before he arrived. Certainly he could have written this prayer by the power of the Lord's Spirit so that it appeared to be spoken by an exile. We believe that God gave his prophet the ability to see into the future. The same assumption persists throughout the entire commentary, and we see no reason to change at this point.

Certainly the prayer fits the situation an exile would confront in Babylon, but the prayer also fits the situation every believer faces while living in this world. The great promises of God lie in the future, beyond the apparent world of sin, death, violence, toil, and trouble. Whenever God's people have experienced such things throughout the centuries, they turned to God in prayer. This prayer provides a model and breathes human sighs of anguish.

Like all prayers by God's faithful, it is grounded in deep faith. The one who prays knows the kindnesses of the Lord. These first verses announce the great "kindnesses of the LORD." The history of God's Old Testament people tells how God delivered them from Egypt, an event most Jews still celebrate annually. God fed his people in the wilderness and gave them a land of their own. He gave them victory when they had no hope of victory. He protected them. He claimed them as his people. God desired to create children who would not be false to him (verse 8).

Every child of God treasures verse 9. We can apply it first to the history of God's dealing with his Old Testament people. The Lord was touched by their affliction in Egypt. Moses wrote: "The Israelites groaned in their slavery and cried out, and their cry for help because of their slavery went up to God. God heard their groaning and he remembered his covenant with Abraham, with Isaac and with Jacob. So God looked on the Israelites and was concerned about them" (Exodus 2:23-25). He brought them out of Egypt and carried them through the wilderness and all throughout their history. He sent the angel of his presence before his people. If it had not been for the Lord's grace and mercy, they would have destroyed themselves or been destroyed by their enemies. In Isaiah's day, the miraculous deliverance from the Assyrian army (chapters 36,37) became just the latest chapter in the long history of God's taking care of his people.

While these thoughts fit the situation of an Old Testament believer, they apply as well to every believer of any generation at any time. We are comforted in knowing that the Lord shares our distress and pain. He is not distant, detached, or remote from any of his people. In all our afflictions, God himself is afflicted. There's more. He has redeemed us by the blood of his own dear Son and delivered us from sin, death, and hell. But there is still more. As we retrace the steps we have walked through life, we can also say that the Lord has lifted us up and carried us all along the way. Our prayers flow from the deep faith in what the grace and mercy of God has already done for us.

> ¹⁰ **Yet they rebelled**
> **and grieved his Holy Spirit.**
> **So he turned and became their enemy**
> **and he himself fought against them.**
>
> ¹¹ **Then his people recalled the days of old,**
> **the days of Moses and his people—**
> **where is he who brought them through the sea,**
> **with the shepherd of his flock?**
> **Where is he who set**
> **his Holy Spirit among them,**
> ¹² **who sent his glorious arm of power**
> **to be at Moses' right hand,**
> **who divided the waters before them,**
> **to gain for himself everlasting renown,**
> ¹³ **who led them through the depths?**
> **Like a horse in open country,**
> **they did not stumble;**
> ¹⁴ **like cattle that go down to the plain,**
> **they were given rest by the Spirit of the LORD.**
> **This is how you guided your people**
> **to make for yourself a glorious name.**

As confident as we may be of the Lord's grace, we are just as sure that our sins have grieved him. The human spirit is perverse. When it notes all the blessings that flow from the grace of God, it rebels against God. Illustrations of that basic, persistent flaw can be found on the pages of Israelite history as they wandered through the wilderness. They complained about the bread that God miraculously gave them. At the foot of Mount Sinai, they made and worshiped a golden calf. The Lord was not happy with his people, "and the LORD struck the people with a plague because of what they did with the calf Aaron had made" (Exodus 32:35). Because of their sin, God became their enemy.

The human spirit has not improved over the centuries. Sin still throttles our joy and turns us away from God to ourselves. We claim to achieve and succeed by our own power. We want to bask in the glow of our own achievements and imagine that they are good enough to deserve God's notice and reward. Yet our behavior reveals the depth of sin and the stranglehold it has on our hearts and minds. Paul wrote: "Do not grieve the Holy Spirit of God. . . . Get rid of all bitterness, rage and anger, brawling and slander, along with every form of malice" (Ephesians 4:30,31).

The perversity of sinful human nature infects us all. God called his Old Testament people to repentance again and again. He remained the same God who delivered them from Egypt in the days of Moses. He had led them through the Red Sea and delivered them safely from the threat of Pharaoh's army. God called them to repentance again and again. We are also infected by sin and often turn away from God. But he calls us to repentance just as he called his Old Testament people to repentance. When we stray, God calls us to return to the loving arms that have guided us, redeemed us, and delivered us. Like prodigal sons and daughters, believers remember the grace of God and return to him in repentance (see Luke 15:11-32). We renew our connection with the God of grace through our daily contrition and repentance. When we renew our connection with the Lord, we can turn to him in prayer with all our troubles.

> ¹⁵ **Look down from heaven and see**
> **from your lofty throne, holy and glorious.**
> **Where are your zeal and your might?**
> **Your tenderness and compassion are withheld from us.**
> ¹⁶ **But you are our Father,**
> **though Abraham does not know us**

or Israel acknowledge us;
you, O LORD, are our Father,
our Redeemer from of old is your name.
¹⁷ Why, O LORD, do you make us wander from your ways
and harden our hearts so we do not revere you?
Return for the sake of your servants,
the tribes that are your inheritance.

At times God does appear to be remote and distant from human troubles. Isaiah taught us that God remains hidden at times (45:15). He does not always reveal himself, nor does he always explain to us what he does in our own personal history or why. Nevertheless, his love for sinners has been clearly revealed to us in Christ and the blessings we have in Christ. Still we often scratch our heads in wonder at why God allows pain and misery to afflict us and others. This prayer expresses that human puzzlement at God's wondrous ways. "Look down" becomes almost a complaint. "God, don't you see what's happening here on earth?" "Where are your zeal and your might?" the prophet prays. At times God appears to withhold his tenderness and compassion.

Yet faithful believers cling to the promises of God. They know that the way of God is always good and that he will make everything work out for the best. That confidence filled the hearts of countless believers during the tragedies of Old Testament history, including the captivity in Babylon. How often God's people might well have wondered why God had allowed such terrible things to happen. But in the midst of the worst of times, they trusted in God.

Verse 16 is remarkable for two reasons. First, it is among the few passages in the Old Testament that refer to God as Father. For the Old Testament believer, that idea stretched back to creation. God had created the world and all humans. He is the Father of God's people in another way too. According to his promise, God called Abraham and gave him and

Sarah a son. Old Testament believers could remember how God had chosen Jacob, or Israel, from whom the nation received its name. The idea that God was their Father gathered together all the promises God had made to their forefathers. They were people of Israel because of God's promises and power. Like a father, God nurtured the growth of his people. He had endured their rebellious years and his power had sustained them. He was their Father. As their Father, he had the responsibility for taking care of them. So this prayer turns to God, expecting him, as the believer's heavenly Father, to take care of his believers.

A second reason makes this verse important. The passage turns to God as the source of help because "Abraham does not know us or Israel acknowledge us." Abraham and Israel were dead and resting securely in the heavenly home they both expected (Hebrews 11:13-16). Once believers die, they know the joys of heaven, but they do not know the affairs of the loved ones they leave behind. Both Abraham and Jacob (Israel) could not help the people of Isaiah's day or any of the people of any age. God reveals the profound truth that the saints in glory do not influence the affairs of humans on earth. Only God does that. He alone is the Father of believers.

If verse 16 is remarkable, verse 17 presents difficulties. It asks why God has hardened the hearts of his people. We wonder why God would harden his people and allow them to wander from the truth. The Scriptures tell us again and again that God does harden people's hearts. When people turn away from his gracious invitation, when they persist in despising his love, when they continue to oppose the message of the gospel, God turns their hearts into wood and stone. As a result, they can no longer fear him and can no longer return to him. He did so with Pharaoh in Egypt. God told Isaiah that his ministry would be a ministry of hardening (6:9,10). The beautiful promises we treasure from this prophet of God were only so much babbling to those who had rejected God (28:9-13). Those beautiful and eloquent promises did not penetrate their hearts of stone. God's message through Isaiah only made their hearts harder and more resistant to the gospel.

In great difficulty, believers may be driven to the brink of despair. Yet for believers, despair never comes. Instead, God's children gasp a confession of faith, turn to the Lord, and ask God to return. Believers hold God to his promises. God had promised to care for his servants, Israel. He had promised that deliverance for all the world would come through their nation. This prayer boldly clings to those promises. "Return for the sake of your servants."

¹⁸ For a little while your people possessed your holy place,
but now our enemies have trampled down your
sanctuary.
¹⁹ We are yours from of old;
but you have not ruled over them,
they have not been called by your name.

Why do bad things enter the lives of believers? These verses fit very well into the mouth of an exile in Babylon. The glory days of Israel were past. The people had built a temple during the relatively short time that they controlled Palestine. They had received the blessings of the Lord throughout their history. But that history would come to an abrupt end with the rise of Babylon. An exile might wonder why God had allowed his temple to be trampled by people who did not know the Lord and his promises. Why was the speaker exiled far away from Jerusalem and the temple? He might well have wondered why God appeared to have abandoned all his promises. "We are yours from of old," the people said, but those who had enslaved them had no knowledge of the Lord. It appeared as if a nation that did not know the Lord had destroyed the very nation God had chosen as his own. Why?

These words fit into the mouth of an exile, but, at times, they also fit into our own mouths. When we see evil triumph, we wonder where God is. How many days are darkened by events that challenge us to wonder whether God can still control things? At times our troubles do not disappear even when we take them to the Lord in prayer. We wonder whether God has forgotten us and failed to fulfill his promises. We are God's faithful believers in this evil world, but at times it does indeed seem that he has abandoned us. Many Christians have faced such times. Again and again it appears that our experiences teach us that God somehow sleeps in heaven and remains unresponsive to our troubles and prayers. Evil succeeds and grows worse and worse.

Such situations challenge our faith in the goodness and power of God. The believer who prayed this prayer had come to that point. But he was not driven to despair. Instead, he firmly held on to the promises of God, praying, "Return for the sake of your servants" (verse 17). In spite of the difficulties, he had not given up his hope in the Lord. In faith he grasped the Lord's grace, which had made him and so many others servants of the living Lord, and he asked for help in his difficulties.

When difficulties drive us to the farthest boundary of our faith and we stand at the very frontier of despair and doubt, we, as God's people, turn to him and pray for his help and strength. We do not abandon faith and then cross into despair; we trust. In our difficulties, it may appear as if God does not rule over us or over anything of this world.

God seems to be hiding in the heavens. Remember how Job's difficulties challenged his faith. At first Job confessed, "The LORD gave and the LORD has taken away; may the name of the LORD be praised" (Job 1:21). But his challenges continued. In Job's difficulties, God remained silent to his prayers, and Job found himself at that bleak border between faith and despair. But he did not abandon his faith in the Lord. Even in those difficulties, Job confessed, "Though he slay me, yet will I hope in him" (13:15). In the same way, this prayer does not cross over into despair. The child of God praying this prayer may have been driven to the border, but he still has both feet planted in faith.

64 Oh, that you would rend the heavens and come down,
that the mountains would tremble before you!
² As when fire sets twigs ablaze
and causes water to boil,
come down to make your name known to your enemies
and cause the nations to quake before you!

Faith turns to the Lord in prayer. Even when God appears barricaded in heaven, ignoring the suffering of his people, faith prays. Consider the example of King Hezekiah. When King Hezekiah peered out from behind Jerusalem's walls to see the Assyrian army massed around his city, all appeared to be lost. No nation had been able to resist the military power of Assyria. Although Hezekiah "did what was right in the eyes of the LORD, just as his father David had done" (2 Chronicles 29:2), the Assyrian forces appeared to be irresistible and the destruction of Jerusalem inevitable. Sennacherib, the king of Assyria, had led his forces against several other cities of Judah and had overcome every defense. The Assyrian commander taunted Hezekiah and the people of Jerusalem. In his arrogant speech before the walls of Jerusalem, the enemy commander offered to give King Hezekiah two thousand horses if he could only put riders on them (Isaiah 36). It was a desperate time. Isaiah recorded the response of Hezekiah to these circumstances: "When King Hezekiah heard this, he tore his clothes and put on sackcloth and went into the temple of the LORD" (37:1). The writer of Chronicles recorded, "King Hezekiah and the prophet Isaiah son of Amoz cried out in prayer to heaven about this" (2 Chronicles 32:20).

In such ominous times, God's believers always turn to the Lord in prayer. This prayer serves as another example. All appeared hopeless. God remained silent. Yet faith held to the promises of God. The one praying utters a desperate plea to the God of heaven: "Our Father, our Redeemer from of old" (63:16). "Oh, that you would rend the heavens and come down, that the mountains would tremble before you!" These are the words of a believer facing difficult troubles and yet clinging to God's promises of power and grace. For this believer, all seems to be out of balance. Evil seems to triumph. Good retreats in the face of persecution. God's enemies smugly defy God, and no one can restrain them. The prophet turns to God and asks him to step in and correct the imbalance: "O Lord, come. Assert your power. Protect and deliver your people. Destroy your enemies and the enemies of your people."

> [3] **For when you did awesome things that we did not expect,**
>   **you came down, and the mountains trembled before you.**
> [4] **Since ancient times no one has heard,**
>   **no ear has perceived,**
>   **no eye has seen any God besides you,**
>   **who acts on behalf of those who wait for him.**
> [5] **You come to the help of those who gladly do right,**
>   **who remember your ways.**

The prayer began with a recitation of "the many good things [the LORD] has done for the house of Israel" (63:7). Here the praying prophet pins his prayer onto the grace God had demonstrated to his people in the past. God had done awesome things no one could have expected. The Exodus was one such example. Before God called Moses, who ever would have imagined an entire nation leaving their bondage? Who could have thought God would deliver his people by separating the sea and leading them safely to the other side? Who could have predicted that the pride of Pharaoh's army would be drowned in the Red Sea? If we need an example of the mountains trembling, consider Mount Sinai. When the Lord descended, "the whole mountain trembled violently" (Exodus 19:18). This prayer attaches its hope of future deliverance upon the past grace of God.

What would that deliverance be? How would it come? Just as no one in the past could have imagined the Exodus, so no human could ever imagine the deliverance God has provided for his people. God's entire plan of salvation lay outside the scope of human thought and imagination. Who could imagine that God would send his one and only Son as a substitute to redeem the world from sin and deliver all humanity from death? Who would have ever imagined that God would accomplish this by sacrificing his own Son? What human mind could have anticipated the empty tomb? Would any single human imagine that by faith in God's Servant, Jesus Christ, a man or woman could become an adopted child of God? God reveals these truths to humanity. God proclaimed his plan through the prophets and then recorded the fulfillment of his plan through the evangelists of the New Testament. The wisdom of God's gracious plan lies beyond the imagination and thought of the most gifted human mind. If anyone is to understand God's grace, God himself must impart that understanding to the human mind. The apostle Paul understood. After citing verse 4 of this chapter, he reminded his readers, "God has revealed it to us by his Spirit" (1 Corinthians 2:10).

God's deliverance always goes beyond what the human intellect can imagine by itself. While God's people were captive in Babylon, the faithful turned to the Lord in prayer and asked for deliverance. Without the promises of God through the prophets, including Isaiah, not one of them could have imagined that God would break the power of imperial Babylon and free his people. Those who tenaciously held on to the promises God had spoken knew God's deliverance was to come. Isaiah had even foretold that Cyrus would be their deliverer. But even they did not know exactly how it would happen. The edict by the Persian king, Cyrus, was the answer to their prayers and the fulfillment of God's promises.

In this prayer, Isaiah held fast to the principle that God would act "on behalf of those who wait for him." That principle lies at the base of all Christian prayer. Believers turn to God in prayer, hoping and trusting that God will act to help. All religions teach people to offer prayers to their gods. Yet only the prayers addressed to the Lord Jehovah in faith reach the throne of grace and receive the answer and action of the Lord. All other prayers are only placebos for fear, guilt, and trouble. Isaiah reminds us that God comes "to the help of those who gladly do right, who remember [his] ways."

Who are those who "do right" and "remember [his] ways"? They are the faithful believers who cling to the promises of God—those in whose hearts the Holy Spirit has created faith through the gospel. Such a person becomes happy in the righteousness of the Lord and gladly does as

God desires. A believer understands that he or she has been declared righteous by the Lord and then joyfully responds with a life that conforms to God's will. A faithful believer remembers the ways of God. But the ways of God are not only his laws for love and justice in human behavior but also his wonderful principle of undeserved grace for sinners. Such are God's ways. So believers pray and have the promise of God's action on their behalf.

> **But when we continued to sin against them,**
> **   you were angry.**
> **How then can we be saved?**
> **⁶ All of us have become like one who is unclean,**
> **   and all our righteous acts are like filthy rags;**
> **we all shrivel up like a leaf,**
> **   and like the wind our sins sweep us away.**
> **⁷ No one calls on your name**
> **   or strives to lay hold of you;**
> **for you have hidden your face from us**
> **   and made us waste away because of our sins.**

Why should God respond to this prayer or to any prayer spoken by any human? When we considered the time of the Exodus, we noted God's dramatic and unexpected deliverance of his people. God unexpectedly and graciously acted to provide deliverance for his people. Why should God act in this way? Only a few months after such a dramatic deliverance, the people worshiped a golden image in the wilderness. God in anger told Moses: "I have seen these people, . . . and they are a stiff-necked people. Now leave me alone so that my anger may burn against them and that I may destroy them. Then I will make you into a great nation" (Exodus 32:9,10). Throughout their history, such perversity and rebellion dogged the people God had claimed from Egypt. In view of all their sins, how could they expect God to deliver them? Isaiah had thundered

God's condemnation upon the disobedience and rebellion of God's people of his day. By what right could any of them expect God's help and aid?

Isaiah included himself among the rebellious and sinful. "All of us . . ." he confessed. In those words God's prophet proclaimed a principle that extends to all humanity of all time. He included us as well. "All of us have become like one who is unclean." The word *unclean* means "polluted and defiled." The Levitical laws described many things, such as certain animals, as "unclean." Isaiah confessed that the people themselves were "unclean" and placed himself among the polluted and defiled. Isaiah then emphasized the disgusting and revolting character of sin. The righteous acts of any human are nothing but filthy rags. The translation does not offend our sensitivities, but the original calls these righteous acts menstrual rags. How can we be saved when we are as unclean as such in God's eyes? Why should God deliver us when even our best—"all our righteous acts"—are nothing more than dirty, bloody menstrual rags? Because of sin, we are disgusting in God's eyes. The words convey the true nature of human sinfulness. Why indeed should the Holy One of Israel save anyone?

Isaiah goes on to describe what sin has done to every human. Sin makes us lifeless and dead like a dry leaves that skitter and scrape across the ground in the autumn wind. By ourselves we have no life and can produce nothing of value in God's eyes. Paul wrote, "You were dead in your transgressions and sins" (Ephesians 2:1). Because of sin no human can call upon the Lord. We are helpless. God's anger burns against all who sin. Isaiah describes God as hiding his face from the sinner. The picture grows more severe when he also says that God makes sinners waste away because of their sins. What a sad state of affairs for the sinner! God hides his face and turns the sinner over to his or her own sins. As sinners persist in their sins, God abandons them to their own imaginations. He withdraws himself and his grace and mercy. So Jesus, at times, remained silent in the face of opposition and told parables that persistent unbelievers could not understand. Each sin carries the sinner, step by step, farther away from God and closer to destruction and judgment. By nature, sin chains every human in its bondage and dooms everyone to destruction. By nature, sinners cannot rescue themselves from the inevitable consequences of their sins.

> ⁸ **Yet, O Lord, you are our Father.**
>   **We are the clay, you are the potter;**
>   **we are all the work of your hand.**
> ⁹ **Do not be angry beyond measure, O Lord;**
>   **do not remember our sins forever.**
> **Oh, look upon us, we pray,**
>   **for we are all your people.**

This wonderful prayer turns to the Lord once more and clings to his undeserved grace—"yet," that is, in spite of our sins and in spite of the fact that even our best amounts to nothing but dirty menstrual rags. In spite of the disgusting stains of sin, the prayer expresses faith in the Lord. We find two names for God here: Lord and Father. Lord is the name for the God of free and faithful grace, the God of the covenant who revealed his name to Moses:

> The Lord, the Lord, the compassionate and gracious God, slow to anger, abounding in love and faithfulness, maintaining love to thousands, and forgiving wickedness, rebellion and sin. Yet he does not leave the guilty unpunished; he punishes the children and their children for the sin of the fathers to the third and fourth generation. (Exodus 34:6,7)

The second name, Father, recalls verse 16 of the previous chapter. This God is "*our* Father." This cry of faith claims God as its dearest treasure.

Such faith also recognizes its relationship with this powerful and gracious God. The description of God as the potter certainly fits the history of God's people. He called Abraham and then shaped and molded his descendants into a nation. God made them what they were. But the description also aptly describes God's people individually. God shapes and molds every believer. We are the clay, and God molds us to the shape and for the use that he deems appropriate. We are the work of his hands. The apostle Paul declared that the Ephesians were dead in their sins, but he went on to assure them that God's grace had saved them: "For we are God's workmanship" (2:10).

Our disgusting sins separate us from God, yet faith turns to God and depends on his gracious promises. This turning to God in spite of sin finds power to pray trusting in the promises of God. As believers we have been taught to pray "in Jesus' name." God has no reason to listen to our prayers. Yet, when we come to him, we do not come to him on our own. We come to him in the name of Jesus, who has shed his blood to wash away our sins. God invites us to pray to him as dear children ask their dear Father. We can pray with confidence and boldness because, in Jesus, God is our dear Father. This prayer boldly erupts from the heart of a believer who trusts in the gracious promises of the Lord.

> [10] **Your sacred cities have become a desert;**
> **even Zion is a desert, Jerusalem a desolation.**
> [11] **Our holy and glorious temple, where our fathers praised**
> **you,**
> **has been burned with fire,**
> **and all that we treasured lies in ruins.**

¹² After all this, O Lᴏʀᴅ, will you hold yourself back?
Will you keep silent and punish us beyond measure?

In conclusion, the prayer sets before God the misery of
his people. The conditions described in these two verses fit
the world of the exiles. While they were exiles in Babylon,
their homeland remained a deserted and abandoned wilderness. The temple lay in ruins, a burnt-out shell of its former
glory. "All that we treasured lies in ruins." Because this
lament fits the time of the exile so well, some have suggested that Isaiah could not have written these words. "How
could he have known that the temple would be burned?"
they ask. The problem disappears if we believe that Isaiah
could see into the future by the power of God's Spirit.
Isaiah saw the future of Jerusalem and the consequences of
the unbelief of his own day. Jerusalem and Judea would
become a desolate wasteland.

Believers of all times have called upon God in times that
are quite similar to those of the exile. In times of persecution, God's people are surrounded by their enemies just as
Jerusalem had been in Hezekiah's day. From any human
perspective, all appears lost and hopeless. The end and
destruction appear inevitable and unavoidable. Even the
faithful suffer. Such times occur in the believer's personal
life too. Disaster, pain, misery, and suffering crash into the
daily routine. We sense our helplessness and may wonder
why God has allowed such turmoil to enter our lives. Like
the prophet, we often turn to the Lord and say, "Lord, look
at this situation. Disaster and desolation—heartache and
heartbreak—camp all around me. I am suffering. Where are
you, Lord of grace and love?"

In the final words of the chapter, the prayer sighs its
petition: "After all this, O Lᴏʀᴅ, will you hold yourself back?
Will you keep silent and punish us beyond measure?" In

other words, "Won't you, Lord, please send deliverance and relief?" This cry comes to the very gate of heaven and knocks at the door. Faith in God's grace and his fatherly care fills this prayer. Faith is no stranger to the power of God to save. The question pleads for God's answer with humble insistence. The prayer ends when the believer turns the bleak situation over to God for his gracious action. The remaining chapters of Isaiah give us God's answer.

The Lord responds to the believer's prayer

65 "I revealed myself to those who did not ask for me;
       I was found by those who did not seek me.
   To a nation that did not call on my name,
       I said, 'Here am I, here am I.'
   ² All day long I have held out my hands
       to an obstinate people,
   who walk in ways not good,
       pursuing their own imaginations—
   ³ a people who continually provoke me
       to my very face,
   offering sacrifices in gardens
       and burning incense on altars of brick;
   ⁴ who sit among the graves
       and spend their nights keeping secret vigil;
   who eat the flesh of pigs,
       and whose pots hold broth of unclean meat;
   ⁵ who say, 'Keep away; don't come near me,
       for I am too sacred for you!'
   Such people are smoke in my nostrils,
       a fire that keeps burning all day.

   ⁶ "See, it stands written before me:
       I will not keep silent but will pay back in full;
       I will pay it back into their laps—
   ⁷ both your sins and the sins of your fathers,"
       says the LORD.
   "Because they burned sacrifices on the mountains
       and defied me on the hills,

**I will measure into their laps
the full payment for their former deeds."**

The prayer recorded in the previous two chapters began with a recitation of God's compassion and kindness—his grace to his people. Although they did not deserve anything from the Lord of heaven, yet he had made them his people, rescued them from Egypt, and fashioned them to be his people throughout their history. The exile caused great difficulty. The faithful wondered if God had forgotten his people and abandoned them. The prayer asked, "Where are your zeal and your might?" (63:15) and, "Why, O LORD, do you make us wander from your ways and harden our hearts so we do not revere you?" (63:17). God's people are often confronted with misery and trouble. At such times God often appears to be silent and uninterested in helping his faithful. Some people abandon faith in the Lord, while others pray, "Lord, where are you?"

This prayer asked God to respond. "Look down from heaven and see" (63:15); "Oh, that you would rend the heavens and come down" (64:1); "Do not be angry beyond measure. . . . Oh, look upon us, we pray" (64:9). The prayer concluded with two questions, "Will you hold yourself back? Will you keep silent and punish us beyond measure?" (64:12). The questions anticipate an answer. They plead for an answer from the Lord. The two final chapters are God's answer to the prayer of his people, expressed by his prophet Isaiah. Some commentators today claim that these chapters do not address the issues raised in the prayer and cannot be considered an answer to the fervent prayer of the previous chapters. Yet the section does explain a great deal and provides a more profound answer than we would at first imagine. That will become evident as we study the Lord's response.

God's answer to the prayer of the previous chapter begins with a fundamental truth of God's approach to humanity: "I revealed myself to those who did not ask for me." By nature, no human can know anything about God and his grace unless God reveals it to humans. His ways are far above anything we might imagine (chapter 55). In order for any human to understand God, he must reveal himself and allow himself to be found. August Pieper wrote of this principle, "Had He [God] waited until He had been sought after, there would never have been a revelation of God's grace" (*Isaiah II*, page 662). Luther confessed, "I believe that I cannot by own thinking or choosing believe in Jesus Christ, my Lord, or come to him" (Small Catechism, Explanation to the Third Article). Paul put it a bit differently but just as clearly: "No one knows the thoughts of God except the Spirit of God" (1 Corinthians 2:11) and, "You were dead in your transgressions and sins" (Ephesians 2:1). Dead is dead. Dead means without the ability to move, breathe, or think. Because of their natural condition of sin, all humans find themselves in this condition.

God, of course, in love reveals himself to humanity. He communicates the message of heaven in the language of earth. The Lord says, "Here am I, here am I." In response to his revealed Word, some believe, that is, they find God. Luther's Small Catechism explains, "The Holy Spirit has called me by the gospel, enlightened me with his gifts, sanctified and kept me in the true faith" (Explanation to the Third Article). Paul speaks the same language when he says, "God has revealed it to us by his Spirit" (1 Corinthians 2:10) and, "Faith comes from hearing the message" (Romans 10:17). If God does not tell us of his grace, we will never find him or understand his love.

Who are the people in verse 1 to whom God reveals himself and says, "Here am I"? The apostle Paul quoted these words and applied them to the gentile nations (Romans 10:20). Isaiah tells us that the people to whom the Lord speaks in this first verse are people who "did not call on my name." The phrase applies to Gentiles who could not claim to be God's special people the way the people of Israel were. But the principle that God expresses here also applies to all humanity, even to the people of Israel. Before the people of Israel became a nation, God revealed himself to them and made them his own. Abraham had no knowledge that God would make him an ancestor of Christ until God called him and revealed his promises to the forefather of the nation Israel. In the same way, Gentiles, who were not part of the nation of Israel, also came to faith through the great promises of God. The Aramean Naaman was led to believe (2 Kings 5).

The apostle Paul applied verse 2 more pointedly to the people of Israel. They had received the special revelation of God and had entered into a special relationship with the Lord. Yet they squandered their special blessings and privileges. At Mount Sinai, God revealed his will for these people. Moses descended from the mount with the tablets of stones and eventually wrote down all that God had revealed to him. The first five books of the Old Testament come from the hand of Moses, and Jews still revere those books. In spite of those special messages from God himself, God's chosen people turned away from his revelation, that is, from his Word.

Instead of obeying and remaining faithful to God's Word, the people of Israel pursued "their own imaginations." God identified some of the departures from his Word in his opening comments. God had given his people specific instructions about where they were to worship and how. At first they worshiped at the tabernacle in the wilderness and later at the temple in Jerusalem. But God's people decided to change their worship. They offered their sacrifices "in gardens" and burned incense on "altars of brick" instead of worshiping the Lord as he had prescribed. Worse yet, they worshiped false gods like Baal at these places.

Israel's perverted worship appeared everywhere. God had clearly told his people: "Let no one be found among you who sacrifices his son or daughter in the fire, who practices divination or sorcery, interprets omens, engages in witchcraft, or casts spells, or who is a medium or spiritist or who consults the dead. Anyone who does these things is detestable to the LORD" (Deuteronomy 18:10-12). In these verses from Isaiah, God tells us that his people sat among the graves and kept secret vigils, no doubt consulting the dead for information or enlightenment. God also said: "The pig . . . is unclean for you. You must not eat their meat or touch their carcasses; they are unclean for you" (Leviticus 11:7,8). Instead of avoiding the flesh of pigs, the people ate pork. They had abandoned God's revelation in favor of their own preferences. Even though they thought that they were worshiping the true God by their religious practices, they insulted him because they failed to honor what he had told them.

In so many ways, the people of Israel turned away from God and did exactly what he had told them not to do. They even thought that by their pious and religious efforts, they had achieved a special elite status. Some thought that they were "too sacred" for common people. What an astounding affront to the Holy One of Israel, who alone is holy and who sanctified his people only through the blood of sacrifice! How could they be holy unless God cleansed them (Isaiah 1:18)? The Lord promised to cleanse them and remove their sins through the sacrifice of the Servant (chapter 53). But they chose to achieve such a holy status by their own religious sacrifices and vigils, which God had expressly forbidden.

It is no wonder that God says that he had recorded all their perversions and would bring judgment upon them for their sins. And God did not even list the sins of bloodshed, injustice, dishonesty, or sexual perversion here. The people chose to abandon God's revealed truth and follow their own imaginations, their own religious feelings, their own hearts. In the process they set themselves against God and were like smoke in his nostrils. His judgment would follow.

What does all this have to do with the prayer of the previous two chapters? Isaiah had wondered if God would punish his people beyond measure (64:12). God answers that he would punish the people because they had so thoroughly and wantonly abandoned him and his Word. God was justly displeased with their sins. Clearly, they could offer no excuse and all deserved his judgment in full measure. But God's response did not end on such a negative note.

⁸**This is what the LORD says:**

"As when juice is still found in a cluster of grapes
  and men say, 'Don't destroy it,
    there is yet some good in it,'
so will I do in behalf of my servants;
  I will not destroy them all.
⁹ **I will bring forth descendants from Jacob,**
  and from Judah those who will possess my mountains;
my chosen people will inherit them,
  and there will my servants live.
¹⁰ **Sharon will become a pasture for flocks,**
  and the Valley of Achor a resting place for herds,
    for my people who seek me.
¹¹ **"But as for you who forsake the LORD**
  and forget my holy mountain,

> who spread a table for Fortune
> and fill bowls of mixed wine for Destiny,
> [12] I will destine you for the sword,
> and you will all bend down for the slaughter;
> for I called but you did not answer,
> I spoke but you did not listen.
> You did evil in my sight
> and chose what displeases me."

[13]Therefore this is what the Sovereign LORD says:

> "My servants will eat,
> but you will go hungry;
> my servants will drink,
> but you will go thirsty;
> my servants will rejoice,
> but you will be put to shame.
> [14] My servants will sing
> out of the joy of their hearts,
> but you will cry out
> from anguish of heart
> and wail in brokenness of spirit.
> [15] You will leave your name
> to my chosen ones as a curse;
> the Sovereign LORD will put you to death,
> but to his servants he will give another name.
> [16] Whoever invokes a blessing in the land
> will do so by the God of truth;
> he who takes an oath in the land
> will swear by the God of truth.
> For the past troubles will be forgotten
> and hidden from my eyes.

The Lord had chosen the descendants of Abraham to be his special people, but they had abandoned what the Lord had revealed to them through his prophets. They had followed their own thoughts and opinions about spirituality and religion, and therefore they clearly deserved the judgment of the Sovereign Lord. But the Lord is a God of grace and mercy. He will "not leave the guilty unpunished"

(Exodus 34:7), but he has revealed himself to be "the LORD, the LORD, the compassionate and gracious God, slow to anger, abounding in love and faithfulness, maintaining love to thousands, and forgiving wickedness, rebellion and sin" (verses 6,7). This section begins with the solemn announcement that this compassionate and gracious LORD has something more to say: "This is what the LORD says."

The Lord compared his people to a cluster of grapes. Perhaps in the hot, dry air, a cluster would shrivel up and seem worthless, but the grapes would still possess some juice. Just as the grape harvesters would not destroy such a cluster as long as juice still remained in it, so the Lord "will not destroy them all." The Lord provides a direct answer to the question at the end of Isaiah's prayer: "Will you keep silent and punish us beyond measure?" (64:12). The Lord pledged not to punish these people beyond measure but to save his servants. He promised that a remnant of the people would be saved. God's prophet had referred to this remnant in the very first chapter of his prophecy. He had written, "Unless the LORD Almighty had left us some survivors, we would have become like Sodom, we would have been like Gomorrah" (1:9).

Why would the Lord take such a step and withhold judgment? What good could anyone find in this cluster of rebellious grapes? The Lord had promised to bring deliverance to all the world through these descendants of Abraham. He had promised to send the Servant at some point in the future. If he destroyed the nation completely, his promise could not have been fulfilled. If the Lord had not saved some of them, no one on earth could be rescued from sin and death, as Isaiah had foretold so eloquently earlier. The whole Old Testament Scripture had issued the same gracious promises. So God refused to utterly destroy these people.

He would withhold judgment upon some, not because some were more worthy or better than others but only because of his gracious promises. We find the reason not in the people, not in the faithfulness of some, but in God, who graciously promised to send the Servant.

Because this Servant would come, God would rescue some out of their own sinfulness and rebellion. But the plan of God extended beyond the Jewish people. He would create a new Israel, a new people—the church. The Savior came from a Jewish family that could trace its ancestry back to King David. He would come from the tribe of Judah (Genesis 49:10). He was the valuable juice in this cluster of grapes. Often Isaiah announced that the nations of the earth would also be interested in the coming of the Messiah. He wrote that the Messiah would be the banner that would beckon the nations (11:10,12; 18:3; 49:22; 62:10; John 3:14,15). Because of the promised Redeemer, Israel would be transformed, changed, and reconstructed. The Lord would gather a group of believers who would inherit all the blessings God promised to his people. These "chosen people" would be "my servants," God said. They would inherit the gracious blessings God had promised. Here the blessings are described in terms that might suggest that the land of Palestine would be transformed into a pleasant and peaceful garden. But the description calls to mind the spiritual blessings promised in the green pastures and quiet waters of Psalm 23 rather than those one might find in a resort or retreat.

The Lord is both a God of grace and a God of judgment. He proclaims law and gospel. We have just learned an important and comforting truth: God would preserve a remnant in order to fulfill all his gracious promises. That's gospel. On the other hand, the Lord could not and would not forget his threats. His judgment would come, and the Lord proceeds to turn our attention to those who reject him and remain in unbelief. We now hear the law. Judgment will fall upon those who forsake the Lord and forget his mountain, that is, his temple and the worship that takes place there.

The objects of God's judgment have abandoned the revelation of the Lord and adopted religious and spiritual practices that the Lord had forbidden. Here the Lord describes these people as those who are ensnared in idolatry. The practice described appears to be a kind of festival in which the gods were laid out on cushions while worshipers placed wine and food before them. The two gods, Fortune and Destiny, imply that by this practice the people were trying to assure their future. Instead of depending on the Lord to secure their future and trusting in his promises, the people had resorted to nothing more than trusting luck and fate.

On these people, the judgment of God would fall. "I will destine you for the sword, and you will all bend down for the slaughter." The Hebrew word for *destine* is a play on words for the name of the god they worshiped, Destiny. The people had bowed down to Destiny and Fortune, but they would receive no help from those gods. Instead, they would bow down to receive death and judgment.

The Lord repeated the reason for his judgment. The people had refused to accept the Lord and follow his Word. The Lord called to them; they didn't respond. The Lord revealed his truth to them, but they chose to follow their own opinions and thoughts. Instead of honoring the will of the Lord, they wanted what they considered good and right. The great sin of these people was their refusal to follow the Word of God. It remains a great sin—a form of unbelief. Whenever human minds consider God's words to be foolish, impractical, harsh, unreasonable, old-fashioned, and out of step with current human thought, the danger of abandoning God's Word lurks as it did for these ancient people. God continues to call to us all in his Word. He continues to speak to us in his Word. We either listen or close our ears. We either cling to the words of God, or we adopt human theories, opinions, and insights. We either receive the blessings of God, or we are destined "for the sword." The Lord clearly announces both the gospel and the law. These people had forsaken God's revelation, in effect telling God, "Leave us alone."

God saw the difference between those who believed him and those who had forsaken him. He did not keep his will a secret; he did not hide how he would respond to both. He promised that his faithful servants would come under his gracious protection and care. They would eat and drink, while the unfaithful would go hungry and thirsty. His servants will rejoice and sing. Jesus promised that the faithful would have enough food and clothing to satisfy their needs and encouraged them not to worry (Matthew 6:25-34). Again and again the New Testament tells us to rejoice—to rejoice even in our troubles (for example, Romans 5:3; Philippians 4:4; 1 Peter 1:6). On the other side, the unfaithful who have forsaken the Lord will suffer and have no reason to rejoice. Instead, they will "wail in brokenness of spirit."

The difference between the Lord's faithful servants and the unfaithful extends even to the names they have. The unfaithful leave their names as a curse. Perhaps the passage means that when God's elect remember the unfaithful, they will remember the curse they called down on themselves. Perhaps it means that whenever God's faithful want to express a wish for all who reject the Lord, they will use the name of these people as a curse. The name of the unfaithful may even serve as a byword or maxim for God's judgment. However one chooses to interpret the phrase, the name of the unfaithful finds a place in curses, not in blessings. The faithful have another name. This may be a reference to the end of chapter 62, where God's people are called "the Holy People, the Redeemed of the LORD; . . . Sought After, the City No Longer Deserted" (verse 12). The faithful cling to the God of truth and use his name as he has required in the Second Commandment. They use God's name to invoke blessings and to take proper oaths. In addition, the past troubles will be forgotten.

Will the Lord keep silent and punish his people without measure? God answers clearly. He will absolutely and thoroughly punish those who forsake him. But he will rescue a remnant. Through that remnant, God's greatest blessing would come. The Messiah would rescue the world, and God would gather his people anew and transform them into the gathering of all believers. The Lord will reveal more about that in the verses ahead. Here the Lord promises that he will richly bless his faithful servants and bring them under his special care. He is a God of grace and mercy to all who believe; at the same time, he is nevertheless a God of judgment to all who forsake his Word.

> ¹⁷ **"Behold, I will create**
> **new heavens and a new earth.**
> **The former things will not be remembered,**
> **nor will they come to mind.**
> ¹⁸ **But be glad and rejoice forever**
> **in what I will create,**
> **for I will create Jerusalem to be a delight**
> **and its people a joy.**
> ¹⁹ **I will rejoice over Jerusalem**
> **and take delight in my people;**
> **the sound of weeping and of crying**
> **will be heard in it no more.**

²⁰ "Never again will there be in it
    an infant who lives but a few days,
    or an old man who does not live out his years;
he who dies at a hundred
    will be thought a mere youth;
he who fails to reach a hundred
    will be considered accursed.
²¹ They will build houses and dwell in them;
    they will plant vineyards and eat their fruit.
²² No longer will they build houses and others live in them,
    or plant and others eat.
For as the days of a tree,
    so will be the days of my people;
my chosen ones will long enjoy
    the works of their hands.
²³ They will not toil in vain
    or bear children doomed to misfortune;
for they will be a people blessed by the LORD,
    they and their descendants with them.
²⁴ Before they call I will answer;
    while they are still speaking I will hear.
²⁵ The wolf and the lamb will feed together,
    and the lion will eat straw like the ox,
    but dust will be the serpent's food.
They will neither harm nor destroy
    on all my holy mountain,"

says the LORD.

Behold always calls attention to something unexpected. Here the Lord informed his people of the wonders he would still perform for them in the future. What the Lord describes here mixes the New Testament church in this world with the church triumphant in eternity. Old Testament prophets often viewed the future without distinctly specifying the first or second coming of the Messiah (see the prophetic vision illustration in *Isaiah 1–39*, in The People's Bible series, page 46). It is as if Isaiah saw the church as a great mansion with a massive courtyard. The mansion itself represents the home of the church triumphant, the eternal Jerusalem waiting for all believers. The courtyard is gated and walled because the Lord protects all within. Yet those in the courtyard have not yet entered the mansion. They wait because they represent the church militant, believers still in this world. God's prophets see them both at once. On the mural of the future of the church, Isaiah paints wonderful blessings.

We focus our attention first on the new heaven and new earth. The first three verses of this section of the prophecy anticipate the new heaven and earth, which the apostle John saw in Revelation chapter 21. The faithful do not remember their former troubles and difficulties. They will "be glad and rejoice forever." So God pictures eternal life and bliss with him in heaven. God's Old Testament people anticipated that joy, and so do we as New Testament believers. God created this new place for his faithful. We know that it exists because God has said so and because his power has made it so. Although we wonder about it in the midst of earth's trials and difficulties, God assures us that it waits for us just beyond time and earthly life. Believers do not hear weeping and crying there. One precious thought should not escape our attention. Not only will God's people rejoice, but God himself will rejoice over his people. In heaven he will delight in his faithful.

Looking into the future, Isaiah and the Old Testament believers could not see the distinction as clearly as we New Testament believers can. God told them that a mansion, the new Jerusalem, stood ready and waiting for them. In the Old Testament, God did not always carefully distinguish between the New Testament church and the church triumphant in heaven. We see that in these verses. In verses

20 to 23, God describes something other than the perfect bliss of heaven. Death is not completely vanquished but only limited. An infant will not die after only a few days of life. A man who does die at the age of 100 will be considered only a youth. And God's people will be allowed to enjoy the fruits of their labors. God here tells about the future church of the New Testament. The people whom God would gather together in that church would be "a people blessed by the LORD." They would come under his special care and protection.

We must be careful not to force this passage beyond its meaning. God tells us that the New Testament believers would come under his care and protection. Yet at times, he does allow young men and women who are part of his New Testament church to die suddenly. Even infants among God's faithful people die and pass from the courtyard into the mansion. Remember that God's ways are not our ways, and we do not always understand why he does things. Isaiah had also written, "The righteous perish, and no one ponders it in his heart; devout men are taken away, and no one understands that the righteous are taken away to be spared from evil" (57:1). God does not promise here that every believer will live to the ripe old age of 100 but that every believer in the church is "blessed by the LORD" and comes under his special watchful eye. He will work in all things for the good of all those who love him (Romans 8:28).

Believers live by prayer and the Word of God. They listen to the Lord as he speaks to them in his Word. When they face trouble, heartache, and danger, they pray. Verse 24 provides powerful encouragement to pray. As believers wait in that courtyard, they call upon the Lord in every trouble. The Lord promises to hear and to respond. In connection with this verse, Luther comments:

Our prayer pleases God because He has commanded it, made promises, and given form to our prayer. For that reason He is pleased with our prayer, He requires it and delights in it, because He promises, commands, and shapes it. . . . God cannot get enough of the prayers of the godly. Therefore the prayer of the godly is likened to the most attractive odor which one cannot smell enough. . . . When the godly pray, it is already guaranteed in heaven and on earth. Therefore we must bring our prayer to a close with Amen. So it is done. (LW, Volume 17, page 393)

The final verse reminds us of the peace that dominates God's rule in the hearts of his people. Both the church on earth and the saints in heaven fall under the peace of God, which surpasses all understanding (Philippians 4:7). The Savior's peace is forgiveness. Believers have perfect peace. Even though our time on earth may be filled with tears and afflictions, we have peace with God. We know that when we leave behind all of life's troubles, God will welcome us into his mansion and wipe the tears from our cheeks with his tender and loving hand. Those things that we endured in the courtyard of his church, waiting to enter his mansion, will all be forgotten. So now we endure, waiting for our turn to walk into his presence.

66 This is what the LORD says:
"Heaven is my throne,
    and the earth is my footstool.
Where is the house you will build for me?
    Where will my resting place be?
² Has not my hand made all these things,
    and so they came into being?"

                    declares the LORD.

The Lord emphatically asserts the appropriate relationship between himself and the earth. The assertion begins, "This is what the LORD says," and ends with "declares the LORD" before going on to the next point. The two phrases stand as exclamation points on both sides of this assertion. Simply stated, the Lord asserts his superiority and authority over the earth and all who live there. God dwells in the heavens. The earth is his footstool. The Lord is infinite, eternal, all powerful, all knowing, and holy—superior to all that is human. He rules all the earth, as Psalm 103:19 says, "The LORD has established his throne in heaven, and his kingdom rules over all." Jesus asserted the same principle in his Sermon on the Mount (Matthew 5:34,35).

God created the earth. The elements of the heavens and the earth, as well as all who inhabit the earth, are not on the same level as God. Where God is infinite, the earth is finite. Where God is eternal, the earth has a beginning and will have an end; it is temporary. God knows all things, past and future; humans may know a great deal, but gaps and boundaries limit their knowledge. God is almighty; humans may wield great power, including the nuclear power of mass destruction, but they are no match for God. Even the powerful forces of nature demonstrated in a thunderstorm, an earthquake, a tornado, or a hurricane are small compared to the power of God. God is holy, perfect, separate from all sin and imperfection; humans are flawed, imperfect, and perverse. Yes, the Lord is above. His throne is in heaven. The earth is only his footstool.

The understanding of our relationship to God begins with this fundamental principle: God is greater than we are. If that is true, then what could we offer to God? We can't give him anything that he does not already have. God asks, "Where is the house you will build for me? Where will my resting place be?" No building could house God and confine his presence. At the dedication of the temple, Solomon exclaimed: "Will God really dwell on earth? The heavens, even the highest heaven, cannot contain you. How much less this temple I have built!" (1 Kings 8:27).

God, however, chooses to be concerned with the earth and his creation even after humanity has soiled it with its imperfection and sin. He chooses to love all humanity. He chose to descend to earth in order to rescue its inhabitants from their own rebellion and sin. He chose birth in a stable and death on a cross, and not because any human was so noble as to deserve it or because anyone could offer God something that would move him to love us so. Isaiah had written earlier, "I, even I, am he who blots out your transgressions, *for my own sake*, and remembers your sins no more" (43:25). Grace—undeserved love for his wayward creatures—moves God to direct his attention to earth and prompts every action toward its inhabitants. By his grace, God chose Abraham and from him shaped the special people of Israel. By his grace, God promised the redemption that eventually came through the Messiah. By his grace, God carefully revealed in his Word all that any human needs to know. Heaven is his throne, and earth is his footstool. God is God, and we are not God.

Some commentators suggest that the reference here to the house of God that the returning exiles would build thrusts these words into the time after the exile. When the remnant returned, they carried out the plan to rebuild the temple. Isaiah by inspiration certainly could have seen that moment in history and written these words to fit the event. In that case the building of the temple by the returning exiles was only an outward expression of their faith.

Yet, in the prayer to God in the previous chapters, Isaiah

had referred to the temple: "Our holy and glorious temple, where our fathers praised you, has been burned with fire, and all that we treasured lies in ruins" (64:11). These words may be considered to be God's answer to that anguished cry. God reminded his faithful that he could not be confined by earthly temples made by human hands. He did not need a temple. Building a temple would not move him to love, cherish, or even notice those who built it. God loves, cherishes, and notices humans because it is his will, not because of any human activity, even the building of a temple.

> **"This is the one I esteem:**
> **he who is humble and contrite in spirit,**
> **and trembles at my word.**
> **³ But whoever sacrifices a bull**
> **is like one who kills a man,**
> **and whoever offers a lamb,**
> **like one who breaks a dog's neck;**
> **whoever makes a grain offering**
> **is like one who presents pig's blood,**
> **and whoever burns memorial incense,**
> **like one who worships an idol.**
> **They have chosen their own ways,**
> **and their souls delight in their abominations;**
> **⁴ so I also will choose harsh treatment for them**
> **and will bring upon them what they dread.**
> **For when I called, no one answered,**
> **when I spoke, no one listened.**
> **They did evil in my sight**
> **and chose what displeases me."**

If we understand that God is God and that we are not, then the proper human response to God can only be humility, reverence, and penitence. God tells us that he values these traits in people. Humility recognizes the superiority of God and his authority and then submits to God. It does not presume to tell God what to say or think. Rather, the humble adopt the attitude of a meek, mild, and obedient servant. The second response is to be "contrite in spirit." Human sin pervades every aspect of our lives, but humans resist the knowledge of their own sin and imperfection. Some even violently oppose anyone who accuses them of sin. The contrite know the depth of their own depravity. They understand the words used in chapter 59 for sin (iniquity, transgression, and rebellion) and apply such words to themselves. A contrite soul has his or her head bowed before the perfect, holy Lord. God looks for a third response: reverence. In this verse God applies the attitude of reverence specifically to the words he has revealed. God is God, and he has revealed himself and all we need to know in the Scriptures, his Word. When humans read the Scriptures, they should treat the words as the very words of God. One who trembles at God's Word will pay careful attention to what God says and will not alter it by adding to it or subtracting from it (Revelation 22:18,19).

Of course, by nature humans do not want to submit to God. Instead, they want to make themselves gods. Satan's temptation in the Garden of Eden urged Eve to consider herself like God. Satan said, "God knows that when you eat of it your eyes will be opened, and *you will be like God,* knowing good and evil" (Genesis 3:5). That temptation echoes in every human heart. We think that we know better than God. Many see no reason to be contrite and conclude that they are just as good as everyone else. Others do not follow the revelation God has given us in the Scriptures, choosing instead to follow their own thoughts or the thoughts of some human philosopher. God's grace in Jesus Christ remains his central revelation. Grace denies human effort and turns the human heart solely toward God. Many cannot accept redemption through Christ as the only way into the family of

God and the mansions above. Surely, they imagine, humans must do something to earn a place with God above.

God says, however, that human effort does not earn redemption and a place at the heavenly feast. Yet humans persist in their imaginations. God therefore once again threatened all those who thought that their sacrifices and offerings could earn his blessings. Without faith, even one who offered an expensive sacrifice like a bull found no approval from God. Instead, he appeared to God "like one who kills a man." Offering a lamb or a grain offering received no recognition from God. Neither did burning memorial incense. All such efforts done to curry God's favor were worthless. God said, "They have chosen their own ways, . . . so I also will choose harsh treatment for them."

God warns against all human effort that seeks to earn his blessings. Such behavior results when humans fail to listen to God's message and invent their own way to God. Verse 4 repeats the thought of 65:12. God has called and spoken. God reveals his message clearly in the words of Scripture. When people choose their own ways, they cannot please God, and they invite his judgment. What else is God to do? He calls. He speaks. He sends his prophets. His Word is accessible to every human. When people refuse to believe, discard God's thoughts, and follow their own, God must follow through on his threats of punishment.

> ⁵ Hear the word of the LORD,
>   you who tremble at his word:
> "Your brothers who hate you,
>   and exclude you because of my name, have said,
> 'Let the LORD be glorified,
>   that we may see your joy!'
>   Yet they will be put to shame.
> ⁶ Hear that uproar from the city,
>   hear that noise from the temple!

It is the sound of the Lord
    repaying his enemies all they deserve.
7 "Before she goes into labor,
    she gives birth;
before the pains come upon her,
    she delivers a son.
8 Who has ever heard of such a thing?
    Who has ever seen such things?
Can a country be born in a day
    or a nation be brought forth in a moment?
Yet no sooner is Zion in labor
    than she gives birth to her children.
9 Do I bring to the moment of birth
    and not give delivery?" says the Lord.
"Do I close up the womb
    when I bring to delivery?" says your God.

In these verses, God turned his attention away from those who rejected him and his grace in order to focus on his faithful. He encouraged those who valued his Word and treated it with reverence to listen. These faithful servants were hounded by the ungodly. Their own brothers hated them. Because they believed that Jehovah redeemed the world through his Servant, the faithful were persecuted. They remained loyal to the Lord and were made to feel like outsiders, excluded because of God's name. The phrase "Let the Lord be glorified, that we may see your joy!" was a taunt on the lips of the unbelievers. The taunts sound similar to those hurled at Jesus on the cross: "Let this Christ, this King of Israel, come down now from the cross, that we may see and believe" (Mark 15:32). God will not forget the jeers the ungodly shouted at his faithful people. "They will be put to shame." God's judgment will come.

"Hear that uproar from the city"! The Lord invites us to hear the evidence of his action against his enemies. The tumultuous noise, like the roar of rushing water, signals the advance of God's judgment. The noise comes from the city and from the temple. Isaiah tells us what to make of the sound: "It is the sound of the LORD repaying his enemies all they deserve." God's enemies rebelled against him and oppressed his people. God's judgment descends upon them.

The noise of judgment signals not only the destruction of God's enemies, but it also ushers in the birth of a new nation. God tells us that suddenly, even before the woman goes into labor, she gives birth. A miracle birth takes place almost at the same time that the city is destroyed. Clearly, the Lord himself brings forth this new nation; he gives it birth. Delivering his people had always been his plan, and he would not close up the womb when he stood ready to deliver Zion's children.

What's happening here? What do these words prophesy? Who is being destroyed, and who are the children that are miraculously and suddenly born? The noise of judgment refers to the coming of the Roman army and the destruction of Jerusalem and the temple. After the coming of Jesus, the Jews revolted against Rome. As a result, the Romans completely destroyed Jerusalem, as Jesus had predicted three days before his death (Matthew 24:1,2). The Old Testament came to an end in the noise of the Roman legions under Titus in A.D. 70. God's judgment came upon those who had rejected the Messiah and rebelled against the Lord.

But almost at the same time, something new and miraculous took place. A new people came forth out of the Old Testament—the church of the New Testament. The Zion and Jerusalem of old were gone, but a new Zion and a new Jerusalem emerged. At the time the Romans destroyed Jerusalem, people had already begun to turn to the Lord. Luke records that three thousand Jews came to faith in Jesus and were baptized on Pentecost (Acts 2). In the words of his prophet Isaiah, God told his people that the time would come when he would put an end to the old covenant and create a new one.

This thought provides an appropriate conclusion for the end of Isaiah's prophecy. In addition, it serves as God's answer to the prayer of chapters 63 and 64. God promises that he will not punish Israel beyond measure. His judgment would come fierce and certain, but not only would a remnant survive from the rubble of judgment, but an entirely new nation would arise—the church, believers in the Servant, Jesus Christ.

> [10] "Rejoice with Jerusalem and be glad for her,
>> all you who love her;
> rejoice greatly with her,
>> all you who mourn over her.
> [11] For you will nurse and be satisfied
>> at her comforting breasts;
> you will drink deeply
>> and delight in her overflowing abundance."
>
> [12]For this is what the LORD says:
>
> "I will extend peace to her like a river,
>> and the wealth of nations like a flooding stream;
> you will nurse and be carried on her arm
>> and dandled on her knees.
> [13] As a mother comforts her child,
>> so will I comfort you;
>> and you will be comforted over Jerusalem."
> [14] When you see this, your heart will rejoice
>> and you will flourish like grass;
> the hand of the LORD will be made known to his servants,
>> but his fury will be shown to his foes.

The church has always been the gathering of believers. Scripture refers to that gathering as "Jerusalem" and "Zion." The Lord addressed his believers and encouraged them to rejoice. They were to rejoice at the birth and transformation of Jerusalem. The Lord promised that the church would reemerge and the New Testament era would dawn with glorious and gracious light. Rejoice greatly!

"Rejoice with Jerusalem . . . all you who mourn over her." How can those who mourn over Jerusalem rejoice? In what sense do they mourn? Through the ages, believers have encountered sorrow as they witnessed the troubles of the church. Those in Isaiah's day saw the hypocrisy, unbelief, and idolatry among their own people. Such realities troubled them deeply. When they saw the Assyrians destroy the Northern Kingdom and invade Judah, they mourned. Later on, their hearts melted as the Babylonians carried believers and unbelievers away as captives. They mourned because they knew that the sins of God's people had brought about the exile. Jesus wept over Jerusalem because of its unbelief (Luke 19:41). The church has been persecuted over the centuries, and believers still suffer for their faith in Jesus. We note the erosion of morality and the abandonment of the gospel of Jesus Christ by so many in our own age. We too mourn over the condition of the visible church. The church on earth remains a faithful little flock battered and ridiculed by the world and even by some who claim to be Christian. Yet even the very gates of hell will not triumph over the church of Christ (Matthew 16:18). Rejoice, all who mourn over the church!

The next few verses give us the reason for the joy of believers. The gathering of believers will find nourishment, comfort, and abundance for their souls. The gospel will give believers all the comfort they need. Peter wrote, "Like newborn babies, crave pure spiritual milk, so that by it you may grow up in your salvation" (1 Peter 2:2). Luther wrote: "The church's glory is the cross which remains despised and wicked in the eyes of the world. Yet through the Holy Spirit the breasts of the church comfort many hearts with peace and the security of faith" (LW, Volume 17, page 408). As believers have gathered together, they have found strength through the gospel in Word and sacrament. God has richly nourished the church through the means of grace and will continue to satisfy his saints during the difficulties and tears of their earthly pilgrimage.

The Lord underscores the blessings he provides for believers with a reminder of the source of this promise: "For this is what the LORD says." We find another reason to rejoice in the peace that flows to God's people. Jesus assured his followers: "Peace I leave with you; my peace I give you. I do not give to you as the world gives. Do not let your hearts be troubled and do not be afraid" (John 14:27). The peace of forgiveness flows to the church and through the church. That peace comes from God. The angels announced it at the birth of the Savior.

But God's people have more reason to rejoice. The wealth of nations also flows into the church. The Gentiles will bring into the church their power, their intellectual gifts, and all their resources. The church will benefit from all the best the nations have to offer.

Isaiah's prophecy drips rich with comfort and beauty. The Lord will take his people and carry them and tenderly rock them as a mother rocks her small child on her knees. The Lord himself promises such comfort and care. No wonder he encourages us to rejoice.

The prophet's prayer of chapters 63 and 64 voiced dismay over the desolation of Jerusalem and the temple. God answers the dismay, concern, and anguish with the promise of the new Jerusalem. It will rise from the remnant of the old. God will fill it with peace and wealth. God's people trust that God will make it wonderful. God himself will nourish his faithful with the gospel and comfort them with his presence and care.

All this is an appropriate response to the prayer of God's Old Testament faithful. As we note these comforting and reassuring promises, God reminds us of the sober reality that will confront all who have followed their own imaginations and become his enemies. As we have had so often, side by side we have rich, beautiful gospel and stern, terrifying law.

> ¹⁵ See, the LORD is coming with fire,
>   and his chariots are like a whirlwind;
> he will bring down his anger with fury,
>   and his rebuke with flames of fire.
> ¹⁶ For with fire and with his sword
>   the LORD will execute judgment upon all men,
>   and many will be those slain by the LORD.

¹⁷"Those who consecrate and purify themselves to go into the gardens, following the one in the midst of those who eat the flesh of pigs and rats and other abominable things—they will meet their end together," declares the LORD.

¹⁸"And I, because of their actions and their imaginations, am about to come and gather all nations and tongues, and they will come and see my glory.

¹⁹"I will set a sign among them, and I will send some of those who survive to the nations—to Tarshish, to the Libyans and Lydians (famous as archers), to Tubal and Greece, and to the distant islands that have not heard of my fame or seen my glory. They will proclaim my glory among the nations.

When Jesus told his disciples that Jerusalem would be destroyed and not one stone would be left on another, he went on to speak of the final judgment (Matthew 24, Mark 13, Luke 21). Jesus wove both the destruction of Jerusalem and the final judgment together in his prophecy. Isaiah does the same here. On the one hand, we see the Lord coming in judgment upon those among his people who had followed their own thoughts and abandoned God's clear Word. They would experience the fury of his anger and the fire of his rebuke.

The judgment upon Jerusalem by the Romans anticipated the final judgment God would visit upon all the world. Jesus said that when he returns, "All the nations of the earth will mourn. They will see the Son of Man coming on the clouds of the sky, with power and great glory" (Matthew 24:30). The words of Isaiah's prophecy speak of the judgment God will bring upon all people. He will come with fire and sword. God's two judgments blend together. The destruction of Jerusalem would signal the end of the Old Testament era and would come upon those of the Jewish nation who had rejected the Lord's Messiah. The final judgment on the Last Day will descend upon "all men" and "all nations and tongues."

At the destruction of Jerusalem, the Lord would allow some from the Jewish nation to survive. Not all Jews would be destroyed. God directs us to see what he would do with the believers that survive the judgment of Jerusalem. God would send some of the believers to be his missionaries. They would go to Tarshish, perhaps Spain; to the Libyans and Lydians, people of northern Africa; to Tubal, the region we know as Asia Minor; to Greece; and to the distant islands, the Mediterranean world. Those whom God would send out would "proclaim [his] glory among the nations." As we read the book of Acts in the New Testament, we can see the fulfillment of this prophecy. Paul and the early Christians were all Jewish by birth. God sent them out into the world to gather the nations into his church. The gospel transformed Jerusalem into a gathering of believers from all nations.

[20]And they will bring all your brothers, from all the nations, to my holy mountain in Jerusalem as an offering to the LORD—on horses, in chariots and wagons, and on mules and camels," says the LORD. "They will bring them, as the Israelites bring their grain offerings, to the temple of the LORD in ceremonially clean vessels. [21]And I will select some of them also to be priests and Levites," says the LORD.

The mission activity of these Jewish believers will be successful. They will bring scattered Jews to faith in Jesus. They will convert Gentiles from all nations and gather them into the church as well. Through their work, the Holy Spirit will gather believers into the church of Jesus Christ. The church will not be confined only to Jews, but all believers will be related by their faith in Jesus. Regardless of their nationalities and origins, they will be brothers and sisters in Jesus Christ.

The Lord's response to Isaiah's prayer challenged the prophet and all the Old Testament faithful to look beyond the history of Judah and the Old Testament. Some of the Jews were selected for special service to the Lord as priests and Levites. In the new Jerusalem, some of the Gentiles will be elevated to this honor. Such a thought repelled Jews who had been taught to avoid everything gentile. But the new Jerusalem would be different. God would select some of his gentile believers to serve as ministers of the gospel, as special public ambassadors of the gospel. Today we do not have many Jews serving as called servants of God's people. Instead, God has called some among the Gentiles into the public ministry in order to serve his people.

²²"As the new heavens and the new earth that I make will endure before me," declares the LORD, "so will your name and descendants endure. ²³From one New Moon to another and from one Sabbath to another, all mankind will come and bow down before me," says the LORD. ²⁴"And they will go out and look upon the dead bodies of those who rebelled against me; their worm will not die, nor will their fire be quenched, and they will be loathsome to all mankind."

What remains to be said? Isaiah had foretold the coming of the Babylonians to carry the Jews off into captivity. He had announced the coming of Cyrus to release them from their exile. Most important, Isaiah had encouraged the faithful of the Lord to look beyond the release from Babylon to a greater redemption and a more profound deliverance. He had assured them that the Servant would come. That Servant would suffer and be humiliated for the sins of the people, but he would accomplish his purpose of redeeming them from sin and death. Yet the people would follow their own imaginations and abandon the Lord's Word. Isaiah announced God's judgment upon the unbelieving people and upon all who remained in unbelief. In chapters 65 and 66, God had responded to the prayer of his people as Isaiah recorded it. He foretold the coming of a new Jerusalem where peace and comfort would dominate. The Gentiles would be a part of that new gathering of believers—the church—and some of them would serve as special servants of the Lord and his people.

What's left? A peek into eternity. The church on earth is the courtyard connected to the glorious eternal mansion of heaven. In that sense, the church on earth anticipates the new heavens and new earth God will create. It will endure before God in time until the Lord calls an end to time and makes the church on earth the church triumphant and eternal. In the church, believers will worship the Lord as he commanded, observing New Moons and Sabbaths. These were Jewish festival commanded by God, and here they represent the proper worship of the Lord. The church worships the Lord in time and will worship the Lord forever in eternity, singing the praises of the Lord Jehovah, the God of free and faithful grace.

The vision into the future that Isaiah presents remains incomplete if we see only the bliss of the faithful. The unfaithful are excluded from the happy worship of the church and the bliss of heaven. Instead, they experience only the fury of God's judgment. They have rebelled against the Lord and are dead. Yet they still suffer: "Their worm will not die, nor will their fire be quenched." Jesus quoted these words when he talked about the torments of hell (Mark 9:48). Isaiah reminds us that after their judgment, the unbelievers will be repulsive and abhorrent to the believers. Isaiah's prophecy ends with the reminder that all who rebel against the Lord will meet a "loathsome" end under God's judgment. Indirectly, we hear a reminder to cling tenaciously to the grace of God in Christ. God has concluded his response.

We have noted the highlights of the previous sections throughout the commentary. As we finish the remaining section of Isaiah's prophecy, we find some additional thoughts to remember.

- God's people pray in the midst of their darkest hours. But they never lose hope, and at the very brink of despair, they turn to their heavenly Father and trust in his promises.

- God responds to the prayers of his people. He remains faithful to all his promises. He asserts that he is the God of heaven and far superior to all that we know on earth. In Christ, we have all the blessings God planned for his people.

- The faithful are those who are humble and contrite and who revere God's Word.

- This last section, beginning at 63:7, mirrors the ending of the first portion of Isaiah's prophecy. When Isaiah concluded that portion, he added the history of the Assyrian invasion, Hezekiah's prayer, and God's response. This second portion of his prophecy concludes with a prayer and response as well. On one level we may read it as the prayer of an exile waiting for the return to Jerusalem. On another level we can read it as the prayer of God's people enduring the troubles of life, waiting to enter the glorious heavenly Jerusalem.

- The last words of chapter 66 conclude with a variation on the words that ended each of the previous nine chapter sections. Chapters 48 and 57 both ended with similar words: "'There is no peace,' says the LORD, 'for the wicked'" (48:22) and "'There is no peace,' says my God, 'for the wicked'" (57:21). This nine-chapter section ends with a look at the wicked, whose "worm will not die, nor will their fire be quenched." The wicked have no eternal peace. Thus the three nine-chapter segments come to a carefully and similarly constructed close.

When Jews read the prophecy of Isaiah in the synagogue, they repeated verse 23 after 24 so that the reading might conclude with words of consolation. But verse 24 concludes the second half of Isaiah's prophecy so well. Isaiah had concluded the first two nine-chapter sections with the words "There is no peace . . . for the wicked" (48:22; 57:21). Thus the last verse of chapter 66 ties the entire second half of Isaiah into a completed package. Of special note, chapter 53 occupies the very center of the last 27 chapters. Chapter 53 foretells the suffering of the Servant, Jesus Christ. The cross of Christ stands at the center, around which all these precious truths revolve. All who abandon the cross of Christ will be outside the glorious heavenly home that God has prepared for his believers.

May the Lord Jehovah preserve us as a part of the remnant of believers who tremble at his Word until he returns to take all believers to the new Jerusalem!

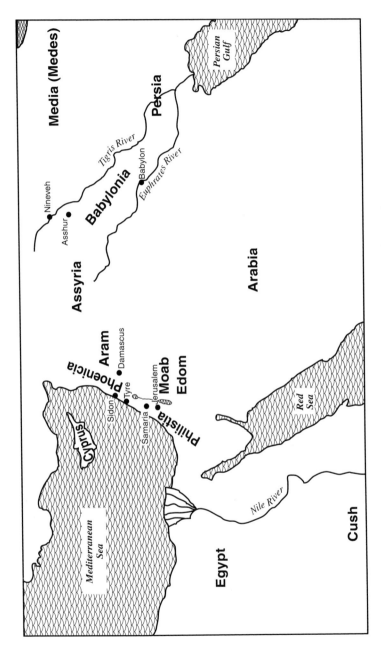

The Middle East at the time of Isaiah